FAITH LESSONS

ON THE death & resurrection OF THE Messiah

LEADER'S GUIDE

Also available from Ray Vander Laan

Video and Group Resources

Faith Lessons on the Life and Ministry of the Messiah
Faith Lessons on the Promised Land
Faith Lessons on the Prophets and Kings of Israel

Book and Audiocassette

Echoes of His Presence

FAITH LESSONS

ON THE death & resurrection OF THE Messiah

LEADER'S GUIDE

Ray Vander Laan

with
Stephen and Amanda Sorenson

ZondervanPublishingHouse
Grand Rapids, Michigan

A Division of HarperCollinsPublishers

Faith Lessons on the Death and Resurrection of the Messiah Leader's Guide
Copyright © 1999 by Ray Vander Laan

Requests for information should be addressed to:

 ZondervanPublishingHouse
Grand Rapids, Michigan 49530

ISBN 0-310-67859-5

Note to Leaders: The videos for this series were originally published under the title *That the World May Know, Faith Lessons 19–27*. If you are using this guide with the original video series, you will have one video on Jerusalem, which is titled "City of the Great King." To use that video with this guide, stop viewing for Session 4 when Mr. Vander Laan moves outside to Robinson's Arch. Begin viewing at that point for Session 5.

Interior design by Sherri Hoffman

Printed in the United States of America

05 / VG / 10 9 8 7 6

contents

introduction

Because God speaks to us through the Scriptures, studying them is a rewarding experience. The inspired human authors of the Bible, as well as those to whom the words were originally given, were primarily Jews living in the Near East. God's words and actions spoke to them with such power, clarity, and purpose that they wrote them down and carefully preserved them as an authoritative body of literature.

God's use of human servants in revealing Himself resulted in writings that clearly bear the stamp of time and place. The message of the Scriptures is, of course, eternal and unchanging—but the circumstances and conditions of the people of the Bible are unique to their times. Consequently, we most clearly understand God's truth when we know the cultural context within which He spoke and acted and the perception of the people with whom He communicated. This does not mean that God's revelation is unclear if we don't know the cultural context. Rather, by learning how to think and approach life as Abraham, Moses, Ruth, Esther, and Paul did, modern Christians will deepen their appreciation of God's Word. To fully apply the message of the Bible, we must enter the world of the Hebrews and familiarize ourselves with their culture.

That is the purpose of this study. The events and characters of the Bible are presented in their original settings. Although the videos offer the latest archaeological research, this series is not intended to be a definitive cultural and geographical study of the lands of the Bible. No original scientific discoveries are revealed here. The purpose of this study is to help us better understand God's revealed mission for our lives by enabling us to hear and see His words in their original context.

understanding the world of the Hebrews

More than 3,800 years ago, God spoke to His servant Abraham: "Go, walk through the length and breadth of the land, for I am giving it to you" (Genesis 13:17). From the outset, God's choice of a Hebrew nomad to begin His plan of salvation (that is still unfolding) was linked to the selection of a specific land where His redemptive work would begin. The nature of God's covenant relationship with His people demanded a place where their faith could be exercised and displayed to all nations so that the world would know of *Yahweh*, the true and faithful God. God showed the same care in preparing a land for His chosen people as He did in preparing a people to live in that land. For us to fully understand God's plan and purpose for His people, we must first understand the nature of the place He selected for them.

By New Testament times, the Jewish people had been removed from the Promised Land by the Babylonians due to Israel's failure to live obediently before God (Jeremiah 25:4–11). The exile lasted seventy years, but its impact upon God's people was astounding. New patterns of worship developed, and scribes and experts in God's law shaped the new commitment to be faithful to Him. The prophets predicted the appearance of a Messiah like King David who would revive the kingdom of the Hebrew people.

But the Promised Land was now home to many other groups of people whose religious practices, moral values, and lifestyles conflicted with those of the Jews. Living as God's witnesses took on added difficulty as Greek, Roman, and Samaritan worldviews mingled with that of the Israelites. The Promised Land was divided between kings and governors, usually under the authority of one foreign empire or another. But the mission of God's people did not change. They were still to live *so that the world would know that their God was the true God.* And the land continued to provide them opportunity to encounter the world that desperately needed to know this reality.

The Promised Land was the arena within which God's people were to serve Him faithfully as the world watched. The land God chose for His people was on the crossroads of the world. A major trade route, the Via Maris, ran through it. God intended for the Israelites to take control of the cities along this route and thereby exert influence on the nations around them. Through their righteous living, the Hebrews were to reveal the one true God, *Yahweh,* to the world. They failed to accomplish this mission, however, because of their unfaithfulness.

Western Christianity tends to spiritualize the concept of the Promised Land as it is presented in the Bible. Instead of seeing it as a crossroads from which to influence the world, modern Christians view it as a distant, heavenly city, a glorious "Canaan" toward which we are traveling as we ignore the world around us. We are focused on the destination, not the journey. We have unconsciously separated our walk with God from our responsibility to the world in which He has placed us. In one sense, our earthly experience is simply preparation for an eternity in the "promised land." Preoccupation with this idea, however, distorts the mission God has set for us.

Living by faith is not a vague, otherworldly experience; rather, it is being faithful to God right now, in the place and time in which He has put us. This truth is emphasized by God's choice of Canaan, a crossroads of the ancient world, as the Promised Land for the Israelites. God wants His people to be in the game, not on the bench. Our mission, as Christians today, is the same one He gave to the Israelites. We are to live obediently *within* the world so that through us *the world may know that our God is the one true God.*

The Assumptions of Biblical Writers

Biblical writers assumed that their readers were familiar with Near Eastern geography. The geography of Canaan shaped the culture of the people living there. Their settlements began near sources of water and food. Climate and raw materials shaped their choice of occupation, dress, weapons, diet, and even artistic expression. As their cities grew, they interacted politically. Trade developed, and trade routes were established.

During New Testament times, the Promised Land was called Palestine or Judea. *Judea* (which means "Jewish") technically referred to the land that had been the nation of Judah. Because of the influence that the people of Judea had over the rest of the land, the land itself was called Judea. The Romans divided the land into several provinces, including Judea, Samaria, and Galilee (the three main divisions during Jesus' time); Gaulanitis, the Decapolis, and Perea (east of the Jordan River); and Idumaea (Edom) and Nabatea (in the south). These further divisions of Israel added to the rich historical and cultural background God prepared for the coming of Jesus and the beginning of His church.

Today the names *Israel* and *Palestine* are often used to designate the land God gave to Abraham. Both terms are politically charged. *Palestine* is used by the Arabs living in the central part of the country, while *Israel* is used by the Jews to indicate the State of Israel. In this study, *Israel* is used in the biblical sense. This choice does not indicate a political statement regarding the current struggle in the Middle East but instead is chosen to best reflect the biblical designation for the land.

Unfortunately, many Christians do not have even a basic geographical knowledge of the region. This series is designed to help solve that problem. We will be studying the people and events of the Bible in their geographical and historical contexts. Once we know the *who*, *what*, and *where* of a Bible story, we will be able to understand the *why*. By deepening our understanding of God's Word, we can strengthen our relationship with God.

The biblical writers also used a language that, like all languages, is bound by culture and time. Therefore, understanding the Scriptures involves more than knowing what the words mean. We need to also understand those words from the perspective of the people who used them.

The people whom God chose as His instruments—the people to whom He revealed Himself—were Hebrews living in the Near East. These people described their world and themselves in concrete terms. Their language was one of pictures, metaphors, and examples rather than ideas, definitions, and abstractions. Whereas we might describe God as omniscient or omnipresent (knowing everything and present everywhere), a Hebrew would have preferred to describe God by saying, "The Lord is my shepherd." Thus, the Bible is filled with concrete images from Hebrew culture: God is our Father, and we are His children; God is the potter, and we are the clay; Jesus is the Lamb killed on Passover; heaven is an oasis in the desert, and hell is the city sewage dump; the Last Judgment will be in the Eastern Gate of the heavenly Jerusalem and will include sheep and goats.

These people had an Eastern mindset rather than a Western mindset. Eastern thought emphasizes the process of learning as much or more than the end result. Whereas Westerners tend to collect information to find the right answer, Hebrew thought stresses the process of discovery as well as the answer. Thus in the Leader's Guide we have included *suggested responses* to the questions. These are provided primarily to help the leader determine the area(s) on which the participants should focus in discovering the answer(s). These suggested responses are not intended to be the final answers or provide an exhaustive list of possible responses. So, the effective leader will allow the participants to process the information and will stress the learning value of that process.

How to use this guide

This Leader's Guide is divided into ten sessions approximately 50–55 minutes in length. Each session corresponds to a videotaped presentation by Ray Vander Laan.

For each session, *the leader* will need:

- Leader's Guide
- Bible
- Video player, monitor, stand, extension cord, etc.
- Videotape

Note: For some sessions, the leader may also want to use an overhead projector, chalk board, or marker board.

For each session, *the participant* will need:

- Participant's Guide
- Bible
- Pen or pencil

Directions to the leader are enclosed in the shaded boxes and are not meant to be spoken.

Each session is divided into six main parts: **Before You Lead**, **Introduction**, **Video Presentation**, **Group Discovery**, **Faith Lesson**, and **Closing Prayer**. A brief explanation of each part follows.

1. Before You Lead

Synopsis
This material is presented for the leader's information. It summarizes the material presented in each of the videos.

Key Points of This Lesson
Highlights the key points you'll want to emphasize.

Session Outline
Provides an overview of the content and activities to be covered throughout the session.

Materials
The materials listed above are critical for both the leader and each participant. Additional materials (optional) are listed when appropriate.

2. Introduction

Welcome

Welcomes participants to the session.

What's to Come

A brief summary you may choose to use as you begin the session.

Questions to Think About

Designed to help everyone begin thinking about the theme or topics that will be covered. A corresponding page is included in the Participant's Guide.

3. Video Presentation

This is the time during which you and the participants will watch the video and write down appropriate notes. Key themes have been indicated.

4. Group Discovery

In this section, you'll guide participants in thinking through materials and themes related to the video you've just seen. You may want to read the material word for word, or simply highlight key words and phrases. Feel free to amplify various points with your own material or illustrations.

The Leader's Guide includes a copy of the corresponding pages in the Participant's Guide. Space is also provided in which to write additional planning notes. Having the Participant's Guide pages in front of you allows you to view the pages the participants are seeing as you talk without having to hold two books at the same time. It also lets you know where the participants are in their book when someone asks you a question.

Video Highlights

Use these questions and suggested responses with the entire group. This will guide participants in verbally responding to key points/themes covered in the video.

Small Group Bible Discovery

At this time, if your group has more than seven participants you will break the group into small groups (three to five people) and assign each group a topic. (If you have more groups than topics, assign some topics to more than one group.) Participants will use their Bibles and write down suggested responses to the questions. At the end of this discovery time, participants will reassemble as a large group. As time allows, small group representatives can share key ideas their groups discussed.

Quite often supplementary material—called *Data File*, *Profile*, etc.—has been inserted near the topics. This material complements the themes but is not required reading to complete the session. Suggest that the participants read and study the supplementary material on their own.

5. faith Lesson

Time for Reflection

At this time, participants will read selected Scripture passages on their own and think about questions that encourage them to apply what they've just discovered to their own lives.

Action Points

At this time, you'll summarize key points (provided for you) with the entire group and encourage participants to act on what they have learned.

6. closing prayer

Close the session with the material or prayer provided.

Before the first session

- Watch the video session.
- Obtain the necessary Participant's Guides for all participants.
- Make sure you have the necessary equipment.

Tips for Leading and promoting Group Discussion

1. Allow group members to participate at their own comfort level. Everyone need not answer every question.
2. Ask questions with interest and warmth and then listen carefully to individual responses. Remember: it is important for participants to think through the questions and ideas presented. The *process* is more important than specific *answers*, which is why *suggested responses* are provided.
3. Be flexible. Reword questions if necessary. Choose to spend more time on a topic. Add or delete questions to accommodate the needs of your group members—and your time frame.
4. Suggest that participants, during the coming week, do the Small Group Bible Discovery topics that their individual small groups may not have had the opportunity to do.
5. Allow for (and expect) differences of opinion and experience.
6. Gently guide all participants into discussion. Do not allow any person(s) to monopolize discussion.
7. Should a heated discussion begin on a theological topic, suggest that the participants involved continue their discussion after the session is over.
8. Do not be afraid of silence. Allow people time to think—don't panic. Sometimes ten seconds of silence seems like an eternity. Remember, some of this material requires time to process—so allow people time to digest a question and *then* respond.

when storms come

Before You Lead

Synopsis

Water has always been an important source of life to people in the Middle East. In biblical times, cities rose up near fresh water sources such as lakes and springs. The people built cisterns, aqueducts, and tunnels to preserve and utilize this precious resource. Bible stories often mention events, discussions, and disputes concerning water.

But in the minds of the Jewish people—the descendants of desert nomads— this highly valued commodity also had a darker side. Large bodies of water, particularly the sea, often represented death and chaos—some of the worst things in life. Believing that stormy seas were caused by evil forces, the people viewed such storms with fear. Only God, they thought, could calm the chaos of stormy water because only He could control evil.

The Sea of Galilee was beautiful, and it provided a means of transportation and source of food. But sometimes cool winds blow off the hills of what people today call the Golan Heights. This cool air sinks rapidly onto the sea, displacing the warmer air and causing sudden storms. So the darker side of the Sea of Galilee was never far from the minds of the Jews who lived nearby.

It is interesting that Jesus deliberately chose the region on the north shore of the Sea of Galilee—the largest body of fresh water in Israel—as the base for His teaching ministry. Jesus called Himself the "living water." He performed miracles on and near the water. And from the shores of the Sea of Galilee, He called fishermen to be His first disciples.

This video focuses on an event that happened to Jesus' disciples on the Sea of Galilee. You'll guide participants in taking a fresh look at the disciples as they endured a terrifying nighttime storm. During this night, Jesus allowed His disciples to strain alone at the oars for many hours, then He nearly walked right by them until they called out to Him for help. While they were stuck in the middle of the Sea of Galilee, rowing against towering waves, they learned more about faith. In this story there is much for us to learn as well.

Key Points of This Lesson

1. *God's power is greater than any evil—any of the storms of life—we face.* Jesus clearly demonstrated His power over evil to His disciples when He commanded the forces of nature and calmed the stormy Sea of Galilee, which represented the power of evil in the minds of His disciples.

2. *Even though God is always watching over us, He sometimes allows us to struggle—just as He allowed the disciples to struggle against the storm-swept waves before He came to their rescue. God uses the storms in our lives to accomplish His work.*

3. *God wants us to follow Him courageously and call out to Him for help as we seek to carry out His purposes.*

Session Outline (52 minutes)

I. Introduction (5 minutes)
Welcome

What's to Come

Questions to Think About

II. Video Presentation "When Storms Come" (16 minutes)

III. Group Discovery (20 minutes)
Video Highlights

Small Group Bible Discovery

IV. Faith Lesson (10 minutes)
Time for Reflection

Action Points

V. Closing Prayer (1 minute)

Materials

If desired, have a marker board, overhead projector, or chalkboard available to record participants' responses to the **Questions to Think About.** No additional materials are required for this session. Simply view the video prior to leading the session so you are familiar with its main points.

when storms come

introduction

Welcome

> Assemble the participants together. Welcome them to session one of *Faith Lessons on the Death and Resurrection of the Messiah.*

What's to Come

Sometimes the life of faith is tough, isn't it? At times we face frightening obstacles as we seek to do that which we believe God would have us do. And sometimes in the midst of the battle, it seems as if God has left us to struggle on our own. But God is never far away when we confront the storms of life. In today's session we will:

- Learn about Jesus' ministry in the regions surrounding the Sea of Galilee and discover insights that will help us face the storms of life.
- See that God is more powerful than any evil, than any storms we face.
- Realize that He sometimes allows us to struggle during a storm but is always ready to answer when we call out to Him.
- Be drawn to step out in faith and live more courageously for Him.

Let's start by thinking about some tough things people face in life.

Questions to Think About

> *Participant's Guide page 11.*

Turn to page 11 of your Participant's Guide. Let's consider several questions that will prepare us for the video we'll see in a few moments.

> Ask each question and solicit a few responses from group members. You may want to record responses to questions one and three on a marker board, chalkboard, or overhead projector so they are visible to the group.

1. Each of us faces difficulties—what we could label "storms"—in life. Which "storms" do people today face? Just give one- or two-word answers.

   Suggested Responses: financial setbacks, divorce, loss of loved ones, sickness, crime, lawsuits, auto accidents, serious injuries, loss of work, children who go astray, natural disasters, fire, etc.

SESSION ONE

when storms come

questions to think about

1. Each of us faces difficulties—what we could label "storms"—in life. Which "storms" do people today face? Just give one- or two-word answers.

2. What difficulties or "storms" frighten you most deeply? To what underlying spiritual force do you attribute those storms?

3. In what ways do evil forces impact your life? Where do you see Satan's power influencing your life?

11

✏ 2.   What difficulties or "storms" frighten you most deeply? To what underlying spiritual force do you attribute those storms?

Suggested Responses: Allow participants who are willing to share their fears and their understanding of what causes those storms.

✏ 3.   In what ways do evil forces impact your life? Where do you see Satan's power influencing your life?

Suggested Responses: See if participants attribute some of their difficulties to the forces of evil. List the difficulties that they believe have spiritual significance or a spiritual source. Try to prepare them to personalize the mindset of the disciples, who viewed the storm they faced on the Sea of Galilee as more than just bad weather.

Let's continue to keep these ideas in mind as we watch the video.

video presentation

16 minutes

Participant's Guide page 12.

On page 12 of your Participant's Guide, you will find a space in which to take notes on key points as we watch this video.

Leader's Video Observations

Perceptions of Water

The Disciples' Catch

The Disciples' Terrifying Night

Peter's Courage

PLANNING NOTES:

SESSION ONE

when storms come

questions to think about

1. Each of us faces difficulties—what we could label "storms"—in life. Which "storms" do people today face? Just give one- or two-word answers.

2. What difficulties or "storms" frighten you most deeply? To what underlying spiritual force do you attribute those storms?

3. In what ways do evil forces impact your life? Where do you see Satan's power influencing your life?

---

12   The Death and Resurrection of the Messiah

video notes

Perceptions of Water

The Disciples' Catch

The Disciples' Terrifying Night

Peter's Courage

Group Discovery

20 minutes

> If your group has seven or more members, use the **Video Highlights** with the entire group (five minutes), then break into small groups of three to five to discuss the **Small Group Bible Discovery** (ten minutes). Then reassemble the group to discuss the key points discovered (five minutes).
>
> If your group has fewer than seven members, begin with the **Video Highlights** (five minutes), then do one or more of the topics found in the **Small Group Bible Discovery** as a group (ten minutes). Finally, spend five minutes at the end discussing points that had an impact on participants.

Video Highlights (5 minutes)

> For this overview, refer to the map of the Sea of Galilee on page 13 of the Participant's Guide.

Please turn to the map of the Sea of Galilee on page 13 of your Participant's Guide. Note the location of Capernaum (the departure point for Jesus' disciples) and Bethsaida (their destination). Also note the location of Gennesaret, about seven miles away, where they finally ended up the next morning.

> Ask one or more of the following questions that relate to the video the participants have just seen.

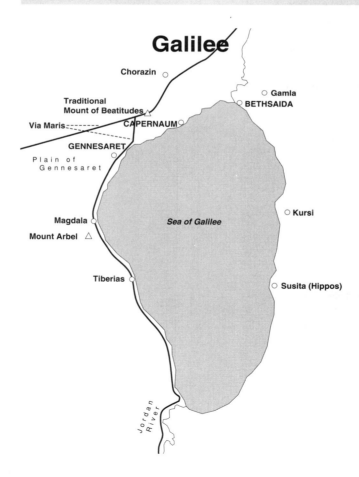

Session One: When Storms Come   13

video Highlights

On the map of the Sea of Galilee note the location of Capernaum (the departure point for Jesus' disciples) and Bethsaida (their destination). Also note the location of Gennesaret, about seven miles away, where they finally ended up the next morning.

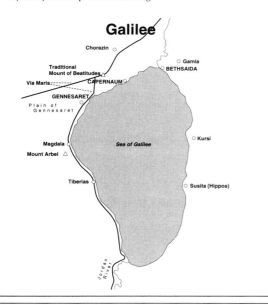

14   The Death and Resurrection of the Messiah

1. In the video, Ray Vander Laan said, "We need to row in the direction we think God wants us to go. But there will be times we'll end up in different places than we expected Him to take us." If you can, briefly describe a time in your life when you did your best to follow Jesus toward a specific goal, but ended up in a very different situation.

2. Why do you think Jesus allowed the disciples to row against the threatening waves for hours without the relief He could have provided? What might we learn from that?

3. A first-century disciple wanted more than anything to be like his rabbi. In light of his desire to be like Jesus, what do you think went through Peter's mind when he stepped out of the boat? When he started to sink and he called out to Jesus for help?

4. Toward the end of the video, the Israeli fisherman demonstrated how to use a fishing net correctly. What does practice have to do with bringing Jesus' love to people?

PLANNING NOTES:

✏ 1. In the video, Ray Vander Laan said, "We need to row in the direction we think God wants us to go. But there will be times we'll end up in different places than we expected Him to take us." If you can, briefly describe a time in your life when you did your best to follow Jesus toward a specific goal, but ended up in a very different situation.

Suggested Responses may reflect: God's faithfulness, God's commitment to accomplish His good work, the differences between our ways and God's ways, the plan He has for each of our lives, the ways in which He teaches us, why our faith grows during difficult times when we can't rely on our own strength, etc.

✏ 2. Why do you think Jesus allowed the disciples to row against the threatening waves for hours without the relief He could have provided? What might we learn from that?

Suggested Responses: wanted to teach them more about faith, wanted them to call upon Him for help instead of trying to do things on their own, etc. We can learn that doing what Jesus wants is worth whatever struggle is required, that Jesus is always watching over us and ready to help us, that God's plans may turn out to be different from ours, and that we need to accept His results, etc.

✏ 3. A first-century disciple wanted more than anything to be like his rabbi. In light of his desire to be like Jesus, what do you think went through Peter's mind when he stepped out of the boat? When he started to sink and he called out to Jesus for help?

Suggested Responses: He probably remembered the miracles Jesus had done, didn't think about the danger because Jesus had invited Him to step out, truly wanted to become what Jesus was, trusted Jesus, etc. He probably thought he should have stayed in the boat, that he misjudged Jesus, that he would die, that Jesus would have to save Him, etc.

✏ 4. Toward the end of the video, the Israeli fisherman demonstrated how to use a fishing net correctly. What does practice have to do with bringing Jesus' love to people?

Suggested Responses: God calls us to reach out to different kinds of people; we will learn more about sharing His love as we do it; it's easy to wait until we think we'll be ready, which may mean we never really commit ourselves to doing it; just as the fishermen used different kinds of nets, we need to use different methods to share Jesus; etc.

Small Group Bible Discovery (15 minutes)

Participant's Guide pages 15–21.

During this time, a group with fewer than seven participants will stay together. A group larger than seven participants will break into small groups and reassemble as a large group during the final five minutes. Assign each group one of the following topics. If you have more than four small groups, assign some topics to more than one group.

14   The Death and Resurrection of the Messiah

1. In the video, Ray Vander Laan said, "We need to row in the direction we think God wants us to go. But there will be times we'll end up in different places than we expected Him to take us." If you can, briefly describe a time in your life when you did your best to follow Jesus toward a specific goal, but ended up in a very different situation.

2. Why do you think Jesus allowed the disciples to row against the threatening waves for hours without the relief He could have provided? What might we learn from that?

3. A first-century disciple wanted more than anything to be like his rabbi. In light of his desire to be like Jesus, what do you think went through Peter's mind when he stepped out of the boat? When he started to sink and he called out to Jesus for help?

4. Toward the end of the video, the Israeli fisherman demonstrated how to use a fishing net correctly. What does practice have to do with bringing Jesus' love to people?

Session One: When Storms Come   15

small group bible discovery

Topic A: A New Calling for Fishermen

1. In fulfillment of the prophecy found in Isaiah 9:1–2, in which region did Jesus focus His preaching ministry? (See Matthew 4:12–17; refer to map on page 17.)

PROFILE OF TWO KINDS OF FISHERMEN	
Fishermen of Galilee	**Fishermen of God**
Fishermen used different kinds of nets and methods (seine nets, circular cast nets, trammel nets, hook and line, spears) to catch different kinds of fish (Job 18:8; Ecclesiastes 9:12; Isaiah 19:8; Matthew 17:24–27; John 21:6–7).	God wants us to use care, dedication, and skill in "fishing" for people who are not yet Christians (Matthew 13:47; Mark 1:16–18; Luke 5:10).
Fishermen fished in the heat of summer and the cold of winter, and at different times of the day to catch different types of fish (John 21:3–6; Luke 5:5–6).	God wants us to vary our approaches to sharing Jesus in order to reach different types of people and guide them into the kingdom of God.
Sometimes fishermen caught fish, sometimes they didn't (John 21:3–6; Luke 5:5–6).	When we share Christ, people respond to Him at some times, at other times they don't.
Fishermen fished from the shore and from boats.	As "fishers of men," we use different means to "fish"—radio, television, one-to-one evangelism, etc.
Fishermen threw away the bad fish they caught (Matthew 13:48).	One day, God's angels will separate the righteous from the unrighteous and throw the unrighteous into the fiery furnace (Matthew 13:49–50).

Let's break into groups of three to five—people sitting near you—and study some of the Bible passages and truths mentioned in the video.

Turn to pages 15–21 in your Participant's Guide. There you'll find a list of four topics. You'll have ten minutes to read and discuss the topic I'll assign to you. Choose one person in your group to be a spokesperson for your group when we discuss these topics later.

> Assign each group a topic.

I'll signal you when one minute is left.

> After nine minutes, let participants know that they have one minute remaining. Then reassemble the entire group. After everyone is back together, begin asking one person from each small group to briefly share a key idea with the larger group. In some cases, you may not have time for every group to share their discoveries.

As time allows, let's briefly share the key ideas that your group discussed.

Topic A: A New Calling for Fishermen

✎ 1. In fulfillment of the prophecy found in Isaiah 9:1–2, in which region did Jesus focus His preaching ministry? (See Matthew 4:12–17; refer to map on page 17.)

Suggested Responses: Jesus went to Capernaum, by the Sea of Galilee. The Via Maris, the Way of the Sea, was the international trade route that ran through this area.

PROFILE OF TWO KINDS OF FISHERMEN	
Fishermen of Galilee	**Fishermen of God**
Fishermen used different kinds of nets and methods (seine nets, circular cast nets, trammel nets, hook and line, spears) to catch different kinds of fish (Job 18:8; Ecclesiastes 9:12; Isaiah 19:8; Matthew 17:24–27; John 21:6–7).	God wants us to use care, dedication, and skill in "fishing" for people who are not yet Christians (Matthew 13:47; Mark 1:16–18; Luke 5:10).
Fishermen fished in the heat of summer and the cold of winter, and at different times of the day to catch different types of fish (John 21:3–6; Luke 5:5–6).	God wants us to vary our approaches to sharing Jesus in order to reach different types of people and guide them into the kingdom of God.
Sometimes fishermen caught fish, sometimes they didn't (John 21:3–6; Luke 5:5–6).	When we share Christ, people respond to Him at some times, at other times they don't.
Fishermen fished from the shore and from boats.	As "fishers of men," we use different means to "fish"—radio, television, one-to-one evangelism, etc.
Fishermen threw away the bad fish they caught (Matthew 13:48).	One day, God's angels will separate the righteous from the unrighteous and throw the unrighteous into the fiery furnace (Matthew 13:49–50).

small group bible discovery

Topic A: A New Calling for Fishermen

1. In fulfillment of the prophecy found in Isaiah 9:1–2, in which region did Jesus focus His preaching ministry? (See Matthew 4:12–17; refer to map on page 17.)

PROFILE OF TWO KINDS OF FISHERMEN	
Fishermen of Galilee	**Fishermen of God**
Fishermen used different kinds of nets and methods (seine nets, circular cast nets, trammel nets, hook and line, spears) to catch different kinds of fish (Job 18:8; Ecclesiastes 9:12; Isaiah 19:8; Matthew 17:24–27; John 21:6–7).	God wants us to use care, dedication, and skill in "fishing" for people who are not yet Christians (Matthew 13:47; Mark 1:16–18; Luke 5:10).
Fishermen fished in the heat of summer and the cold of winter, and at different times of the day to catch different types of fish (John 21:3–6; Luke 5:5–6).	God wants us to vary our approaches to sharing Jesus in order to reach different types of people and guide them into the kingdom of God.
Sometimes fishermen caught fish, sometimes they didn't (John 21:3–6; Luke 5:5–6).	When we share Christ, people respond to Him at some times, at other times they don't.
Fishermen fished from the shore and from boats.	As "fishers of men," we use different means to "fish"—radio, television, one-to-one evangelism, etc.
Fishermen threw away the bad fish they caught (Matthew 13:48).	One day, God's angels will separate the righteous from the unrighteous and throw the unrighteous into the fiery furnace (Matthew 13:49–50).

2. What did Jesus ask the two brothers to do, and how did they respond? (See Matthew 4:18–20; Mark 1:16–18.)

3. How did the two sons of Zebedee respond to Jesus' call? What does their response reveal about their attitude toward Jesus and their commitment to Him? (See Matthew 4:21–22.)

4. In what ways had the brothers' occupation prepared them to understand and fulfill the mission Jesus had in store for them—that of becoming "fishers of men"? (See Mark 1:16–18; Luke 5:1–11.)

5. How does the commitment shown by Peter, Andrew, James, and John when they heard Jesus' call differ from that of many would-be disciples? (See Matthew 4:20, 22.)

2. What did Jesus ask the two brothers to do, and how did they respond? (See Matthew 4:18–20; Mark 1:16–18.)

    Suggested Responses: Jesus asked them to "come, follow me" and "become fishers of men." Immediately they left their nets and followed Him.

3. How did the two sons of Zebedee respond to Jesus' call? What does their response reveal about their attitude toward Jesus and their commitment to Him? (See Matthew 4:21–22.)

DATA FILE

The Sea of Galilee

- Is more than twelve miles long from north to south and nearly eight miles wide at its widest point. The surface is nearly 700 feet below sea level, and it is more than 150 feet deep in some places.
- Is subject to sudden storms caused by an east wind that brings cool air over the warmer blanket of air that covers the lake. The heavier cold air drops as the warm air rises, which causes great air turbulence and violent storms.
- Is the locale where Jesus lived and conducted most of His ministry. He performed ten of His thirty-three recorded miracles in the region.
- Although called a "sea," is really a freshwater lake, fed primarily by the Jordan River in the north. The Sea of Galilee teems with fish today, just as it did during Jesus' time.
- Is deep blue in color and is surrounded by fertile hills and mountains where several hot mineral springs can be found.

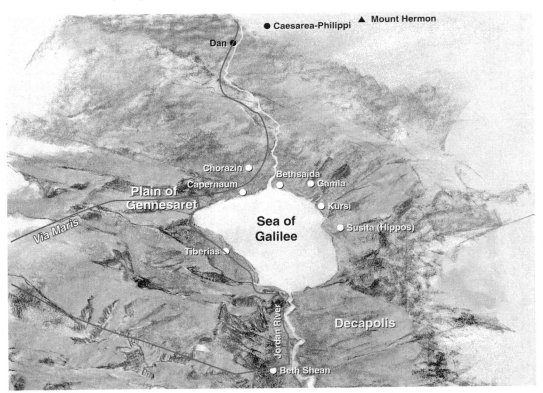

---

2. What did Jesus ask the two brothers to do, and how did they respond? (See Matthew 4:18–20; Mark 1:16–18.)

3. How did the two sons of Zebedee respond to Jesus' call? What does their response reveal about their attitude toward Jesus and their commitment to Him? (See Matthew 4:21–22.)

4. In what ways had the brothers' occupation prepared them to understand and fulfill the mission Jesus had in store for them—that of becoming "fishers of men"? (See Mark 1:16–18; Luke 5:1–11.)

5. How does the commitment shown by Peter, Andrew, James, and John when they heard Jesus' call differ from that of many would-be disciples? (See Matthew 4:20, 22.)

DATA FILE

The Sea of Galilee

- Is more than twelve miles long from north to south and nearly eight miles wide at its widest point. The surface is nearly 700 feet below sea level, and it is more than 150 feet deep in some places.
- Is subject to sudden storms caused by an east wind that brings cool air over the warmer blanket of air that covers the lake. The heavier cold air drops as the warm air rises, which causes great air turbulence and violent storms.
- Is the locale where Jesus lived and conducted most of His ministry. He performed ten of His thirty-three recorded miracles in the region.
- Although called a "sea," is really a freshwater lake, fed primarily by the Jordan River in the north. The Sea of Galilee teems with fish today, just as it did during Jesus' time.
- Is deep blue in color and is surrounded by fertile hills and mountains where several hot mineral springs can be found.

Suggested Responses: Both James and John recognized Jesus as a respected rabbi and immediately followed Him. Clearly they were committed to Him and believed strongly in Him—they left their father standing in the boat!

4. In what ways had the brothers' occupation prepared them to understand and fulfill the mission Jesus had in store for them—that of becoming "fishers of men"? (See Mark 1:16–18; Luke 5:1–11.)

Suggested Responses: They knew how to work long hours, sometimes catching few fish; knew how to attract fish and now would attract people to Jesus' message; had learned to be disciplined in dealing with routine but vitally important tasks such as washing linen nets; didn't give up when things became difficult and would face many difficult times as Jesus' disciples; faced the Abyss as a part of daily life; etc.

5. How does the commitment shown by Peter, Andrew, James, and John when they heard Jesus' call differ from that of many would-be disciples? (See Matthew 4:20, 22.)

Suggested Responses: They left everything, would-be disciples tend to hold onto their possessions; they immediately left what they were doing, would-be disciples tend to hesitate when God calls; they recognized the voice of God, would-be disciples may be too busy to hear it; etc.

Topic B: The Symbols of the Sea

To the Jewish mind in biblical times, the sea represented evil. So in Scripture the sea was used to symbolize the forces of evil in much the same way that a shepherd, rock, and living water were used to represent God. Let's take a look at the symbolic significance of the sea in Scripture.

1. Describe how the evil of the "sea" is personified in these verses:

Psalm 74:13–14	*a multi-headed monster*
Isaiah 27:1	*leviathan—a slithering, coiling serpent; the monster of the sea*
Daniel 7:2–7	*the four winds of heaven churned up the sea and four great evil beasts came up out of the sea*
Revelation 13:1–2	*a beast that resembled a leopard, bear, and lion that had ten horns, seven heads (each with a blasphemous name), and ten crowns on his horns*

2. What are some of the similarities between the Abyss and the sea? (See Revelation 11:3–7; 17:8; 20:1–3.)

Suggested Responses: The Abyss is the residence of the beast; enemies of God will rise up from the Abyss; Satan will be locked into the Abyss; etc.

3. In Matthew 11:20–24, what condemnation did Jesus promise to those people who lived in Capernaum, at the edge of the sea, and had heard His message but did not repent?

Suggested Responses: He promised that they would "go down to the depths," into the Abyss, and that the judgment on Sodom would be easier to bear than the judgment they would receive.

16   The Death and Resurrection of the Messiah

2. What did Jesus ask the two brothers to do, and how did they respond? (See Matthew 4:18–20; Mark 1:16–18.)

3. How did the two sons of Zebedee respond to Jesus' call? What does their response reveal about their attitude toward Jesus and their commitment to Him? (See Matthew 4:21–22.)

4. In what ways had the brothers' occupation prepared them to understand and fulfill the mission Jesus had in store for them—that of becoming "fishers of men"? (See Mark 1:16–18; Luke 5:1–11.)

5. How does the commitment shown by Peter, Andrew, James, and John when they heard Jesus' call differ from that of many would-be disciples? (See Matthew 4:20, 22.)

---

18   The Death and Resurrection of the Messiah

Topic B: The Symbols of the Sea

To the Jewish mind in biblical times, the sea represented evil. So in Scripture the sea was used to symbolize the forces of evil in much the same way that a shepherd, rock, and living water were used to represent God. Let's take a look at the symbolic significance of the sea in Scripture.

1. Describe how the evil of the "sea" is personified in these verses:

    Psalm 74:13–14

    Isaiah 27:1

    Daniel 7:2–7

    Revelation 13:1–2

2. What are some of the similarities between the Abyss and the sea? (See Revelation 11:3–7; 17:8; 20:1–3.)

3. In Matthew 11:20–24, what condemnation did Jesus promise to those people who lived in Capernaum, at the edge of the sea, and had heard His message but did not repent?

✍ 4.   Read Luke 8:27–33, which records an incident involving Jesus, the forces of evil, and the sea.

   a. When Jesus confronted the demon-possessed man, where did the demons beg Jesus not to send them?

       Suggested Response: the Abyss.

   b. Where did the demons want to go instead?

       Suggested Response: into a herd of pigs.

   c. What happened when Jesus gave the demons permission to go there?

       Suggested Response: The pigs rushed into the sea, which represents the Abyss, and were drowned.

Topic C: God Is the Deliverer and Tamer of the Sea

The people of Jesus' day believed that God alone could rescue them from the evil of the sea.

✍ 1.   What do we learn about water in Psalm 24:1–2 and Genesis 1:2, 6–10?

       Suggested Responses: From the beginning, God had power over the formless, watery chaos; He brought order to the chaos; He gathered the seas together to form dry land; and He saw that it was good; etc.

✍ 2.   How did God use water to punish sinful people? (See Genesis 7; Exodus 14:23–28.)

       Suggested Responses: He used it to remove sinful people from the earth during the great flood; He used it to kill Pharaoh's soldiers as they pursued the Israelites.

✍ 3.   When did God use water to save His people? (See Exodus 14:5–9, 27–30; Psalm 77:19–20; Isaiah 51:10.)

       Suggested Responses: God helped the Israelites as they fled Egypt by turning part of the Red Sea into a pathway so they could cross to the other side and by drowning Pharaoh's soldiers.

✍ 4.   Which water-related terms in the following verses are used to describe difficulties and despair or the way in which God brought miraculous deliverance when people called on Him for help?

Psalm 30:1	*lifted me out of the depths*
Psalm 69:1–3	*waters up to my neck, sank in the miry depths where there is no foothold, deep waters, engulfing floods*
Psalm 65:5–7	*God stilled the roaring seas, the roaring waves, the turmoil of nations*
Psalm 77:16–20	*the waters saw God and writhed, the depths convulsed; God's path led through the mighty waters*
Isaiah 51:10	*God dried up the sea, the waters of the great deep*

4. Read Luke 8:27–33, which records an incident involving Jesus, the forces of evil, and the sea.

   a. When Jesus confronted the demon-possessed man, where did the demons beg Jesus not to send them?

   b. Where did the demons want to go instead?

   c. What happened when Jesus gave the demons permission to go there?

Topic C: God Is the Deliverer and Tamer of the Sea
The people of Jesus' day believed that God alone could rescue them from the evil of the sea.

1. What do we learn about water in Psalm 24:1–2 and Genesis 1:2, 6–10?

2. How did God use water to punish sinful people? (See Genesis 7; Exodus 14:23–28.)

3. When did God use water to save His people? (See Exodus 14:5–9, 27–30; Psalm 77:19–20; Isaiah 51:10.)

4. Which water-related terms in the following verses are used to describe difficulties and despair or the way in which God brought miraculous deliverance when people called on Him for help?

   Psalm 30:1

   Psalm 69:1–3

   Psalm 65:5–7

   Psalm 77:16–20

   Isaiah 51:10

   Jonah 2:1–6

Topic D: The Value of Seeking God in a Solitary Place
In this video, we learned that Jesus went to a solitary place to be with His Father while His disciples set out to cross the Sea of Galilee. He often sought a solitary place to pray—sometimes alone, sometimes with His disciples. Although He was divine, Jesus was also human, so He experienced the same things we experience. He became weary

PLANNING NOTES:

Jonah 2:1–6   *depths of the grave, threatened by engulfing waters, currents swirled about Jonah, waves and breakers swept over him, the deep surrounded him; from the depths of the grave he called to the Lord and He answered.*

Topic D: The Value of Seeking God in a Solitary Place

In this video, we learned that Jesus went to a solitary place to be with His Father while His disciples set out to cross the Sea of Galilee. He often sought a solitary place to pray—sometimes alone, sometimes with His disciples. Although He was divine, Jesus was also human, so He experienced the same things we experience. He became weary physically and emotionally and needed the strength and encouragement of His heavenly Father.

1. Why was it vitally important for Jesus to spend time alone with His Father as he faced the following situations?

   Matthew 14:6–13

   Suggested Responses: He needed to grieve for John the Baptist, a special messenger of God and friend whom Herod beheaded.

   Matthew 14:14–23

   Suggested Responses: Jesus tried to find a place by himself, but the multitudes followed Him. He felt compassion for them and healed their sick. Then, because it was late, He fed the five thousand men plus women and children. After all that, He needed time away from the demands of the crowds to pray.

   Mark 1:23–25, 29–38

   Suggested Responses: In one day, Jesus had driven out an evil spirit, healed Simon's mother-in-law, and after sunset healed many other people who had crowded by the door of the home in which He was staying. He left the home early in the morning so He could find a quiet place and would not be followed. When His disciples found Him and told him that people were looking for Him, He announced that He and His disciples must go to a different place in order to fulfill His purpose.

   Luke 6:12

   Suggested Responses: Jesus went to a mountain and prayed all night, then He selected His twelve disciples.

   Luke 22:39–46

   Suggested Responses: Jesus knew that soon He would be arrested and crucified. He felt the weight of the world's sins pressing down on Him. So, He sought the strength and fellowship of His Father in heaven.

2. Why did Jesus go to such "lonely places"? (See Mark 1:40–45.)

   Suggested Responses: Jesus was beset by crowds of people wherever He went. So He had to get away in order to sleep, pray, and gather strength to do His Father's will. Even then, the crowds searched for Him.

20   The Death and Resurrection of the Messiah

3. When did God use water to save His people? (See Exodus 14:5–9, 27–30; Psalm 77:19–20; Isaiah 51:10.)

4. Which water-related terms in the following verses are used to describe difficulties and despair or the way in which God brought miraculous deliverance when people called on Him for help?

   Psalm 30:1

   Psalm 69:1–3

   Psalm 65:5–7

   Psalm 77:16–20

   Isaiah 51:10

   Jonah 2:1–6

Topic D: The Value of Seeking God in a Solitary Place
In this video, we learned that Jesus went to a solitary place to be with His Father while His disciples set out to cross the Sea of Galilee. He often sought a solitary place to pray—sometimes alone, sometimes with His disciples. Although He was divine, Jesus was also human, so He experienced the same things we experience. He became weary

Session One: When Storms Come   21

physically and emotionally and needed the strength and encouragement of His heavenly Father.

1. Why was it vitally important for Jesus to spend time alone with His Father as he faced the following situations?

   Matthew 14:6–13

   Matthew 14:14–23

   Mark 1:23–25, 29–38

   Luke 6:12

   Luke 22:39–46

2. Why did Jesus go to such "lonely places"? (See Mark 1:40–45.)

3. After Jesus spent time alone with His Father, what did He usually do? (See Matthew 14:13–14, 19–21, 34–36; Mark 1:35–42.)

4. If you spent more time alone with God in a "lonely place," how might your life be different?

✏ 3.   After Jesus spent time alone with His Father, what did He usually do? (See Matthew 14:13–14, 19–21, 34–36; Mark 1:35–42.)

   Suggested Responses: Jesus usually ministered to people immediately afterward. Apparently, the strength to minister to other people came from the time He spent alone with His Father.

✏ 4.   If you spent more time alone with God in a "lonely place," how might your life be different?

   Suggested Responses: would have a better relationship with God; would know God's will better; would experience less fear, anger; would make wiser decisions; would be more conformed to the character of Jesus; etc.

faith Lesson

IO minutes   **Time for Reflection (4 minutes)**

It's time for each of us to think quietly about how we can apply what we've learned today. On page 22 of the Participant's Guide, you'll find a passage of Scripture. Let's each read this passage silently and take the next few minutes to consider some of the questions that follow.

Please do not talk during this time. It's a time when we all can reflect on how we respond to the storms in our lives.

> *The Scripture passage and questions are reproduced in their entirety in the Participant's Guide on pages 22–23*

Immediately Jesus made his disciples get into the boat and go on ahead of him to Bethsaida, while he dismissed the crowd. After leaving them, he went up on a mountainside to pray. When evening came, the boat was in the middle of the lake, and he was alone on land. He saw the disciples straining at the oars, because the wind was against them. About the fourth watch of the night he went out to them, walking on the lake. He was about to pass by them, but when they saw him walking on the lake, they thought he was a ghost. They cried out, because they all saw him and were terrified. Immediately he spoke to them and said, "Take courage! It is I. Don't be afraid."

MARK 6:45–50

"Lord, if it's you," Peter replied, "tell me to come to you on the water." "Come," he said. Then Peter got down out of the boat, walked on the water and came toward Jesus. But when he saw the wind, he was afraid and, beginning to sink, cried out, "Lord, save me!" Immediately Jesus reached out his hand and caught him. "You of little faith," he said, "why did you doubt?" And when they climbed into the boat, the wind died down. Then those who were in the boat worshiped him, saying, "Truly you are the Son of God." When they had crossed over, they landed at Gennesaret.

MATTHEW 14:28–34

physically and emotionally and needed the strength and encouragement of His heavenly Father.

1. Why was it vitally important for Jesus to spend time alone with His Father as he faced the following situations?

Matthew 14:6–13

Matthew 14:14–23

Mark 1:23–25, 29–38

Luke 6:12

Luke 22:39–46

2. Why did Jesus go to such "lonely places"? (See Mark 1:40–45.)

3. After Jesus spent time alone with His Father, what did He usually do? (See Matthew 14:13–14, 19–21, 34–36; Mark 1:35–42.)

4. If you spent more time alone with God in a "lonely place," how might your life be different?

faith Lesson

Time for Reflection

The following Scripture passage describes the storm the disciples faced on the Sea of Galilee. Read this passage silently and consider how you respond to the storms in your life.

Immediately Jesus made his disciples get into the boat and go on ahead of him to Bethsaida, while he dismissed the crowd. After leaving them, he went up on a mountainside to pray. When evening came, the boat was in the middle of the lake, and he was alone on land. He saw the disciples straining at the oars, because the wind was against them. About the fourth watch of the night he went out to them, walking on the lake. He was about to pass by them, but when they saw him walking on the lake, they thought he was a ghost. They cried out, because they all saw him and were terrified. Immediately he spoke to them and said, "Take courage! It is I. Don't be afraid."

MARK 6:45–50

"Lord, if it's you," Peter replied, "tell me to come to you on the water." "Come," he said. Then Peter got down out of the boat, walked on the water and came toward Jesus. But when he saw the wind, he was afraid and, beginning to sink, cried out, "Lord, save me!" Immediately Jesus reached out his hand and caught him. "You of little faith," he said, "why did you doubt?" And when they climbed into the boat, the wind died down. Then those who were in the boat worshiped him, saying, "Truly you are the Son of God." When they had crossed over, they landed at Gennesaret.

MATTHEW 14:28–34

PLANNING NOTES:

DATA FILE

Galilean Boat

Remains of a first-century boat of the type the disciples would have used have been found in the mud of the Sea of Galilee. Imagine what it would have been like to be one of the disciples on that stormy night!

- The wooden boat is twenty-six feet long and seven-and-one-half feet wide.
- It would have had a crew of five: four members would have rowed at the two pairs of oars, the fifth would have steered. It also carried a small sail.

- The boat could have held several people in addition to the crew.
- A cushion could be placed on the small deck at either end of the boat so a person could sleep.
- The sides of the boat were low to make it easier to cast nets over the side and draw them in. Waves did not have to be high to threaten the boat!

🔊 1.   Given the mindset of their culture—the evil that the storm-swept sea represented to them—can you imagine how terrified the disciples must have been when they first saw Jesus? Which situations and circumstances in your life are frightening to you? How do you respond when you come face-to-face with those fears?

🔊 2.   As you face difficult "storms" in your life that threaten to overwhelm you, which truths about God's knowledge, power, and care for you that we explored in this lesson encourage you to persevere?

🔊 3.   The disciples had already seen Jesus' power demonstrated in many ways, yet when Jesus calmed the sea, they exclaimed, "Truly you are the Son of God" (Matthew 14:33). What have you seen God do that causes you to marvel and worship Him?

> As soon as participants have spent four minutes reflecting on the above questions, get the entire group's attention and move to the next section.

Action Points (6 minutes)

The following points are reproduced on pages 25–26 of the Participant's Guide:

Now it's time to wrap up our session.

Session One: When Storms Come   23

1. Given the mindset of their culture—the evil that the storm-swept sea represented to them—can you imagine how terrified the disciples must have been when they first saw Jesus? Which situations and circumstances in your life are frightening to you? How do you respond when you come face-to-face with those fears?

2. As you face difficult "storms" in your life that threaten to overwhelm you, which truths about God's knowledge, power, and care for you that we explored in this lesson encourage you to persevere?

3. The disciples had already seen Jesus' power demonstrated in many ways, yet when Jesus calmed the sea, they exclaimed, "Truly you are the Son of God" (Matthew 14:33). What have you seen God do that causes you to marvel and worship Him?

---

24   The Death and Resurrection of the Messiah

DATA FILE

Galilean Boat
Remains of a first-century boat of the type the disciples would have used have been found in the mud of the Sea of Galilee. Imagine what it would have been like to be one of the disciples on that stormy night!

- The wooden boat is twenty-six feet long and seven-and-one-half feet wide.
- It would have had a crew of five: four members would have rowed at the two pairs of oars, the fifth would have steered. It also carried a small sail.
- The boat could have held several people in addition to the crew.
- A cushion could be placed on the small deck at either end of the boat so a person could sleep.
- The sides of the boat were low to make it easier to cast nets over the side and draw them in. Waves did not have to be high to threaten the boat!

> Give participants a moment to transition from their own thoughts to giving you their full attention.

I'd like to take a moment to summarize the key points we explored. After I have reviewed these points, I will give you a moment to jot down the action step (or steps) that you will commit to this week as a result of what you have learned today.

> Read each point and pause after each point so that participants can consider and write out their commitment.

📖 1. *God's power is greater than any evil, greater than any of the storms of life that we face.* Jesus demonstrated this truth to His disciples by controlling the forces of nature and calming the stormy Sea of Galilee—which represented the power of evil.

The storm that most frightens me right now is _____
_____.

Each day this week, I will talk to God about this storm. I will praise Him for the power He has over every evil against which I struggle. I will ask Him to help me face the storm and thank Him that I can count on His help.

📖 2. *Even though God is always with us and watching us, He sometimes allows us to struggle—just as He allowed the disciples to struggle against the waves.* God uses storms in our lives as part of His plan. He uses them to teach us:

- to depend on Him.
- to have faith in His plan for our lives.
- to call out to Him for help.
- to remind us that we need Him and can't handle everything on our own.
- to commit ourselves to practice and persevere—to do whatever it takes to accomplish that which He has given us to do.

List several storms of life that you have faced (or are facing). Next to each write out the lesson God has taught you.

My Storms	God's Lessons

📖 3. *God wants us to follow Him courageously, to step out in faith and do His will.* Just as Peter stepped out of the boat in faith, we have the opportunity to courageously pursue God and do what He calls us to do. Doing so may take us into entirely new directions than what we expect—in relationships, career, evangelism, etc.—just as it took the disciples to Gennesaret instead of Bethsaida.

Peter took a courageous step of faith—right into the raging waves—when he approached Jesus.

Which courageous step is God calling you to take?

Action Points

Take a moment to review the key points you explored today. Then write down the action step (or steps) that you will commit to this week as a result of what you have discovered.

1. *God's power is greater than any evil, greater than any of the storms of life that we face.* Jesus demonstrated this truth to His disciples by controlling the forces of nature and calming the stormy Sea of Galilee—which represented the power of evil.

   The storm that most frightens me right now is _____
   _____
   _____.

   Each day this week, I will talk to God about this storm. I will praise Him for the power He has over every evil against which I struggle. I will ask Him to help me face the storm and thank Him that I can count on His help.

2. *Even though God is always with us and watching us, He sometimes allows us to struggle—just as He allowed the disciples to struggle against the waves.* God uses storms in our lives as part of His plan. He uses them to teach us:
   - to depend on Him.
   - to have faith in His plan for our lives.
   - to call out to Him for help.
   - to remind us that we need Him and can't handle everything on our own.
   - to commit ourselves to practice and persevere—to do whatever it takes to accomplish that which He has given us to do.

   List several storms of life that you have faced (or are facing). Next to each write out the lesson God has taught you.

My Storms	God's Lessons

3. *God wants us to follow Him courageously, to step out in faith and do His will.* Just as Peter stepped out of the boat in faith, we have the opportunity to courageously pursue God and do what He calls us to do. Doing so may take us into entirely new directions than what we expect—in relationships, career, evangelism, etc.—just as it took the disciples to Gennesaret instead of Bethsaida.

   Peter took a courageous step of faith—right into the raging waves—when he approached Jesus.

   Which courageous step is God calling you to take?

   What do you fear as you consider where that step will take you?

   What does it mean to you that God is more powerful than any evil you may face?

   From what do you need to ask Him to save you?

PLANNING NOTES:

What do you fear as you consider where that step will take you?

What does it mean to you that God is more powerful than any evil you may face?

From what do you need to ask Him to save you?

closing prayer

I minute

I hope that this session has strengthened your confidence in God's power over evil and given you courage to step out and face the storms of life, knowing that He will be with you. Let's pray.

Thank You, Lord, for watching over us during life's storms, for hearing us when we call out to You. Even when it seems like we are rowing as hard as we can and not going anywhere, You are still watching over us, You still know where we will land. Please give us more faith to act courageously in doing what You want us to do. Amen.

26   The Death and Resurrection of the Messiah

My Storms	God's Lessons

3. *God wants us to follow Him courageously, to step out in faith and do His will.* Just as Peter stepped out of the boat in faith, we have the opportunity to courageously pursue God and do what He calls us to do. Doing so may take us into entirely new directions than what we expect—in relationships, career, evangelism, etc.—just as it took the disciples to Gennesaret instead of Bethsaida.

Peter took a courageous step of faith—right into the raging waves—when he approached Jesus.

Which courageous step is God calling you to take?

What do you fear as you consider where that step will take you?

What does it mean to you that God is more powerful than any evil you may face?

From what do you need to ask Him to save you?

piercing the Darkness

Before You Lead

Synopsis

From the eastern shore of the Sea of Galilee, a district named the Decapolis spread to the south and east. It originally comprised ten sophisticated cities that were founded by the Greeks, but it had grown to eighteen cities by the time of Jesus. According to one rabbinic tradition, the inhabitants of the Decapolis descended from the seven Canaanite nations that Joshua drove out of the Promised Land (Joshua 3:10; Acts 13:17–19). Although some Jews lived there, its historic Canaanite and Hellenistic influences made it thoroughly pagan. The people living there were involved in fertility cults and considered the pig to be their sacred animal—a stark contrast to the Jews who considered pigs to be unclean. The Decapolis—the place "across the sea"—was so evil that religious Jews believed that Beelzebub himself lived there.

In this session, you'll help participants understand the significance of Jesus' decision to sail across the Sea of Galilee to the sophisticated and pagan Decapolis. That day, Jesus performed at least two miracles. He calmed the furious storm on the lake. He healed the dangerous, demon-possessed man on the eastern shore of the Sea of Galilee in the Decapolis. But these demonstrations of His divine power conveyed an even more significant message.

Jesus came to give life to both the Jew and the Gentile. Thus He interacted with many different kinds of people during His ministry—Jews who were satisfied with the Romans; Jewish zealots who hated the Romans; religious Jews; and yes, even pagans who lived east of the Sea of Galilee. This video emphasizes Jesus' compassion for and ministry to people who had never before been a part of the ministry of God and who did not honor Him. It also highlights Jesus' commitment to actively confront the power of evil.

Jesus—the light of the world—deliberately, righteously, and actively confronted the spiritual darkness of His day. He confronted the sea, which symbolized evil's power and influence. He then confronted the power of Satan, as evidenced by the demon-possessed man who immediately met Jesus when His boat reached shore. Interestingly, Jesus cast the demons into pigs—the very animals the pagan inhabitants of that land considered to be sacred. The pigs then drowned in the lake—the symbol of the Abyss. In response to these actions, the local people pleaded with Jesus to leave their territory.

The man Jesus healed, however, wanted to accompany Jesus. But Jesus had something else in mind. Jesus told him to go home and tell other people in the Decapolis what had happened and how much the Lord had done for him. Evidently the man did just that. As a result of Jesus' willingness to reach out and save just one man who was trapped in Satan's evil, many pagans in the Decapolis became Christians. In fact, the area became a cornerstone of the early Christian church. Christians from this area played a key role in the early church councils that defined the differences between heresy and orthodox Christian doctrine and established the canon, the books that are in the Bible today.

Key Points of This Lesson

1. *Jesus—the light of the world (John 8:12)—deliberately and boldly pierced the spiritual darkness of pagan Decapolis.* With great authority, He appropriated God's power to confront and defeat the devil on his own turf—on the sea and among the pagan people of the Decapolis. As a result, many people wanted Him to leave, but one man was delivered into a new life.

2. *The ministry of one person is powerful!* After healing the demon-possessed man, Jesus told him to go home and tell people what God had done for him. As a result of the man's obedience, many people were drawn to Christ, and a strong Christian community developed in the Decapolis.

Session Outline (53 minutes)

    I. Introduction (5 minutes)
      Welcome
      What's to Come
      Questions to Think About

    II. Video Presentation "Piercing the Darkness" (17 minutes)

    III. Group Discovery (20 minutes)
      Video Highlights
      Small Group Bible Discovery

    IV. Faith Lesson (10 minutes)
      Time for Reflection
      Action Points

    V. Closing Prayer (1 minute)

Materials

If desired, have a marker board, overhead projector, or chalkboard available to record participants' responses to question two of the **Questions to Think About.** No additional materials are needed for this session. Simply view the video prior to leading the session so you are familiar with its main points.

piercing the darkness

introduction

5 minutes

Welcome

> Assemble the participants together. Welcome them to session two of *Faith Lessons on the Death and Resurrection of the Messiah.*

What's to Come

In this session, we'll see how Jesus confronted the power of evil in His world—both on the Sea of Galilee and in a pagan, Gentile community where a man was demon possessed. We'll see that God calls us, as Christians, to confront evil in our culture and to share what He has done in our lives with people who don't yet have a personal relationship with Him.

Questions to Think About

> *Participant's Guide page 27.*

Before we view the video, let's think for a moment about the challenges and fears we must overcome if we are to pierce the strongholds of spiritual darkness in our culture. Several questions to consider are on page 27 of your Participant's Guide.

> Ask each question and solicit a few responses from group members. It may be helpful to record responses to question two on a marker board, chalkboard, or overhead projector so they can be visible to the group throughout the lesson.

✏ 1. Why do you think many Christians keep company with other Christians instead of going to where non-Christians are and sharing Christ with them?

Suggested Responses: fear, don't want to be rejected, don't think they are prepared enough to share Christ with non-Christians, spiritual laziness, too busy with other things, fear of being around non-Christians because of their own weakness or inability to resist temptation, don't feel comfortable around non-Christians, think non-Christians should come to them, etc.

✏ 2. In which segments of our culture do you think Satan and his evil influence is particularly active?

Suggested Responses: the New Age movement, prisons, abortion clinics, runaway kids, entertainment industry, humanistic seminaries, Christian communities in which Christians are always fighting among themselves, affluent communities in which people don't think they need God, etc.

SESSION TWO

piercing the darkness

questions to think about

1. Why do you think many Christians keep company with other Christians instead of going to where non-Christians are and sharing Christ with them?

2. In which segments of our culture do you think Satan and his evil influence is particularly active?

3. What one place seems so evil to you that you would never want to go to it?

4. What would go through your mind if you were walking next to Jesus one day and He announced: "Today, we're going to *that* place"?

✏ 3. What one place seems so evil to you that you would never want to go to it?

Suggested Responses: Ask several participants to name their "evil place" and share it with the group.

✏ 4. What would go through your mind if you were walking next to Jesus one day and He announced: "Today, we're going to *that* place"?

Suggested Responses: Ask several participants to share their responses, or ask everyone to ponder their response silently and write it down.

Let's keep these ideas in mind as we view the video.

video presentation

17 minutes   *Participant's Guide page 28.*

On page 28 of your Participant's Guide, you will find a space in which to take notes on key points as we watch this video.

Leader's Video Observations

The Decapolis

Jesus' Feeding of the 5,000 and 4,000

The Trip "Across the Sea"

The Demon-Possessed Man

Jesus' Call to Confront Evil

SESSION TWO

piercing the darkness

questions to think about

1. Why do you think many Christians keep company with other Christians instead of going to where non-Christians are and sharing Christ with them?

2. In which segments of our culture do you think Satan and his evil influence is particularly active?

3. What one place seems so evil to you that you would never want to go to it?

4. What would go through your mind if you were walking next to Jesus one day and He announced: "Today, we're going to *that* place"?

---

28   The Death and Resurrection of the Messiah

video notes

The Decapolis

Jesus' Feeding of the 5,000 and 4,000

The Trip "Across the Sea"

The Demon-Possessed Man

Jesus' Call to Confront Evil

group discovery

20 minutes

If your group has seven or more members, use the **Video Highlights** with the entire group (five minutes), then break into small groups of three to five to discuss the **Small Group Bible Discovery** (ten minutes). Then reassemble the group to discuss the key points discovered (five minutes).

If your group has fewer than seven members, begin with the **Video Highlights** (five minutes), then do one or more of the topics found in the **Small Group Bible Discovery** as a group (ten minutes). Finally, spend five minutes at the end discussing points that had an impact on participants.

Video Highlights (5 minutes)

Here you'll review the geography of the Decapolis (map on page 29 of the Participant's Guide), and ask one or more of the following questions that directly relate to the video the participants have just seen.

Look at the map on page 29 of your Participant's Guide. Note the area of the Decapolis in relationship to Capernaum and the Sea of Galilee. Note the location of Beth Shan, Susita, Gadara, Gerasa (Jerash)—several key cities of the Decapolis district.

✏ 1.   From whom, according to one rabbinic tradition, did the people of the Decapolis descend?

Suggested Response: One Jewish tradition says that the seven Canaanite nations mentioned in Joshua 3:10 and Acts 13:19 moved there after Joshua forced them out of the Promised Land.

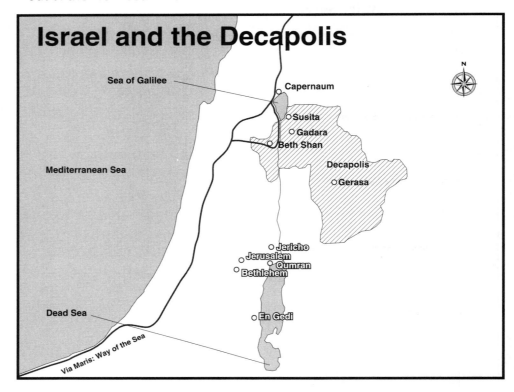

Piercing the Darkness

Session Two: Piercing the Darkness

video highlights

Look at the map of the land of Israel and the Decapolis. Note the area of the Decapolis in relationship to Capernaum and the Sea of Galilee. Note the location of Beth Shan, Susita, Gadara, Gerasa (Jerash)—several key cities of the Decapolis district.

1. From whom, according to one rabbinic tradition, did the people of the Decapolis descend?

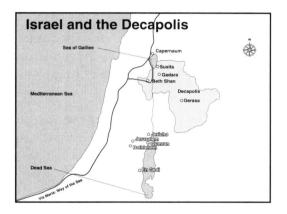

PLANNING NOTES:

2. What did the Jews think about the Decapolis district? Why?

Suggested Responses: They thought the people there were evil and that Satan lived there. The cities there had been founded by pagan Greeks and Romans, its inhabitants practiced fertility cults, the people considered pigs to be their sacred animals, everything about the area was an affront to a religious Jew, etc.

3. Why did the disciples think of the Decapolis as "the other side"?

Suggested Responses: geographically it was on the other side of the lake, the other side of the Jordan; culturally the people were pagan, not Jewish; spiritually it was the dwelling place of Satan, not God; the people worshiped pigs, which to the Jews were unclean; etc.

4. Why did Jesus sail to the Decapolis district? What can we learn from His desire to take His disciples into the most pagan area of His world?

Suggested Responses: to heal the demoniac, because He cared about the pagan people, He knew that God would do a mighty work there, so his disciples could have the same experiences and desires He had. Jesus desires to save all people, even those who appear to be totally consumed by evil.

5. How do you think the disciples felt about going across the sea to "the other side"? Do you think they were surprised that a demon-possessed man met them almost immediately after Jesus calmed the storm? Why or why not?

Suggested Responses: They were probably afraid, irritated, uncertain, questioning, etc. The disciples were probably not surprised by the man who greeted them. After all, they were challenging Satan on his own turf—the Decapolis—the home, they believed, of Beelzebub.

Small Group Bible Discovery (15 minutes)

Participant's Guide pages 31–38.

During this time, a group with fewer than seven participants will stay together. A group larger than seven participants will break into small groups and reassemble as a large group during the final five minutes. Assign each group one of the following topics. If you have more than four small groups, assign some topics to more than one group.

Let's break into groups of three to five and study some of the Bible passages and truths mentioned in the video.

Turn to pages 31–38 in your Participant's Guide. There you'll find a list of four topics. You'll have ten minutes to read and discuss the topic I'll assign to you. Choose one person in your group to be a spokesperson for your group when we discuss these topics later.

Assign each group a topic.

I'll signal you when one minute is left.

After nine minutes, let participants know that they have one minute remaining. Then reassemble the entire group. After everyone is back together, begin

30   The Death and Resurrection of the Messiah

2. What did the Jews think about the Decapolis district? Why?

3. Why did the disciples think of the Decapolis as "the other side"?

4. Why did Jesus sail to the Decapolis district? What can we learn from His desire to take His disciples into the most pagan area of His world?

5. How do you think the disciples felt about going across the sea to "the other side"? Do you think they were surprised that a demon-possessed man met them almost immediately after Jesus calmed the storm? Why or why not?

Session Two: Piercing the Darkness   31

small Group bible discovery

Topic A: The Power of One

1. What kind of a response did Jesus and His disciples receive when they returned to "the other side" a while after Jesus healed the demon-possessed man? (See Mark 7:31–36; Matthew 15:30.)

2. How had the people in the entire Decapolis district heard about Jesus? (See Luke 8:38–39; Mark 5:18–20.)

3. What, according to this biblical story, is the key to evangelism?

4. What seems unusual or surprising to you about the way in which God used this one man to establish a strong Christian community in a pagan culture?

5. What can we learn from the spiritual impact of one formerly demon-possessed man who knew no theology yet became an effective missionary in this most pagan area of first-century Israel?

PLANNING NOTES:

asking one person from each small group to briefly share a key idea with the larger group. In some cases, you may not have time for every group to share their discoveries.

As time allows, let's briefly share the key ideas that your group discussed.

Topic A: The Power of One

1. What kind of a response did Jesus and His disciples receive when they returned to "the other side" a while after Jesus healed the demon-possessed man? (See Mark 7:31–36; Matthew 15:30.)

    Suggested Responses: The people came to them in droves, bringing many sick people to be healed.

2. How had the people in the entire Decapolis district heard about Jesus? (See Luke 8:38–39; Mark 5:18–20.)

    Suggested Responses: from the former demon-possessed man, whom Jesus had healed. The man had returned home and told others what God had done for him. Then he went from city to city until he reached the entire district.

3. What, according to this biblical story, is the key to evangelism?

    Suggested Response: telling people what Christ has done in our lives.

4. What seems unusual or surprising to you about the way in which God used this one man to establish a strong Christian community in a pagan culture?

    Suggested Responses: will vary, but may focus on the difference one person can make, the fact that the man had no theological training, that Jesus sent him out alone, that the people listened to him.

5. What can we learn from the spiritual impact of one formerly demon-possessed man who knew no theology yet became an effective missionary in this most pagan area of first-century Israel?

    Suggested Responses: In God's power, any of us can make a great spiritual impact; we don't have to know lots of theology or attend seminary in order to make an impact on our communities; when we simply share the truth of what God has done for us, He can use our lives in special ways; no matter how tough the mission field may be, God can use us; witnessing is simply sharing Jesus with those whom we meet in everyday life; etc.

Topic B: Jesus' Commitment to Confronting Evil

1. Immediately after Jesus defeated the storm—the power of evil manifested by the sea—whom did He meet? Explain the possible link between these two events. (See Mark 5:1–13; Luke 8:26–33.)

    Suggested Responses: Jesus met the uncontrollable man who was possessed by a "legion" of demons. Jesus had just defeated the power of the sea that threatened His disciples, demonstrating His authority over evil. When He stepped ashore, He faced yet another confrontation with the forces of evil, this time on

small Group Bible Discovery

Topic A: The Power of One

1. What kind of a response did Jesus and His disciples receive when they returned to "the other side" a while after Jesus healed the demon-possessed man? (See Mark 7:31–36; Matthew 15:30.)

2. How had the people in the entire Decapolis district heard about Jesus? (See Luke 8:38–39; Mark 5:18–20.)

3. What, according to this biblical story, is the key to evangelism?

4. What seems unusual or surprising to you about the way in which God used this one man to establish a strong Christian community in a pagan culture?

5. What can we learn from the spiritual impact of one formerly demon-possessed man who knew no theology yet became an effective missionary in this most pagan area of first-century Israel?

Topic B: Jesus' Commitment to Confronting Evil

1. Immediately after Jesus defeated the storm—the power of evil manifested by the sea—whom did He meet? Explain the possible link between these two events. (See Mark 5:1–13; Luke 8:26–33.)

2. In Luke 8:30–33, the sea into which the demonized pigs ran is referred to as what region?

   a. What does the word *Abyss* symbolize in the book of Revelation? (See Revelation 9:1–3, 11; 11:7; 17:8; 20:1–4.)

   b. What, then, is the significance of the pigs rushing into the sea and drowning?

3. Jesus had demonstrated His power over demons many times. Two such accounts are recorded in Mark 1:21–28 and Mark 9:14–29. Please read these accounts and answer the following questions.

   a. Did the demons recognize who Jesus was? How did they respond to Him?

DATA FILE

The History of the Decapolis

Alexander the Great established a Greek presence in the Decapolis in 330 B.C. The Roman general Pompey organized that league of city-states and assumed control of the area in 64–63 B.C. in order to control the trade route from Arabia to Damascus and to protect the eastern frontier. Although the Decapolis comprised more than ten city-states during much of its history, it retained the original name. During New Testament times, the pagan cities in the Decapolis—located to the south and east of the Sea of Galilee—remained a league of free city-states under the umbrella of Roman authority.

The Glory of the Decapolis

Today the ruins of the Decapolis district (derived from the Greek word *Decapolis* that meant "ten cities") still provide evidence of its Greek splendor and seductive, Hellenistic allure:

- A fifteen-mile-long aqueduct brought water to Susita, a city built on a thirty-five-acre plateau. One of the modern Hellenistic cities of the Decapolis, Susita boasted pagan temples, magnificent examples of Greek architecture, paved streets, and fountains.
- In other cities, temples honored local gods and glorified the excesses of pleasure.
- Located about five miles from the Sea of Galilee, the beautiful bath complex at Hammat Gader used hot mineral springs from the nearby Gilead Mountains. At least eight pools—including one more than 100 feet long that featured thirty-two marble fountains—soothed bathers, who no doubt came to the region to find healing in the warm baths and to worship their gods of healing.
- Colonnaded streets, running water, and marble fountains were common in the cities of the Decapolis, as were buildings such as theaters, stadiums, and temples that represented Greek ideals.

The Culture of the Decapolis

The cities of the Decapolis were fully immersed in Greek culture. Hellenism—the humanistic religion of the Greeks—glorified sexuality, the human form, and the excesses of pleasure, violence, and wealth. It preached that truth could be known only through the human mind and that pleasure was a crucial goal in life. Festivals that celebrated pagan holidays and theaters that portrayed erotic themes were a part of daily life in the Decapolis.

Although the religious Jews of Jesus' day opposed the values and practices of Hellenism, the Greek educational system of the region had instilled Greek ideas into generations of young Jewish people. Young Jews read Greek mythology and philosophy and learned to draw and sculpt the forms of Greek gods. The Pharisees, who were devoted to keeping God's people faithful to Torah, constantly admonished young Jews who were intrigued by Greek culture.

Hope for the Decapolis

Jesus deliberately brought the gospel to the people in this region because they needed the "therapy" that He alone could provide. The pagan gods and ideals of Hellenism provided only a false hope.

- After Jesus met a demon-possessed man and drove out his demons, the man told the inhabitants of a nearby city (probably Susita) what had happened to him (Mark 5:1–20). Perhaps as a result of seeing the demon-possessed man healed, a number of people became Christians, making the city a center of early Christianity. Remains of at least five large churches have been found in Susita.
- When people found no cure in the baths at Hammat Gader, some of them turned to Jesus, whose healing powers were known in the Decapolis (Mark 7:31–37). Even though the culture of the Decapolis was sophisticated and offered "healing" for some people, the people needed Jesus' healing power most of all.

DATA FILE

The History of the Decapolis

Alexander the Great established a Greek presence in the Decapolis in 330 B.C. The Roman general Pompey organized that league of city-states and assumed control of the area in 64–63 B.C. in order to control the trade route from Arabia to Damascus and to protect the eastern frontier. Although the Decapolis comprised more than ten city-states during much of its history, it retained the original name. During New Testament times, the pagan cities in the Decapolis—located to the south and east of the Sea of Galilee—remained a league of free city-states under the umbrella of Roman authority.

The Glory of the Decapolis

Today the ruins of the Decapolis district (derived from the Greek word *Decapolis* that meant "ten cities") still provide evidence of its Greek splendor and seductive, Hellenistic allure:

- A fifteen-mile-long aqueduct brought water to Susita, a city built on a thirty-five-acre plateau. One of the modern Hellenistic cities of the Decapolis, Susita boasted pagan temples, magnificent examples of Greek architecture, paved streets, and fountains.
- In other cities, temples honored local gods and glorified the excesses of pleasure.
- Located about five miles from the Sea of Galilee, the beautiful bath complex at Hammat Gader used hot mineral springs from the nearby Gilead Mountains. At least eight pools—including one more than 100 feet long that featured thirty-two marble fountains—soothed bathers, who no doubt came to the region to find healing in the warm baths and to worship their gods of healing.
- Colonnaded streets, running water, and marble fountains were common in the cities of the Decapolis, as were buildings such as theaters, stadiums, and temples that represented Greek ideals.

The Culture of the Decapolis

The cities of the Decapolis were fully immersed in Greek culture. Hellenism—the humanistic religion of the Greeks—glorified sexuality, the human form, and the excesses of pleasure, violence, and wealth. It preached that truth could be known only through the human mind and that pleasure was a crucial goal in life. Festivals that celebrated pagan holidays and theaters that portrayed erotic themes were a part of daily life in the Decapolis.

Although the religious Jews of Jesus' day opposed the values and practices of Hellenism, the Greek educational system of the region had instilled Greek ideas into generations of young Jewish people. Young Jews read Greek mythology and philosophy and learned to draw and sculpt the forms of Greek gods. The Pharisees, who were devoted to keeping God's people faithful to Torah, constantly admonished young Jews who were intrigued by Greek culture.

Hope for the Decapolis

Jesus deliberately brought the gospel to the people in this region because they needed the "therapy" that He alone could provide. The pagan gods and ideals of Hellenism provided only a false hope.

- After Jesus met a demon-possessed man and drove out his demons, the man told the inhabitants of a nearby city (probably Susita) what had happened to him (Mark 5:1–20). Perhaps as a result of seeing the demon-possessed man healed, a number of people became Christians, making the city a center of early Christianity. Remains of at least five large churches have been found in Susita.
- When people found no cure in the baths at Hammat Gader, some of them turned to Jesus, whose healing powers were known in the Decapolis (Mark 7:31–37). Even though the culture of the Decapolis was sophisticated and offered "healing" for some people, the people needed Jesus' healing power most of all.

PLANNING NOTES:

land against demons that controlled an unsaved man. Once again, He demonstrated His power over evil.

✏ 2. In Luke 8:30–33, the sea into which the demonized pigs ran is referred to as what region?

Suggested Response: the Abyss.

a. What does the word *Abyss* symbolize in the book of Revelation? (See Revelation 9:1–3, 11; 11:7; 17:8; 20:1–4.)

Suggested Responses: It symbolizes a place of great evil where Satan and his demonic beings live and where God will cast Satan and his angels.

b. What, then, is the significance of the pigs rushing into the sea and drowning?

Suggested Responses: the demons were defeated and were sent to the place that God had reserved for them, where they could no longer work their evil on humankind.

✏ 3. Jesus had demonstrated His power over demons many times. Two such accounts are recorded in Mark 1:21–28 and Mark 9:14–29. Please read these accounts and answer the following questions.

a. Did the demons recognize who Jesus was? How did they respond to Him?

Suggested Responses: In each case, they recognized Him immediately. One demon cried out a fearful challenge, the other threw its victim into a violent seizure.

b. How did Jesus confront the demons? What was the result?

Suggested Responses: Jesus commanded each demon to come out, and the demons responded immediately by shrieking and causing their victims to convulse as they left.

c. What was the people's response?

Suggested Responses: They were amazed by Jesus' power and authority over evil spirits.

d. What difficulty had the disciples faced in casting out the demon that possessed the boy? What was the solution?

Suggested Responses: They had failed to cast out the demon and did not know why; the father appears to have had some difficulty in believing in God's power. Jesus explained to His disciples that that particular demon could only be cast out by prayer.

✏ 4. What can we learn from Jesus' confrontation with evil that applies to our lives today? (See Matthew 4:23–25.)

Suggested Responses: God's power is stronger than evil, we can count on Jesus when we face evil, Satan appears to be stronger than he really is, Jesus holds the key to victory over Satan, we are to take the message and power of Christ to centers of evil, only the power of God can overcome evil, etc.

32 The Death and Resurrection of the Messiah

Topic B: Jesus' Commitment to Confronting Evil

1. Immediately after Jesus defeated the storm—the power of evil manifested by the sea—whom did He meet? Explain the possible link between these two events. (See Mark 5:1–13; Luke 8:26–33.)

2. In Luke 8:30–33, the sea into which the demonized pigs ran is referred to as what region?

   a. What does the word *Abyss* symbolize in the book of Revelation? (See Revelation 9:1–3, 11; 11:7; 17:8; 20:1–4.)

   b. What, then, is the significance of the pigs rushing into the sea and drowning?

3. Jesus had demonstrated His power over demons many times. Two such accounts are recorded in Mark 1:21–28 and Mark 9:14–29. Please read these accounts and answer the following questions.

   a. Did the demons recognize who Jesus was? How did they respond to Him?

Session Two: Piercing the Darkness 33

   b. How did Jesus confront the demons? What was the result?

   c. What was the people's response?

   d. What difficulty had the disciples faced in casting out the demon that possessed the boy? What was the solution?

4. What can we learn from Jesus' confrontation with evil that applies to our lives today? (See Matthew 4:23–25.)

Topic C: A Man Who Had Deep Needs

1. Describe the condition of the demon-possessed man. In what way(s) might he have posed a threat to Jesus and His disciples? (See Mark 5:1–5.)

2. How did the man react to Jesus? Why? (See Mark 5:6–8; Luke 8:28.)

Topic C: A Man Who Had Deep Needs

✎ 1. Describe the condition of the demon-possessed man. In what way(s) might he have posed a threat to Jesus and His disciples? (See Mark 5:1–5.)

Suggested Responses: He was wild, couldn't be held by chains, and nobody could control him; he roamed the hills day and night; he lived in the tombs and would cry out and cut himself; he was naked, which indicated that he was under Satan's control. Certainly he was unpredictable. His unrestrained physical strength was a threat to any individual or even group of people who crossed his path.

✎ 2. How did the man react to Jesus? Why? (See Mark 5:6–8; Luke 8:28.)

Suggested Responses: The man noticed Jesus from a far distance, ran to Jesus, fell on his knees before Him, and shouted at Jesus about not wanting to be tortured because Jesus had commanded the evil spirit to come out of him. Clearly the demons recognized who Jesus was and were fearful of their fate in His hands.

✎ 3. What was the name of the demons? (See Mark 5:9.)

Suggested Responses: Legion. (This word may have a double meaning. It can mean a large number. Also, a legion of 6,000 Roman soldiers were stationed at the Decapolis, and in Scripture "Rome" sometimes symbolized evil and even the devil himself. Furthermore, the symbol of that Roman legion was a boar's head.)

DATA FILE

Who is Beelzebub?
- Baal-Zebul was the god of the Philistines and means "Exalted Baal" or "Prince Baal."
- The Hebrew name *Baal-Zebub* is a parody of Baal-Zebul and means "Lord of the Flies" (2 Kings 1:2–4).
- In the Greek language of the New Testament, the name becomes *Beelzebub*. Jesus used the name *Beelzebub* for Satan, the prince of demons. (See Matthew 10:25; 12:24–27; Mark 3:22; Luke 11:14–26.) This usage seems to indicate that Old Testament Baal worship was satanic—a tool Satan used to draw the Israelite people away from God.

What Is His Goal?
- First and foremost, Satan is the enemy of God's plan of salvation.
- He has devoted himself to destroying God's plan of salvation since the temptation of Adam and Eve in the Garden of Eden (Genesis 3).
- He tried to use Herod to kill baby Jesus (Matthew 2:13–18).
- He tempted Jesus at the beginning of His ministry, hoping that Jesus would compromise His mission (Matthew 4:1–11).

How Did Jesus Confront Him?
Jesus confronted Satan directly while He was on earth and had numerous confrontations with Satan's demons as well:
- He cast the demon out of the man in the synagogue (Mark 1:23–28).
- He cast a "legion" of demons out of the man of the tombs (Mark 5:1–20).
- He cast a demon out of a boy who couldn't speak and had seizures (Mark 9:14–29).
- He cast many demons out of people after He healed Peter's mother-in-law (Matthew 8:16).

    b. How did Jesus confront the demons? What was the result?

    c. What was the people's response?

    d. What difficulty had the disciples faced in casting out the demon that possessed the boy? What was the solution?

4. What can we learn from Jesus' confrontation with evil that applies to our lives today? (See Matthew 4:23–25.)

Topic C: A Man Who Had Deep Needs

1. Describe the condition of the demon-possessed man. In what way(s) might he have posed a threat to Jesus and His disciples? (See Mark 5:1–5.)

2. How did the man react to Jesus? Why? (See Mark 5:6–8; Luke 8:28.)

3. What was the name of the demons? (See Mark 5:9.)

DATA FILE

Who is Beelzebub?
- Baal-Zebul was the god of the Philistines and means "Exalted Baal" or "Prince Baal."
- The Hebrew name *Baal-Zebub* is a parody of Baal-Zebul and means "Lord of the Flies" (2 Kings 1:2–4).
- In the Greek language of the New Testament, the name becomes *Beelzebub*. Jesus used the name *Beelzebub* for Satan, the prince of demons. (See Matthew 10:25; 12:24–27; Mark 3:22; Luke 11:14–26.) This usage seems to indicate that Old Testament Baal worship was satanic—a tool Satan used to draw the Israelite people away from God.

What Is His Goal?
- First and foremost, Satan is the enemy of God's plan of salvation.
- He has devoted himself to destroying God's plan of salvation since the temptation of Adam and Eve in the Garden of Eden (Genesis 3).
- He tried to use Herod to kill baby Jesus (Matthew 2:13–18).
- He tempted Jesus at the beginning of His ministry, hoping that Jesus would compromise His mission (Matthew 4:1–11).

How Did Jesus Confront Him?
Jesus confronted Satan directly while He was on earth and had numerous confrontations with Satan's demons as well:
- He cast the demon out of the man in the synagogue (Mark 1:23–28).
- He cast a "legion" of demons out of the man of the tombs (Mark 5:1–20).
- He cast a demon out of a boy who couldn't speak and had seizures (Mark 9:14–29).
- He cast many demons out of people after He healed Peter's mother-in-law (Matthew 8:16).

✏ 4.   After Jesus sent the demons away, how did the man change? (See Luke
        8:34–35.)

       Suggested Responses: He sat peacefully at Jesus' feet. He was dressed and think-
       ing clearly again.

✏ 5.   Why do you think the local people reacted as they did to the healing of this
        man? (See Luke 8:35–37.)

       Suggested Responses: The man was utterly hopeless in their eyes, so they were
       afraid of the power that had set him free; they lost 2,000 pigs, which probably
       made a negative impact on the local economy; since the pigs were sacred ani-
       mals to them, they may have sensed the spiritual nature of Jesus' power and
       were afraid of a spiritual power greater than that of their gods. Jesus was upset-
       ting the status quo in a big way!

✏ 6.   How was Jesus received during His second visit? What accounted for the dif-
        ference? (See Mark 5:18–20; 7:31–37; Matthew 15:29–31.)

       Suggested Responses: The people came to Him in droves, bringing many sick
       people to be healed. The former demoniac had obeyed Jesus and told others
       what God had done for him. Clearly his testimony of Jesus' miraculous power
       had opened their hearts and minds.

Topic D: Old Testament Heroes Who Confronted Evil*

✏ 1.   Elijah (See 1 Kings 18:16–40.)

       a.   What was the evil Elijah confronted? What did he say to King Ahab and
            the Israelites? (See 1 Kings 18:16–21.)

            Suggested Responses: The worship of Baal, the strongest supporters of which
            were King Ahab and Queen Jezebel. He told King Ahab to summon the
            Israelites to Mount Carmel, and to bring the 450 prophets of Baal and the
            400 prophets of Asherah who were eating at Queen Jezebel's table. Once
            the Israelites were assembled, he told them they could no longer waver but
            needed to choose which God they would serve.

       b.   What "test" did Elijah propose? (See1 Kings 18:22–25.)

            Suggested Responses: Elijah proposed that the Baal prophets would sacrifice
            a bull, which was Baal's symbol, and so would he. Each side would place their
            bull on an altar of wood and call upon their god. The god who answered with
            fire would be the true God.

       c.   What was the result? (See 1 Kings 18:26–40.)

            Suggested Responses: Although the prophets of Baal cried out long and hard,
            Baal—the god who was portrayed with a lightning bolt in his hand—didn't

---

*Note: Other examples of Old Testament people who confronted evil include: Deb-
orah (Judges 4), Esther (Esther 3:8–11; 4; 5:1–8; 7:1–10), and Josiah (2 Chronicles
34:1–11, 29–33).

4. After Jesus sent the demons away, how did the man change? (See Luke 8:34–35.)

5. Why do you think the local people reacted as they did to the healing of this man? (See Luke 8:35–37.)

6. How was Jesus received during His second visit? What accounted for the difference? (See Mark 5:18–20; 7:31–37; Matthew 15:29–31.)

Topic D: Old Testament Heroes Who Confronted Evil*

1. *Elijah* (See 1 Kings 18:16–40.)

   a. What was the evil Elijah confronted? What did he say to King Ahab and the Israelites? (See 1 Kings 18:16–21.)

   b. What "test" did Elijah propose? (See 1 Kings 18:22–25.)

*Note: Other examples of Old Testament people who confronted evil include: Deborah (Judges 4), Esther (Esther 3:8–11; 4; 5:1–8; 7:1–10), and Josiah (2 Chronicles 34:1–11, 29–33).

   c. What was the result? (See 1 Kings 18:26–40.)

2. *David* (See 1 Samuel 17.)

   a. Who did Satan use to defy Israel and their God? (See 1 Samuel 17:4–10.)

   b. Who battled the giant? Why? By whose power was the giant killed? (See 1 Samuel 17:32–37, 45–50.)

3. *Phinehas* (See Numbers 25:1–13.)

   a. What were the Israelites doing that was evil in the sight of God? (See Numbers 25:1–3.)

   b. What strong measures did God order to confront this evil? (See Numbers 25:4–5.)

   c. What did Phinehas do? What was the result? (See Numbers 25:6–9.)

answer; the God of Israel answered with fire from heaven and burned up every bit of the sacrifice—even the twelve stones representing the twelve tribes of Israel, the water Elijah poured over the sacrifice, and the surrounding soil. Then the Israelites killed all the prophets of Baal.

2. David (See 1 Samuel 17.)

   a. Who did Satan use to defy Israel and their God? (See 1 Samuel 17:4–10.)

   Suggested Response: a Philistine giant named Goliath, who was more than nine feet tall.

   b. Who battled the giant? Why? By whose power was the giant killed? (See 1 Samuel 17:32–37, 45–50.)

   Suggested Responses: a shepherd boy named David. He was greatly offended by Goliath's insults to God. David trusted in God's protection and power and announced that God would deliver the giant into his hand specifically so that God would be honored among the nations.

3. Phinehas (See Numbers 25:1–13.)

   a. What were the Israelites doing that was evil in the sight of God? (See Numbers 25:1–3.)

   Suggested Responses: The men were engaging in sexual immorality with Moabite women and began worshiping Baal.

   b. What strong measures did God order to confront this evil? (See Numbers 25:4–5.)

   Suggested Response: God ordered Moses to kill every man who had worshiped false gods.

   c. What did Phinehas do? What was the result? (See Numbers 25:6–9.)

   Suggested Responses: Even as the people were mourning the evil in which they had engaged, one man brazenly brought a Moabite woman into his tent. Phinehas immediately killed the man and the woman, and a plague that had killed 24,000 Israelites ended.

38   The Death and Resurrection of the Messiah

    c.   What was the result? (See 1 Kings 18:26–40.)

  2. *David* (See 1 Samuel 17.)

    a.   Who did Satan use to defy Israel and their God? (See 1 Samuel 17:4–10.)

    b.   Who battled the giant? Why? By whose power was the giant killed? (See 1 Samuel 17:32–37, 45–50.)

  3. *Phinehas* (See Numbers 25:1–13.)

    a.   What were the Israelites doing that was evil in the sight of God? (See Numbers 25:1–3.)

    b.   What strong measures did God order to confront this evil? (See Numbers 25:4–5.)

    c.   What did Phinehas do? What was the result? (See Numbers 25:6–9.)

PLANNING NOTES:

ғᴀɪᴛʜ ʟᴇѕѕᴏɴ

10 minutes

Time for Reflection (6 minutes)

It's time for each of us to think quietly about how today's lesson applies to each of us. On page 39 of your Participant's Guide, you'll find a passage of Scripture. Let's each read this passage silently and take the next few minutes to consider the questions that follow the Scripture passage.

Please do not talk during this time. It's a time when we all can reflect on how God would have us pierce the darkness of our culture.

The Scripture passage and questions are reproduced in their entirety in the Participant's Guide on pages 39–41.

A furious squall came up, and the waves broke over the boat, so that it was nearly swamped. Jesus was in the stern, sleeping on a cushion. The disciples woke him and said to him, "Teacher, don't you care if we drown?" He got up, rebuked the wind and said to the waves, "Quiet! Be still!" Then the wind died down and it was completely calm. He said to his disciples, "Why are you so afraid? Do you still have no faith?" They were terrified and asked each other, "Who is this? Even the wind and the waves obey him!" They went across the lake to the region of the Gerasenes. When Jesus got out of the boat, a man with an evil spirit came from the tombs to meet him. . . . When he saw Jesus from a distance, he ran and fell on his knees in front of him. He shouted at the top of his voice, "What do you want with me, Jesus, Son of the Most High God? Swear to God that you won't torture me!" For Jesus had said to him, "Come out of this man, you evil spirit!" Then Jesus asked him, "What is your name?" "My name is Legion," he replied, "for we are many." And he begged Jesus again and again not to send them out of the area. A large herd of pigs was feeding on the nearby hillside. The demons begged Jesus, "Send us among the pigs; allow us to go into them." He gave them permission, and the evil spirits came out and went into the pigs. The herd, about two thousand in number, rushed down the steep bank into the lake and were drowned. Those tending the pigs ran off and reported this in the town and countryside, and the people went out to see what had happened. When they came to Jesus, they saw the man who had been possessed by the legion of demons, sitting there, dressed and in his right mind; and they were afraid. . . . As Jesus was getting into the boat, the man who had been demon-possessed begged to go with him. Jesus did not let him, but said, "Go home to your family and tell them how much the Lord has done for you, and how he has had mercy on you." So the man went away and began to tell in the Decapolis how much Jesus had done for him. And all the people were amazed.

MARK 4:37–5:2; 5:6–15, 18–20

1. Life is a spiritual battleground between good and evil—God and Satan. Are you active in the battle, or are you "on the sidelines"?

faith Lesson

Time for Reflection

The following passage of Scripture portrays Jesus as He pierced the darkness of evil in His world. Read this passage silently and take the next few minutes to consider your response to the evil that surrounds you.

A furious squall came up, and the waves broke over the boat, so that it was nearly swamped. Jesus was in the stern, sleeping on a cushion. The disciples woke him and said to him, "Teacher, don't you care if we drown?" He got up, rebuked the wind and said to the waves, "Quiet! Be still!" Then the wind died down and it was completely calm. He said to his disciples, "Why are you so afraid? Do you still have no faith?" They were terrified and asked each other, "Who is this? Even the wind and the waves obey him!" They went across the lake to the region of the Gerasenes. When Jesus got out of the boat, a man with an evil spirit came from the tombs to meet him. . . . When he saw Jesus from a distance, he ran and fell on his knees in front of him. He shouted at the top of his voice, "What do you want with me, Jesus, Son of the Most High God? Swear to God that you won't torture me!" For Jesus had said to him, "Come out of this man, you evil spirit!" Then Jesus asked him, "What is your name?" "My name is Legion," he replied, "for we are many." And he begged Jesus again and again not to send them out of the area. A large herd of pigs was feeding on the nearby hillside. The demons begged Jesus, "Send us among the pigs; allow us to go into them." He gave them permission, and the evil spirits came out and went into the pigs. The herd, about two thousand in number, rushed down the steep bank into the lake and were drowned. Those tending the pigs ran off and reported this in the town and countryside, and the people went out to see what had happened. When they came to Jesus, they saw the man who had been possessed by the legion of

demons, sitting there, dressed and in his right mind; and they were afraid. . . . As Jesus was getting into the boat, the man who had been demon-possessed begged to go with him. Jesus did not let him, but said, "Go home to your family and tell them how much the Lord has done for you, and how he has had mercy on you." So the man went away and began to tell in the Decapolis how much Jesus had done for him. And all the people were amazed.

MARK 4:37–5:2; 5:6–15, 18–20

1. Life is a spiritual battleground between good and evil—God and Satan. Are you active in the battle, or are you "on the sidelines"?

2. When you come face-to-face with evil, are you, like the disciples, afraid that Jesus will allow you to perish? What message from this session can help strengthen your faith and bolster your courage when evil threatens?

3. What does this session teach about the impact that one person can have if he or she has a grateful heart and a desire to serve God?

PLANNING NOTES:

👉 2.   When you come face to face with evil, are you, like the disciples, afraid that Jesus will allow you to perish? What message from this session can help strengthen your faith and bolster your courage when evil threatens?

👉 3.   What does this session teach about the impact that one person can have if he or she has a grateful heart and a desire to serve God?

👉 4.   What keeps you from sharing what Jesus has done for you with the people you see every day? With whom might God want you to share what He has done for you?

👉 5.   What might be the impact on your culture if you were to confront evil whenever you encounter it? If you do not challenge evil?

> As soon as participants have spent six minutes reflecting on the above questions, get the entire group's attention and move to the next section.

Action Points (4 minutes)

> *The following points are reproduced on pages 41–42 of the Participant's Guide.*

Now it's time to wrap up our session.

> Give participants a moment to make the transition from their own thoughts to giving you their full attention.

I'd like to take a moment to summarize the key points we explored. After I have reviewed these points, I will give you a moment to jot down an action step (or steps) that you will commit to this week as a result of what you have learned today.

> Read each point and pause after each so that participants can consider and write out their commitment.

👉 1.   *Jesus—the light of the world (John 8:12)—deliberately and boldly pierced the spiritual darkness of pagan Decapolis.* With great authority, He appropriated God's power to confront and defeat the devil on his own turf—on the sea and among the pagan people of the Decapolis. As a result, many people wanted Him to leave, but one man was delivered into a new life.

Sometimes it is easy to ignore rampant evil around us and hide in our "safe" communities and churches. At other times, it's easy to compromise with sin. God, however, calls His people to boldly confront the power of evil wherever it is. He calls us to be His people in a culture that doesn't hold His values. He calls us to respond compassionately and appropriately to both personal evil—such as immorality, injustice, and hatred—and natural evil—such as death and disease. When we do that, we can expect people to resist and resent us—and the message of Christ that we bring.

Are you willing to step out of your secure environment, to interact with people who hold vastly different values, or to pierce the darkness of a place with which you are unfamiliar and uncomfortable? Armed with the power

demons, sitting there, dressed and in his right mind; and they were afraid. . . . As Jesus was getting into the boat, the man who had been demon-possessed begged to go with him. Jesus did not let him, but said, "Go home to your family and tell them how much the Lord has done for you, and how he has had mercy on you." So the man went away and began to tell in the Decapolis how much Jesus had done for him. And all the people were amazed.

MARK 4:37–5:2; 5:6–15, 18–20

1. Life is a spiritual battleground between good and evil—God and Satan. Are you active in the battle, or are you "on the sidelines"?

2. When you come face-to-face with evil, are you, like the disciples, afraid that Jesus will allow you to perish? What message from this session can help strengthen your faith and bolster your courage when evil threatens?

3. What does this session teach about the impact that one person can have if he or she has a grateful heart and a desire to serve God?

4. What keeps you from sharing what Jesus has done for you with the people you see every day? With whom might God want you to share what He has done for you?

5. What might be the impact on your culture if you were to confront evil whenever you encounter it? If you do not challenge evil?

Action Points

Take a moment to review the key points you explored today. Then write down the action step (or steps) that you will commit to this week as a result of what you have discovered.

1. *Jesus—the light of the world (John 8:12) deliberately and boldly pierced the spiritual darkness of pagan Decapolis.* With great authority, He appropriated God's power to confront and defeat the devil on his own turf—on the sea and among the pagan people of the Decapolis. As a result, many people wanted Him to leave, but one man was delivered into a new life.

Sometimes it is easy to ignore rampant evil around us and hide in our "safe" communities and churches. At other times, it's easy to compromise with sin. God, however, calls His people to boldly confront the power of evil wherever it is. He calls us to be His people in a culture that doesn't hold His values. He calls us to respond compassionately and appropriately to both personal evil—such as immorality, injustice, and hatred—and natural evil—such as death and

PLANNING NOTES:

and name of Jesus, will you allow God to use you to confront immorality, hatred, injustice, and other evils? If so, what might He be calling you to do?

2. *The ministry of one person is powerful!* After healing the demon-possessed man, Jesus told him to go home and tell people what God had done for him. As a result of the man's obedience, many people were drawn to Christ, and a strong Christian community developed in the Decapolis.

In fact, that area of the Decapolis became a cornerstone of the early Christian church. Representatives from the Decapolis served on the early church councils that helped define the important creeds of Christianity and establish the canon, the books that are in the Bible today!

God asks us to tell other people what He has done for us. When we do that, He can work miracles. His light can pierce the darkest evil. Just as that one man made an eternal difference in his pagan community, you can make an eternal difference in your community. What has Jesus done for you that you can share with others? What is your commitment to testify of what God has done for you?

closing prayer
I minute

As we've seen, God cares deeply about people who are enslaved by evil. In His power, we can—like Jesus—go to where evil is and confront it. And, like the man who had been demon possessed, we can simply share what Jesus has done for us and make an eternal impact. Let's close in prayer.

Dear God, help us to realize how truly awesome Your power over evil is. Thank You for giving us that same power to pierce the darkness. Help us to be more aware of what You do for us. Give us a story to share with others. Guide us to people who need to receive the healing only You can provide. Give us the courage to share what You have done for us with other people who are enslaved by evil so they, too, can know You and be set free. Amen.

disease. When we do that, we can expect people to resist and resent us—and the message of Christ that we bring.

Are you willing to step out of your secure environment, to interact with people who hold vastly different values, or to pierce the darkness of a place with which you are unfamiliar and uncomfortable? Armed with the power and name of Jesus, will you allow God to use you to confront immorality, hatred, injustice, and other evils? If so, what might He be calling you to do?

2. *The ministry of one person is powerful!* After healing the demon-possessed man, Jesus told him to go home and tell people what God had done for him. As a result of the man's obedience, many people were drawn to Christ, and a strong Christian community developed in the Decapolis.

In fact, that area of the Decapolis became a cornerstone of the early Christian church. Representatives from the Decapolis served on the early church councils that helped define the important creeds of Christianity and establish the canon, the books that are in the Bible today!

God asks us to tell other people what He has done for us. When we do that, He can work miracles. His light can pierce the darkest evil. Just as that one man made an eternal difference in his pagan community, you can make an eternal difference in your community. What has Jesus done for you that you can share with others? What is your commitment to testify of what God has done for you?

gates of hades (hell)

before you lead

Synopsis

Shortly before His crucifixion, Jesus took his disciples to Caesarea Philippi, a pagan city built by Herod Philip, who was a son of Herod the Great. This city was located in the northeastern part of Israel at the foot of Mount Hermon, Israel's highest mountain. For many years, people in this area had worshiped false gods, including Baal (Joshua 11:16–17; 12:7). And several miles away, in the city of Dan, King Jeroboam had set up the golden calf on a "high place" (1 Kings 12:25–31). During Jesus' time, the people in the region worshiped Greek fertility gods.

Caesarea Philippi was about twenty-five miles away from the area in which Jesus focused His ministry. It may surprise us that Jesus deliberately led His disciples on a two-day walk over mountainous terrain in order to give them fifteen minutes of teaching at this thriving center of pagan religion. Yet this was where He chose to give His disciples their "graduation talk." Here He taught them a profound lesson about His purpose and the mission to which He had called them.

This video was filmed at the base of a cliff that is more than one hundred feet high. There the people built temples and shrines dedicated to various gods, including "Pan," the fertility god of mountains and forests. (In fact, the ancient name of Caesarea Philippi was *Panias*—named after Pan.) This cliff could also be referred to as the "Rock of the Gods," because idols and statues of gods and goddesses were placed into small openings cut into the rock.

In the lush area at the base of this cliff is one of the three springs from which the Jordan River flows. At one time, the spring of water gushed from a cave, which has since collapsed. To the pagan mind, the cave was a "gate of Hades" because the ancient people believed that gods entered the underworld through caves. They also believed that Baal caused the dry season each year by going into caves to enter the underworld.

In this setting, Jesus taught His disciples and asked, "Who do people say the Son of Man is?" After listening to their answers, He asked, "Who do you say that I am?"

Peter, who may have been standing near the pagan shrines, stated, "You are Christ, the Son of the living God."

Jesus then said, "You are Peter, and on this rock I will build my church, and the gates of Hades [hell] will not overcome it."

Different traditions emphasize different aspects of this statement. Catholic tradition emphasizes that the church is built on Peter and his work. Protestant tradition emphasizes that Peter's confession is the rock on which the church is built. In consideration of the setting, Ray Vander Laan suggests that Jesus also intended to communicate a symbolic meaning: that His church would be built on the pagan "rock"—the rock into which idols had been placed, the rock on which the golden calf had been placed, the rock that represented pagan worship and ungodly values.

Jesus was saying, in effect, "My church will come and replace the very power and strength of the devil." Jesus then added that "the gates of Hades" (hell) would not prove stronger than His church. Because gates are designed to keep out enemies, Jesus was saying that His church would overcome even the gates of hell if its faith remained rooted in Him—the Messiah—and its methods remained His methods.

In the powerful setting of an ancient shrine, Ray Vander Laan encourages us to confront ungodly values and not to hide in our safe, secure enclaves. Like Jesus' disciples, who after three years of preparation were ready to "graduate" and begin their ministry, we are to prepare ourselves to confront the gates of hell—the devil's strength and power. In Jesus' power, those gates will fall.

Key Points of This Lesson

You will guide participants in understanding:

1. *The history, geography, and culture of Caesarea Philippi.* The region was a stronghold of Satanic activity. Its people had worshiped false gods—including Baal, whom Jesus called the devil—for many years.
2. *What Jesus taught His disciples during their "graduation talk."* Jesus promised that His church would be stronger than the "gates of Hades." He told the disciples that they were to challenge the most pagan expressions of the power of evil. On that "rock"—at the place where Satan is strongest in society, where ungodly values and beliefs are boldly promoted—Jesus would build His church.
3. *The mission of the church.* As the church of Jesus, we are to prepare ourselves to actively confront the gates of Hades (hell). In the power of God, we are to challenge anything that is not godly—through our attitudes, words, and actions.

Session Outline (55 minutes)

I. Introduction (5 minutes)
Welcome
What's to Come
Questions to Think About

II. Video Presentation "Gates of Hades (Hell)" (19 minutes)

III. Group Discovery (20 minutes)
Video Highlights
Small Group Bible Discovery

IV. Faith Lesson (9 minutes)
Time for Reflection
Action Points

V. Closing Prayer (2 minutes)

Materials

No additional materials are needed for this session. Simply view the video prior to leading the session so you are familiar with its main points.

gates of hades (hell)

introduction

5 minutes

Welcome

> Assemble the participants together. Welcome them to session three of *Faith Lessons on the Death and Resurrection of the Messiah.*

What's to Come

In the region of Caesarea Philippi, a longstanding center of pagan worship, Jesus told His disciples that He would build His church on the very power base of Satan and that even the gates of Hades (hell) could not stand against it. In this session, Ray Vander Laan will encourage us to use the opportunities and power that God has given us to go on the offensive against the gates of hell—meaning any aspects of our culture and society that do not reflect God's ways.

Questions to Think About

> *Participant's Guide page* 43.

Turn to page 43 of your Participant's Guide. Let's consider several questions that will prepare us for the video we'll see in a few moments.

> Ask each question and solicit a few responses from group members.

1. As you consider the Christian church today, would you say that it is on the offensive against evil, or has it taken a defensive position? Explain your answer and give examples to illustrate it.

   Suggested Responses: Allow participants to share their viewpoints so that they begin thinking about the role of the church in culture.

2. Many people through the centuries have boldly attacked the forces of evil for the sake of the gospel. Name some biblical characters or more contemporary people who have made an impact for God by confronting evil in their worlds. Also identify the evil they confronted.

   Suggested Responses: These will vary. Allow people to share examples.

3. Think about what represents evil in your world. What are some of the ways Christians could boldly stand against those evils in the name and power of Jesus—in their neighborhoods, workplaces, or schools?

   Suggested Responses: may include people who stand up for biblical truth in a classroom, challenge injustice, write to companies that promote violence in the media, support certain legislation, etc.

   Let's keep these ideas in mind as we view the video.

SESSION THREE

Gates of Hades (Hell)

Questions to Think About

1. As you consider the Christian church today, would you say that it is on the offensive against evil, or has it taken a defensive position? Explain your answer and give examples to illustrate it.

2. Many people through the centuries have boldly attacked the forces of evil for the sake of the gospel. Name some biblical characters or more contemporary people who have made an impact for God by confronting evil in their worlds. Also identify the evil they confronted.

3. Think about what represents evil in your world. What are some of the ways Christians could boldly stand against those evils in the name and power of Jesus—in their neighborhoods, workplaces, or schools?

43

video presentation

19 minutes

Participant's Guide page 44.

On page 44 of your Participant's Guide, you will find space in which to take notes on key points as we watch this video.

Leader's Video Observations

The Evil of Caesarea Philippi

Jesus' Message to His Disciples

The Mission of the Church

Group Discovery

20 minutes

If your group has seven or more members, use the **Video Highlights** with the entire group (5 minutes), then break into small groups of three to five to discuss the **Small Group Bible Discovery** (10 minutes). Then reassemble the group to discuss the key points discovered (5 minutes).

If your group has fewer than seven members, begin with the **Video Highlights** (5 minutes), then do one or more of the topics found in the **Small Group Bible Discovery** as a group (10 minutes). Finally, spend five minutes at the end discussing points that had an impact on participants.

44   The Death and Resurrection of the Messiah

video Notes

The Evil of Caesarea Philippi

Jesus' Message to His Disciples

The Mission of the Church

Video Highlights (5 minutes)

Here you'll ask one or more of the following questions that directly relate to the video the participants have just seen.

Look at the map on page 45 of your Participant's Guide. Note how far Caesarea Philippi was from Capernaum and the Sea of Galilee. Note also Mount Hermon, the beginnings of the Jordan River, and the city of Dan.

1. What do you think the disciples thought as they traveled with Jesus to Caesarea Philippi?

    Suggested Responses: it was a long way from where they had spent most of their time with Jesus, must have wondered why they were going so far; it was even more pagan than the Decapolis, so they probably couldn't imagine why Jesus would want to go there; they were probably confused and questioning; etc.

2. Which part of the video made the greatest impact on you? Why?

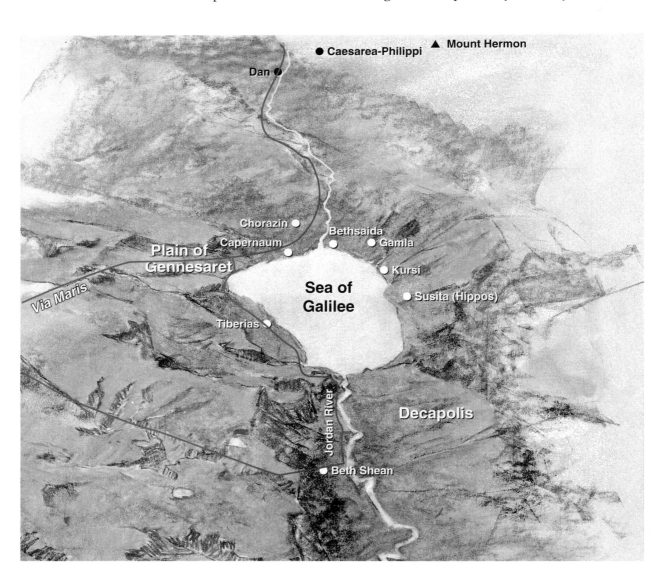

video Highlights

Look at the map of the region around the Sea of Galilee and note how far Caesarea Philippi was from Capernaum and the Sea of Galilee. Note also Mount Hermon, the beginnings of the Jordan River, and the city of Dan.

    1. What do you think the disciples thought as they traveled with Jesus to Caesarea Philippi?

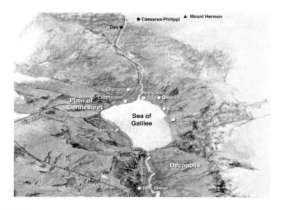

---

    2. Which part of the video made the greatest impact on you? Why?

    3. How does the perspective that the church is to take the offensive rather than the defensive against the "gates of hell" affect your view of ministry? How do you think it affected the disciples' view?

Suggested Responses: Give participants the opportunity to share what touched them.

✏ 3.   How does the perspective that the church is to take the offensive rather than the defensive against the "gates of Hades" affect your view of ministry? How do you think it affected the disciples' view?

Suggested Responses: Allow participants to share their personal views and observations of how the disciples went about fulfilling the mission to which Jesus had called them. Participants may observe that the disciples didn't shy away from confrontation, that they went out into the world, that they didn't hesitate to venture into pagan cultures around them, etc.

Small Group Bible Discovery (15 minutes)

Participant's Guide pages 47–53.

During this time, a group with fewer than seven participants will stay together. A group larger than seven participants will break into small groups and reassemble as a large group during the final five minutes. Assign each group one of the following topics. If you have more than four small groups, assign some topics to more than one group.

Let's break into groups of three to five—people sitting near you—and study some of the Bible passages and truths mentioned in the video.

Turn to pages 47–53 in your Participant's Guide. There you'll find a list of four topics. You'll have ten minutes to read and discuss the topic I'll assign to you. Choose one person in your group to be a spokesperson for your group when we discuss these topics later.

Assign each group a topic.

I'll signal you when one minute is left.

After nine minutes, let participants know that they have one minute remaining. Then reassemble the entire group. After everyone is back together, begin asking one person from each small group to briefly share a key idea with the larger group. In some cases, you may not have time for every group to share their discoveries.

As time allows, let's briefly share the key ideas that your group discussed.

Topic A: Jesus as Messiah

✏ 1.   Which roles, according to the prophet Zechariah, would *the* Messiah fulfill? (See Deuteronomy 18:18; Zechariah 6:13.)

Suggested Responses: He would be a prophet, a king, and a priest.

✏ 2.   After Jesus asked His disciples who people said He was, why do you think He asked His disciples who they thought He was? (See Matthew 16:15; Mark 8:29.)

2. Which part of the video made the greatest impact on you? Why?

3. How does the perspective that the church is to take the offensive rather than the defensive against the "gates of hell" affect your view of ministry? How do you think it affected the disciples' view?

small group bible discovery

Topic A: Jesus as Messiah

1. Which roles, according to the prophet Zechariah, would the Messiah fulfill? (See Deuteronomy 18:18; Zechariah 6:13.)

2. After Jesus asked His disciples who people said He was, why do you think He asked His disciples who they thought He was? (See Matthew 16:15; Mark 8:29.)

3. What was the significance of Peter's response to Jesus' second question? (See Matthew 16:16; Mark 8:29.)

4. After Peter made his profession, what did Jesus do? Why do you think He picked this moment to begin explaining this? (See Matthew 16:21–26.)

5. What kind of life did Isaiah the prophet predict that Jesus would have? (See Isaiah 53:1–12.)

Suggested Responses: They had never before professed that He was the Messiah; He knew how important it was for them to know Him as the Messiah, the Son of the living God; they needed to affirm their belief in Him as the Messiah before He could share with them the events that would soon unfold—His suffering, death, and resurrection.

3. What was the significance of Peter's response to Jesus' second question? (See Matthew 16:16; Mark 8:29.)

Suggested Responses: On behalf of all the disciples, Peter affirmed that Jesus was the Messiah; he stated that Jesus was the Son of the living God—contrasting Jesus with the "dead" idols around them. (Note: It appears that this was the first time during Jesus' teaching ministry that the disciples professed that He was the Messiah.)

4. After Peter made his profession, what did Jesus do? Why do you think He picked this moment to begin explaining this? (See Matthew 16:21–26.)

Suggested Responses: Jesus began to teach them about His coming suffering, death, and resurrection. As God's anointed, Jesus would complete the purposes for which He—the Messiah—had come to earth, but He knew that His disciples expected a different kind of Messiah than He would be. They needed to know that those who would serve Him must also be willing to suffer for Him.

5. What kind of life did Isaiah the prophet predict that Jesus would have? (See Isaiah 53:1–12.)

Suggested Responses: Jesus' life would be difficult. He would suffer greatly. He would carry our sin. Although He was innocent, He would be oppressed and killed.

DATA FILE

Jesus Christ the Messiah

As English-speaking Christians, we refer to our Savior as *Jesus Christ* and *Messiah*. There is great richness of meaning behind these three words.

Jesus is the English form of the name found in Greek versions of the New Testament. The Hebrew name translated *Jesus* was *Yeshua*, a shortened version of the word *Y'hoshua*, which means "Yahweh saves," and in English is translated *Joshua*.

Christ is the English translation of the Greek word *Christos*, which means *Messiah*. Therefore the words *Messiah* and *Christ* are the same, although *Messiah* better reflects the Jewish setting of Jesus' ministry.

Messiah means "anointed" and is rooted in the Old Testament. It refers to the pouring (anointing) of oil on people who were marked by God as uniquely qualified for a task or office. This anointing was a symbol of the authority a person received from God. (That's why Jesus' baptism is so significant—Matthew 3:13–17.) Every anointed person (e.g., prophet, priest, and king) was, in the sense of having been anointed, *a* messiah. The prophets predicted that one day God would send His deliverer—"the ultimate Messiah"—who would combine the roles of prophet, priest, and king. However, the people of Jesus' day emphasized the kingly role of Messiah, whom they believed would deliver them from the political oppression of Rome.

small group bible discovery

Topic A: Jesus as Messiah

1. Which roles, according to the prophet Zechariah, would the Messiah fulfill? (See Deuteronomy 18:18; Zechariah 6:13.)

2. After Jesus asked His disciples who people said He was, why do you think He asked His disciples who they thought He was? (See Matthew 16:15; Mark 8:29.)

3. What was the significance of Peter's response to Jesus' second question? (See Matthew 16:16; Mark 8:29.)

4. After Peter made his profession, what did Jesus do? Why do you think He picked this moment to begin explaining this? (See Matthew 16:21–26.)

5. What kind of life did Isaiah the prophet predict that Jesus would have? (See Isaiah 53:1–12.)

6. In light of Isaiah 53:1–12, why do you think it was so difficult for the people of Jesus' day, including the disciples, to understand what He—the Messiah—was called to do?

DATA FILE

Jesus Christ the Messiah

As English-speaking Christians, we refer to our Savior as *Jesus Christ* and *Messiah*. There is great richness of meaning behind these three words.

Jesus is the English form of the name found in Greek versions of the New Testament. The Hebrew name translated *Jesus* was *Yeshua*, a shortened version of the word *Y'hoshua*, which means "Yahweh saves," and in English is translated *Joshua*.

Christ is the English translation of the Greek word *Christos*, which means *Messiah*. Therefore the words *Messiah* and *Christ* are the same, although *Messiah* better reflects the Jewish setting of Jesus' ministry.

Messiah means "anointed" and is rooted in the Old Testament. It refers to the pouring (anointing) of oil on people who were marked by God as uniquely qualified for a task or office. This anointing was a symbol of the authority a person received from God. (That's why Jesus' baptism is so significant—Matthew 3:13–17.) Every anointed person (e.g., prophet, priest, and king) was, in the sense of having been anointed, *a* messiah. The prophets predicted that one day God would send His deliverer— "the ultimate Messiah"—who would combine the roles of prophet, priest, and king. However, the people of Jesus' day emphasized the kingly role of Messiah, whom they believed would deliver them from the political oppression of Rome.

PLANNING NOTES:

✎ 6.   In light of Isaiah 53:1–12, why do you think it was so difficult for the people of Jesus' day, including the disciples, to understand what He—the Messiah—was called to do?

Suggested Responses: The people were suffering under Roman rule and desperately wanted a political, kingly Messiah to save them from their oppressors rather than to save them from their sin.

Topic B: The Meanings of the Rock

✎ 1.   On what did Jesus promise to build His church? (See Matthew 16:18.)

Suggested Response: Jesus used the phrase "this rock."

✎ 2.   There are two major viewpoints concerning what Jesus meant by the "rock" upon which He would build His church. What does the Bible say about:
   a.   Peter—representing all the disciples—being the "rock"? (See Ephesians 2:20–21.)

   Suggested Responses: that the apostles and prophets were the foundation (rock) of which Jesus Himself was the chief cornerstone.

   b.   Peter's profession—that Jesus is the Christ, the Son of the living God—being the "rock"? (See 1 Corinthians 3:10–15; Acts 4:10–11.)

   Suggested Responses: that Jesus Christ is the foundation, the essential "rock" of the church on which we build our faith.

✎ 3.   What is the significance of the description "*this* rock" in Matthew 16:18?

Suggested Responses: Jesus apparently was referring to the rock cliff at Caesarea Philippi, which was covered with shrines to dead pagan gods. Jesus, the Son of the living God, would build His church on solid rock. His living faith would replace the pagan practices devoted to dead gods. In this sense, His church would replace or be built over or on the shrines to pagan gods. The tall, shrine-covered rock provided a physical image of a "great" rock—illustrating the solid foundation of the church.

✎ 4.   The imagery of the "rock" was not new to the disciples.
   a.   On which "rock" was the nation of Israel built? (See Isaiah 51:1–2.)

   Suggested Response: Abraham.

   b.   Read Psalm 18:2–3. Who is the "rock" whom David praised? How does David describe that "rock"?

   Suggested Responses: The "rock" is the Lord. David describes the Lord as a fortress, deliverer, refuge, shield, stronghold, savior, etc.

Topic C: The Gates of Hades (Hell)

Hades—originally the Greek god of the underworld—is the namesake for the place where departed spirits live and was frequently used in the Bible as a synonym for hell or the grave (Psalm 9:17; 55:15; 116:3). As Jesus used it in

Topic B: The Meanings of the Rock

1. On what did Jesus promise to build His church? (See Matthew 16:18.)

2. There are two major viewpoints concerning what Jesus meant by the "rock" upon which He would build His church. What does the Bible say about:

    a. Peter—representing all the disciples—being the "rock"? (See Ephesians 2:20–21.)

    b. Peter's profession—that Jesus is the Christ, the Son of the living God—being the "rock"? (See 1 Corinthians 3:10–15; Acts 4:10–11.)

3. What is the significance of the description "*this* rock" in Matthew 16:18?

4. The imagery of the "rock" was not new to the disciples.

    a. On which "rock" was the nation of Israel built? (See Isaiah 51:1–2.)

    b. Read Psalm 18:2–3. Who is the "rock" whom David praised? How does David describe that "rock"?

Topic C: The Gates of Hades (Hell)

Hades—originally the Greek god of the underworld—is the namesake for the place where departed spirits live and was frequently used in the Bible as a synonym for hell or the grave (Psalm 9:17; 55:15; 116:3). As Jesus used it in Matthew 16:18, *Hades* seems to refer to the powers of evil that resisted Jesus, including Satan's ultimate weapon—physical death.

1. What did Jesus say His church would have to confront? (See Matthew 16:18.)

    a. What did Jesus say would be the outcome?

    b. How can we be assured of this outcome? (See 1 John 3:7–8; 4:2–4.)

2. What is the significance of the imagery of the "gates" here, as pointed out in the video?

PLANNING NOTES:

Matthew 16:18, *Hades* seems to refer to the powers of evil that resisted Jesus, including Satan's ultimate weapon—physical death.

1. What did Jesus say His church would have to confront? (See Matthew 16:18.)

   Suggested Response: The church would face the "gates of Hades," which probably referred to evil forces—the powers of hell and Satan—arrayed against God.

   a. What did Jesus say would be the outcome?

      Suggested Response: The "gates of Hades" will not be able to stand against the power of God's people.

   b. How can we be assured of this outcome? (See 1 John 3:7–8; 4:2–4.)

      Suggested Responses: The Son of God has destroyed the devil's work; therefore we have already overcome the enemy because Jesus is greater than Satan.

2. What is the significance of the imagery of the "gates" here, as pointed out in the video?

   Suggested Responses: Gates are defensive, not offensive, so gates can never attack; the church must confront the gates of Hades—take the battle to hell itself; the gates of Hades will never be stronger than the church; etc.

3. What was Jesus' method of defeating Satan, sin, and physical death—the "gates of Hades"? (See Matthew 16:21–23; 1 Corinthians 15:26–28.)

   Suggested Responses: He defeated Satan by suffering, dying, and being raised from the dead. He conquered physical death and overcame the devil and all his evil by serving others to the point of death, even by giving His life sacrificially.

4. What is the source of our power to confront evil? (See Ephesians 1:17–23; Acts 1:8; 19:20; Luke 10:17–19; Ephesians 6:10–18; Hebrews 4:12.)

   Suggested Responses: Our power comes from God; the Holy Spirit; the Word of God; the authority God has given us, as His people, over the devil; the armor of God; etc.

Topic D: Dead Gods Versus the Living God

When the Israelites entered Canaan, they found a land of farmers who attributed their fertile land to their god, Baal. So the Jews struggled, wondering whether to worship the God who had guided them to the Promised Land, or to honor the fertility god of the land, or to worship both. Today God's people still face the struggle: Will we be totally committed to God, or will we honor the "gods" of the places we inhabit?

1. What is the difference between the living God and idols such as Pan, the fertility god worshiped in Caesarea Philippi? (See Jeremiah 10:1–16.)

   Suggested Responses: God is great, the true God, the living God, the Eternal King, the king of the nations. He is powerful, wise, and understanding. Even His name is mighty in power. He is the maker of all things. He creates and controls the powers of the earth and the heavens. Idols, on the other hand, are made by human hands

50   The Death and Resurrection of the Messiah

   b. Read Psalm 18:2–3. Who is the "rock" whom David
       praised? How does David describe that "rock"?

Topic C: The Gates of Hades (Hell)

Hades—originally the Greek god of the underworld—is the namesake for the place where departed spirits live and was frequently used
in the Bible as a synonym for hell or the grave (Psalm 9:17; 55:15;
116:3). As Jesus used it in Matthew 16:18, *Hades* seems to refer to the
powers of evil that resisted Jesus, including Satan's ultimate weapon—
physical death.

   1. What did Jesus say His church would have to confront?
       (See Matthew 16:18.)

   a. What did Jesus say would be the outcome?

   b. How can we be assured of this outcome? (See 1 John
       3:7–8; 4:2–4.)

   2. What is the significance of the imagery of the "gates" here,
       as pointed out in the video?

Session Three: Gates of Hades (Hell)   51

   3. What was Jesus' method of defeating Satan, sin, and phys-
       ical death—the "gates of Hades"? (See Matthew 16:21–23;
       1 Corinthians 15:26–28.)

   4. What is the source of our power to confront evil? (See Eph-
       esians 1:17–23; Acts 1:8; 19:20; Luke 10:17–19; Ephesians
       6:10–18; Hebrews 4:12.)

Topic D: Dead Gods Versus the Living God

When the Israelites entered Canaan, they found a land of farmers who
attributed their fertile land to their god, Baal. So the Jews struggled,
wondering whether to worship the God who had guided them to the
Promised Land, or to honor the fertility god of the land, or to worship both. Today God's people still face the struggle: will we be totally
committed to God or will we honor the "gods" of the places we
inhabit?

   1. What is the difference between the living God and idols
       such as Pan, the fertility god worshiped in Caesarea
       Philippi? (See Jeremiah 10:1–16.)

PLANNING NOTES:

and cannot speak or walk. They glorify and exaggerate human sin, which is why they so often portray violence or extreme sexuality. They have no power. They totter if they are not supported by human effort. They cannot do harm or good.

2. Read the following passages and note the ways in which God demonstrated His supremacy over Baal.

Reference	God's Power Demonstrated
Joshua 3:9–17	The Jordan was at flood stage, which the people believed was due to Baal's sending of rain, but the Lord completely stopped the flow of the river to let His people cross.
Judges 5:19–21	The river Kishon swept away the Canaanite enemies of Israel.
1 Kings 17:1; 18:1, 21–45	Through the prophet Elijah, God stopped and started the rain, which the people believed Baal controlled. God also sent fire from heaven to burn up the sacrifice, which the prophets of Baal—no matter how fervently they pleaded—could not do.
2 Kings 2:8, 11–14, 19–22	God demonstrated His power over water by parting the Jordan for Elijah and then Elisha; He also showed it by healing the water of Jericho.

3. Impatient to receive their place to live in the Promised Land, the tribe of Dan refused to remain in the territory God had provided and established the city of Dan on Israel's northern border.

a. For what was the city of Dan known? (See Judges 18:1–2, 23–31; 1 Kings 12:25–31.)

    Suggested Response: idol worship.

b. What was the fate of the city of Dan? (See 1 Kings 15:20.)

    Suggested Response: It was among the first cities to fall to the nations God sent to punish His people for idol worship.

4. What are some of the "gods" that are worshiped in our culture? In what ways do these gods contrast with the true, living God?

    Suggested Responses: Our gods glorify sinful human tendencies and are destructive because they exaggerate the worst in people. Some of the things we make into gods include: wealth, cars, physical beauty, intellect, power, fame, youth, security, relationships, self, sexual pleasure, knowledge, etc. These gods can do nothing, but God is alive, powerful, and active in our lives; He answers prayers, communicates living truth through His Word, gives us eternal life, etc.

52   The Death and Resurrection of the Messiah

2. Read the following passages and note the ways in which God demonstrated His supremacy over Baal.

Reference	God's Power Demonstrated
Joshua 3:9–17	
Judges 5:19–21	
1 Kings 17:1; 18:1, 21–45	
2 Kings 2:8, 11–14, 19–22	

3. Impatient to receive their place to live in the Promised Land, the tribe of Dan refused to remain in the territory God had provided and established the city of Dan on Israel's northern border.

    a. For what was the city of Dan known? (See Judges 18:1–2, 23–31; 1 Kings 12:25–31.)

    b. What was the fate of the city of Dan? (See 1 Kings 15:20.)

Session Three: Gates of Hades (Hell)   53

4. What are some of the "gods" that are worshiped in our culture? In what ways do these gods contrast with the true, living God?

5. In what ways do you see the community of Christians simply coexisting with, rather than confronting, the "gods" of this world?

IDENTITY PROFILE

Who Was Baal?
- The fertility god of the Canaanites.
- Believed to be the supreme god because he had defeated the sea god and so controlled the sea and could prevent storms.
- Believed to have power over weather.
- Often depicted as a man with the head and horns of a bull, carrying a lightning bolt in his hand(s).
- Attractive to his followers because of his supposed ability to provide rain in a dry country.
- Supposedly went to the land of the dead, the underworld, each year and returned to bring rain to the earth and create abundant harvests.
- Appeased through sacrifices, usually animals (1 Kings 18:23), although Baal's followers sometimes, during times of crisis, sacrificed their children (Deuteronomy 12:31; 18:9–11).
- Thought to have a mistress, Asherah—the fertility goddess. Believing that the sexual union of Baal and Asherah produced fertility, pagan worshipers engaged in immoral sex to cause the gods to join together and ensure good harvests.

✏ 5.   In what ways do you see the community of Christians simply coexisting with, rather than confronting, the "gods" of this world?

Suggested Responses: tolerates evil, compromises with evil, "hides" within church walls instead of confronting evil, does not give total allegiance to God, doesn't get involved in key legislative issues, etc.

IDENTITY PROFILE

Who Was Baal?

- The fertility god of the Canaanites.
- Believed to be the supreme god because he had defeated the sea god and so controlled the sea and could prevent storms.
- Believed to have power over weather.
- Often depicted as a man with the head and horns of a bull, carrying a lightning bolt in his hand(s).
- Attractive to his followers because of his supposed ability to provide rain in a dry country.
- Supposedly went to the land of the dead, the underworld, each year and returned to bring rain to the earth and create abundant harvests.
- Appeased through sacrifices, usually animals (1 Kings 18:23), although Baal's followers sometimes, during times of crisis, sacrificed their children (Deuteronomy 12:31; 18:9–11).
- Thought to have a mistress, Asherah—the fertility goddess. Believing that the sexual union of Baal and Asherah produced fertility, pagan worshipers engaged in immoral sex to cause the gods to join together and ensure good harvests.

ꜰɑith ʟᴇsson

9 minutes

Time for Reflection (6 minutes)

It's time for each of us to think quietly about how we can apply what we've learned today. On page 54 of the Participant's Guide, you'll find a passage of Scripture. Let's each read this passage silently and take the next few minutes to consider some of the questions that follow the Scripture passage.

Please do not talk during this time. It's a time when we all can reflect on today's lesson and how it applies to our lives.

The Scripture passage and questions are reproduced in their entirety in the Participant's Guide on pages 54–56.

When Jesus came to the region of Caesarea Philippi, he asked his disciples, "Who do people say the Son of Man is?" They replied, "Some say John the Baptist; others say Elijah; and still others, Jeremiah or one of the prophets." "But what about you?" he asked. "Who do you say I am?" Simon Peter answered, "You are the Christ, the Son of the living God." Jesus replied,

4. What are some of the "gods" that are worshiped in our culture? In what ways do these gods contrast with the true, living God?

5. In what ways do you see the community of Christians simply coexisting with, rather than confronting, the "gods" of this world?

IDENTITY PROFILE

Who Was Baal?
- The fertility god of the Canaanites.
- Believed to be the supreme god because he had defeated the sea god and so controlled the sea and could prevent storms.
- Believed to have power over weather.
- Often depicted as a man with the head and horns of a bull, carrying a lightning bolt in his hand(s).
- Attractive to his followers because of his supposed ability to provide rain in a dry country.
- Supposedly went to the land of the dead, the underworld, each year and returned to bring rain to the earth and create abundant harvests.
- Appeased through sacrifices, usually animals (1 Kings 18:23), although Baal's followers sometimes, during times of crisis, sacrificed their children (Deuteronomy 12:31; 18:9–11).
- Thought to have a mistress, Asherah—the fertility goddess. Believing that the sexual union of Baal and Asherah produced fertility, pagan worshipers engaged in immoral sex to cause the gods to join together and ensure good harvests.

faith Lesson

Time for Reflection

The following passage of Scripture recounts the discussion Jesus had with His disciples concerning His identity. Read this passage silently and take a few minutes to consider who you believe Jesus to be.

> When Jesus came to the region of Caesarea Philippi, he asked his disciples, "Who do people say the Son of Man is?" They replied, "Some say John the Baptist; others say Elijah; and still others, Jeremiah or one of the prophets." "But what about you?" he asked. "Who do you say I am?" Simon Peter answered, "You are the Christ, the Son of the living God." Jesus replied, "Blessed are you, Simon son of Jonah, for this was not revealed to you by man, but by my Father in heaven. And I tell you that you are Peter, and on this rock I will build my church, and the gates of Hades will not overcome it."... From that time on Jesus began to explain to his disciples that he must go to Jerusalem and suffer many things at the hands of the elders, chief priests and teachers of the law, and that he must be killed and on the third day be raised to life. Peter took him aside and began to rebuke him. "Never, Lord!" he said. "This shall never happen to you!" Jesus turned and said to Peter, "Get behind me, Satan! You are a stumbling block to me; you do not have in mind the things of God, but the things of men." Then Jesus said to his disciples, "If anyone would come after me, he must deny himself and take up his cross and follow me. For whoever wants to save his life will lose it, but whoever loses his life for me will find it. What good will it be for a man if he gains the whole world, yet forfeits his soul? Or what can a man give in exchange for his soul?"
>
> MATTHEW 16:13–18, 21–26

1. Have you come to the point in your life when you, like Peter, have said with conviction, "You are the Christ, the Son of the living God"? What impact does that belief have

"Blessed are you, Simon son of Jonah, for this was not revealed to you by man, but by my Father in heaven. And I tell you that you are Peter, and on this rock I will build my church, and the gates of Hades will not overcome it. . . . From that time on Jesus began to explain to his disciples that he must go to Jerusalem and suffer many things at the hands of the elders, chief priests and teachers of the law, and that he must be killed and on the third day be raised to life. Peter took him aside and began to rebuke him. "Never, Lord!" he said. "This shall never happen to you!" Jesus turned and said to Peter, "Get behind me, Satan! You are a stumbling block to me; you do not have in mind the things of God, but the things of men." Then Jesus said to his disciples, "If anyone would come after me, he must deny himself and take up his cross and follow me. For whoever wants to save his life will lose it, but whoever loses his life for me will find it. What good will it be for a man if he gains the whole world, yet forfeits his soul? Or what can a man give in exchange for his soul?

MATTHEW 16:13–18, 21–26

1. Have you come to the point in your life when you, like Peter, have said with conviction, "You are the Christ, the Son of the living God"? What impact does that belief have on your life? In what ways should that belief have a greater impact on your life? Be specific.

2. Where do you see the "gates of Hades" most clearly in your community? In what ways are you seeking opportunities to confront Satan's power?

3. In what ways are you tempted to hide from, rather than challenge, evil? Which steps are you willing to take in order to challenge evil in Jesus' name? Be specific.

4. Which specific form of evil might God be calling you to confront within your sphere of influence? What sacrifices might be required of you to challenge that evil? Are you prepared to pay that cost?

5. Do you know people who are effectively challenging the evil of this world? If so, what can you learn from them and apply to your own life?

As soon as participants have spent six minutes reflecting on the above questions, get the entire group's attention and move to the next section.

The Truth of the Matter
To believe in Jesus (*Yeshua*) is to accept His work of saving sinners from sin and to accept the mission to take on the gates of hell. To believe in Christ (Messiah, *Mashiach*) is to confess that He was chosen and equipped by God for His office as prophet, priest, and king. Jesus accomplished the task he was sent to do by serving others and suffering for them, even unto death. Following Christ means accepting His command to suffer for Him and to serve others on His behalf. When we engage in the process of believing and following, we are truly Christian (Christlike).

on your life? In what ways should that belief have a greater impact on your life? Be specific.

2. Where do you see the "gates of Hades" most clearly in your community? In what ways are you seeking opportunities to confront Satan's power?

3. In what ways are you tempted to hide from, rather than challenge, evil? Which steps are you willing to take in order to challenge evil in Jesus' name? Be specific.

THE TRUTH OF THE MATTER

To believe in Jesus (*Yeshua*) is to accept His work of saving sinners from sin and to accept the mission to take on the gates of hell. To believe in Christ (Messiah, *Mashiach*) is to confess that He was chosen and equipped by God for His office as prophet, priest, and king. Jesus accomplished the task he was sent to do by serving others and suffering for them, even unto death. Following Christ means accepting His command to suffer for Him and to serve others on His behalf. When we engage in the process of believing and following, we are truly Christian (Christlike).

4. Which specific form of evil might God be calling you to confront within your sphere of influence? What sacrifices might be required of you to challenge that evil? Are you prepared to pay that cost?

5. Do you know people who are effectively challenging the evil of this world? If so, what can you learn from them and apply to your own life?

Action Points

Take a moment to review the key points you explored today. Then write down the action step (or steps) that you will commit to this week as a result of what you have discovered.

1. *As Jesus taught His disciples in Caesarea Philippi, He said that they were to challenge the most pagan expressions of the power of evil.* He assured them that on that "rock"—the place where Satan is strongest in society, where ungodly values and beliefs are boldly promoted—He would build His church.

2. *Jesus' message applies to the followers of Jesus—the church—today, just as it did to His disciples in Caesarea Philippi.* We are to go on the offensive and actively confront the "gates of Hades." In the power of God, we are to challenge anything that is not godly—through our attitudes, words, and actions. We can gain confidence from

Action Points (3 minutes)

> The following summary and action points are reproduced on pages 56–57 of the Participant's Guide:

Now it's time to wrap up our session.

> Give participants a moment to transition from their thoughtfulness to giving you their full attention.
>
> Read the following summary and action points and pause afterward so that participants can consider and write out their commitment.

I'd like to take a moment to summarize the key points we explored today. We have gained an understanding of the history and culture of Caesarea Philippi, a stronghold of idolatry. This has given us a perspective from which to better understand Jesus' "graduation talk" to His disciples.

✏ 1. *As Jesus taught His disciples in Caesarea Philippi, He said that they were to challenge the most pagan expressions of the power of evil.* He assured them that on that "rock"—the place where Satan is strongest in society, where ungodly values and beliefs are boldly promoted—He would build His church.

✏ 2. *Jesus' message applies to the followers of Jesus—the church—today, just as it did to His disciples in Caesarea Philippi.* We are to go on the offensive and actively confront the "gates of Hades." In the power of God, we are to challenge anything that is not godly—through our attitudes, words, and actions. We can gain confidence from Jesus' promise to His disciples that the power of evil, the "gates of Hades," cannot prevail against the church of Jesus the Messiah.

Please take a moment to write out an action step (or steps) that you will commit to this week as a result of what you have learned today.

I will prepare myself and actively use _____

_____

(the gifts, abilities, and opportunities God has given me)

to challenge _____

(the evil within my sphere of influence)

in the name and power of Jesus.

closing prayer

2 minutes

I hope that this lesson has challenged you, as it has me, to think about ways in which we can, in the power of Christ, bring His message to people who are not Christians and also confront evil around us. Before we pray I'd like to read a brief passage of Scripture from which we can draw encouragement as we seek to challenge evil in our world:

4. Which specific form of evil might God be calling you to confront within your sphere of influence? What sacrifices might be required of you to challenge that evil? Are you prepared to pay that cost?

5. Do you know people who are effectively challenging the evil of this world? If so, what can you learn from them and apply to your own life?

Action Points

Take a moment to review the key points you explored today. Then write down the action step (or steps) that you will commit to this week as a result of what you have discovered.

1. *As Jesus taught His disciples in Caesarea Philippi, He said that they were to challenge the most pagan expressions of the power of evil.* He assured them that on that "rock"— the place where Satan is strongest in society, where ungodly values and beliefs are boldly promoted—He would build His church.

2. *Jesus' message applies to the followers of Jesus—the church—today, just as it did to His disciples in Caesarea Philippi.* We are to go on the offensive and actively confront the "gates of Hades." In the power of God, we are to challenge anything that is not godly—through our attitudes, words, and actions. We can gain confidence from

Jesus' promise to His disciples that the power of evil, the "gates of Hades," cannot prevail against the church of Jesus the Messiah.

I will prepare myself and actively use _____

_____

(the gifts, abilities, and opportunities God has given me)

to challenge_____
                (the evil within my sphere of influence)

in the name and power of Jesus.

In the power of Christ, we can bring His message to people who are not Christians and also confront evil around us. The following Scripture passage offers encouragement as we seek to challenge evil in our world:

> I write to you, dear children, because your sins have been forgiven on account of his name. . . . I write to you, fathers, because you have known him who is from the beginning. I write to you, young men, because you are strong, and the word of God lives in you, and you have overcome the evil one.

> 1 John 2:12, 14

PLANNING NOTES:

I write to you, dear children, because your sins have been forgiven on account of his name. . . . I write to you, fathers, because you have known him who is from the beginning. I write to you, young men, because you are strong, and the word of God lives in you, and you have overcome the evil one.

1 JOHN 2:12, 14

Let's close in prayer now, asking God to give us the courage to do what He has called us—His people, His church—to do in His name.

Dear God, thank You for coming to earth as Messiah. Truly You are the Son of the living God. Please give us the courage and wisdom we need to be prepared and go out to confront the "gates of Hades"—the pagan values all around us. Please fill us with the Holy Spirit, and help us to use the weapons you've given us to fight evil. Thank You that the gates of hell are powerless before You. In Your name we pray, Jesus. Amen.

Jesus' promise to His disciples that the power of evil, the "gates of Hades," cannot prevail against the church of Jesus the Messiah.

I will prepare myself and actively use _____

_____

(the gifts, abilities, and opportunities God has given me)

to challenge_____

(the evil within my sphere of influence)

in the name and power of Jesus.

In the power of Christ, we can bring His message to people who are not Christians and also confront evil around us. The following Scripture passage offers encouragement as we seek to challenge evil in our world:

> I write to you, dear children, because your sins have been forgiven on account of his name. . . . I write to you, fathers, because you have known him who is from the beginning. I write to you, young men, because you are strong, and the word of God lives in you, and you have overcome the evil one.
>
> 1 JOHN 2:12, 14

city of the great king—the temple

before you lead

Synopsis

To walk down Jerusalem's streets is to experience the unfolding of history that goes back a thousand years before Christ. Truly Jerusalem is a focal point of history. Pivotal events in both Judaism and Christianity have occurred there. As we better understand that vibrant city's history, we gain insights into the ancient land of Israel and the great work of redemption God accomplished there.

Through the years, many people have impacted the city we know as Jerusalem. God commanded Abraham to offer a sacrifice to God in the region of Mount Moriah, where Jerusalem is located. God enabled David to capture the ancient city of Jebus (1 Chronicles 11:4), which became Jerusalem—the religious and political capital of the people and nation of Israel. In obedience to God's leading, David selected the site for God's temple, which his son, Solomon, built. Hezekiah and Herod rebuilt and expanded the temple. Jesus worshiped, learned, and taught in the temple. And empowered by the Spirit given at Pentecost, the Christian faith spread from the temple in Jerusalem to the uttermost ends of the earth.

In this session, you'll guide participants in learning about God's temple in Jerusalem, the place God chose to bear His name and house His presence on earth. Because it was the dwelling place of God, the temple in Jerusalem was the focal point of Jewish worship and culture. Using a large-scale model of what the temple and city of Jerusalem looked like during Jesus' time, Ray Vander Laan explains many fascinating details about the architecture, construction, and layout of the Temple Mount and the biblical events that took place in or near the temple. For example, you'll see:

- Where the city of David was located. Only about ten acres in size, this city played a key role during David's reign.
- Evidence of King Herod's genius. (Hand-hewn rocks his engineers positioned on the Temple Mount weigh more than 500 metric tons each.)
- The site where Peter and John healed the beggar (Acts 3:1–16).
- The location of the "Court of the Gentiles." You'll better understand why Jesus angrily drove the vendors and money changers out of there.

What's most important in this session is helping participants learn about Jewish culture and spirituality in relationship to the temple and the events that transpired there. This is necessary because the material in this session on the temple in Jerusalem and the following session on the city of Jerusalem provides background for the remaining sessions, which focus on events that took place in Jerusalem.

Key Points of this Session

1. *Learning about the temple in Jerusalem—its structures, practices, history—gives us insight into the heart of God's salvation for His people.* It also helps us visualize biblical events that occurred there.

2. *God wanted His temple—the symbol of His presence on earth—to be available to everyone.* He designated it to be a house of prayer for all nations—Jews, Gentiles, even lepers. Ray Vander Laan believes that's why Jesus became so angry when the temple authorities allowed vendors to carry on their trade in the Court of the Gentiles, which would disrupt the Gentiles who had come to worship God. No wonder the chief priest and his assistants who profited greatly from the business of the temple plotted Jesus' death!

Session Outline (58 minutes)

I. Introduction (4 minutes)
Welcome
What's to Come
Questions to Think About

II. Video Presentation "City of the Great King—the Temple" (23 minutes)

III. Group Discovery (20 minutes)
Video Highlights
Small Group Bible Discovery

IV. Faith Lesson (10 minutes)
Time for Reflection
Action Points

V. Closing Prayer (1 minute)

Materials

No additional materials are needed for this session. Simply view the video prior to leading the session so you are familiar with its main points.

city of the great king— the temple

introduction

4 minutes

Welcome

Assemble the participants together. Welcome them to session four of *Faith Lessons on the Death and Resurrection of the Messiah.*

What's to Come

In this session, we'll explore the ancient city of Jerusalem and focus our attention on what the temple—the center of Jewish faith and culture—was like during Jesus' day. We'll see some of Herod the Great's marvelous construction, learn how the temple area was organized, and visualize a great deal more about Jewish worship and culture. Let's begin this session by considering several questions that start us thinking about the subject of this video.

Questions to Think About

Participant's Guide page 58.

Turn to page 58 of your Participant's Guide. Let's consider several questions that will prepare us for the video we'll see in a few moments.

Ask each question and solicit a few responses from group members.

1. When you think about the great cities you have visited or in which you have lived, what thoughts come to mind? What do those cities inspire in you in relationship to history, human accomplishment (or failure), human nature, etc.?

   Suggested Responses: Allow participants to share their ideas with the group. Some cities carry the weight of a long history, some seem energetic and inspire vigor and hope for the future, some reveal the terrible cost of war, some show the results of amazing human accomplishment, others reflect beauty and grandeur, still others speak of man's injustice to man or the vast gulf between wealth and poverty, etc.

2. When you think of Jerusalem, what thoughts come to mind?

   Suggested Responses may include: the Arab/Israeli conflict, the place where Jesus taught in the temple, a special city during biblical times, a city from which Jesus' disciples went out to witness to the world, a city in which God revealed Himself

SESSION FOUR

city of the great king— the temple

questions to think about

1. When you think about the great cities you have visited or in which you have lived, what thoughts come to mind? What do those cities inspire in you in relationship to history, human accomplishment (or failure), human nature, etc.?

2. When you think of Jerusalem, what thoughts come to mind?

3. In what ways have events in Jerusalem affected our Christian faith?

in special ways, the events of Pentecost, a holy city, a city of many faiths, a clash of cultures, an ancient city, a focal point for the end times, etc.

✏ 3.   In what ways have events in Jerusalem affected our Christian faith?

Suggested Responses: without the events there, particularly Jesus' death and resurrection, our Christian faith would not exist; the destruction of Jerusalem created a separation between Jew and Christian; etc.

Let's keep these ideas in mind as we view the video.

video presentation
23 minutes

Participant's Guide page 59.

On page 59 of your Participant's Guide, you will find a space in which to take notes on key points as we watch this video.

Leader's Video Observations

The Topography of Jerusalem

The Temple Mount

Events Within the Temple

A House of Prayer for All Nations

SESSION FOUR

city of the great king— the temple

questions to think about

1. When you think about the great cities you have visited or in which you have lived, what thoughts come to mind? What do those cities inspire in you in relationship to history, human accomplishment (or failure), human nature, etc.?

2. When you think of Jerusalem, what thoughts come to mind?

3. In what ways have events in Jerusalem affected our Christian faith?

Session Four: City of the Great King—the Temple   59

video notes

The Topography of Jerusalem

The Temple Mount

Events Within the Temple

A House of Prayer for All Nations

Group Discovery

20 minutes

If your group has seven or more members, use the **Video Highlights** with the entire group (5 minutes), then break into small groups of three to five to discuss the **Small Group Bible Discovery** (10 minutes). Then reassemble the group to discuss the key points discovered (5 minutes).

If your group has fewer than seven members, begin with the **Video Highlights** (5 minutes), then do one or more of the topics found in the **Small Group Bible Discovery** as a group (10 minutes). Finally, spend five minutes at the end discussing points that had an impact on participants.

Video Highlights (5 minutes)

Here you'll ask one or more of the following questions that directly relate to the video the participants have just seen.

Please turn to the diagram of the city of Jerusalem during Jesus' time, on page 61 of your Participant's Guide. Note the Temple Mount, the Royal Stoa, and David's City on the slope below.

Jerusalem of Jesus' Time

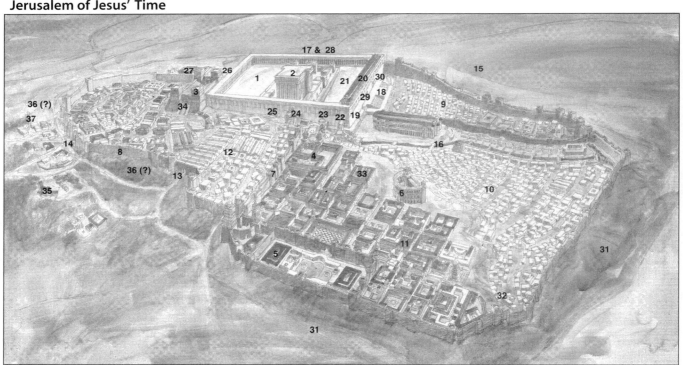

1 Temple Mount	9 David's City	16 Tyropoeon Valley	22 Robinson's Arch	30 Triple Gates
2 Temple	10 Lower City	17 Golden Gate	23 Barclay's Gate	31 Hinnorn Valley
3 Antonia	11 Upper City	18 Southern Stairs	24 Wilson's Arch & Bridge	32 Essene Quarter
4 Hasmonaean Palace	12 Business District	19 South Wall	25 Warren's Gate	33 Mansions
5 Herod's Palace	13 Garden Gate	20 Royal Stoa	26 Tadi Gate	34 Entrance to Antonia
6 Theater	14 Towers	21 Opening of Entrance	27 Pool of Bethesda	35 New City
7 First Wall	(Damascus) Gate	Tunnels on Temple	28 Eastern Gate	36 Golgotha (?)
8 Second Wall	15 Kidron Valley	Mount	29 Double Gates	37 Garden Tomb

video highlights

On the diagram of the city of Jerusalem during Jesus' time, note the location of the Temple Mount, the Royal Stoa, and David's City on the slope below.

1. How have your impressions of Jerusalem changed as a result of seeing this video?

2. Why was the temple in Jerusalem so important to the Jews during Jesus' time?

3. Why is it so significant that the temple even had a court for lepers?

4. Imagine yourself as one of the Sadducean priests who operated the temple and consider what you might have thought and how you might have responded when Jesus forced the buyers and sellers out of the temple.

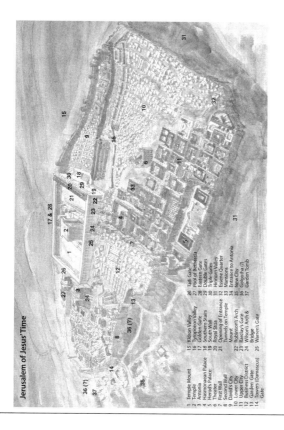

Jerusalem of Jesus' Time

PLANNING NOTES:

✏ 1. How have your impressions of Jerusalem changed as a result of seeing this video?

Suggested Responses: amazed by what Herod accomplished, particularly the size and construction of the Temple Mount; view Jerusalem as a key to understanding God and the Christian faith instead of just a city; realize how important the city, particularly the temple, is to the Jewish faith; etc.

✏ 2. Why was the temple in Jerusalem so important to the Jews during Jesus' time?

Suggested Responses: It was the place God had chosen to put His name and the place He had chosen for His presence to live on earth; it was a place where everyone could worship God; the sacrifices made there symbolized God's forgiveness of sins; it was the foremost symbol of their religious faith that remained intact even during the Roman occupation; Moses had commanded them to appear before the Lord (in Jerusalem) three times each year—on Passover, Pentecost, and the Feast of Tabernacles; the location, Mount Moriah, had been a part of their heritage since the time of Abraham; etc.

✏ 3. Why is it so significant that the temple even had a court for lepers?

Suggested Responses: It shows that God wanted everyone—even the outcasts—to be able to come into His presence and worship Him; He loved the outcasts just as much as He loved other people; He wanted to be accessible to everyone; etc.

✏ 4. Imagine yourself as one of the Sadducean priests who operated the temple and consider what you might have thought and how you might have responded when Jesus forced the buyers and sellers out of the temple.

Suggested Responses: Jesus challenged the temple officials' way of life; He pointed out their lack of sensitivity to the Gentiles' worship; He disrupted their income; He made them look foolish in people's eyes; He questioned the validity of their leadership, even their very right to lead the people. Most of us would have been offended and responded in anger. Perhaps we, too, would have planned revenge.

Small Group Bible Discovery (15 minutes)

Participant's Guide pages 62–76.

During this time, a group with fewer than seven participants will stay together. A group larger than seven participants will break into small groups and reassemble as a large group during the final five minutes. Assign each group one of the following topics. If you have more than five small groups, assign some topics to more than one group.

Let's break into groups of three to five—people sitting near you—and study some Bible passages and truths mentioned in the video today.

Turn to pages 62–76 in your Participant's Guide. There you'll find a list of five topics. You'll have ten minutes to read and discuss the topic I'll assign to you. Choose one person in your group to be a spokesperson for your group when we discuss these topics later.

video Highlights

On the diagram of the city of Jerusalem during Jesus' time, note the location of the Temple Mount, the Royal Stoa, and David's City on the slope below.

1. How have your impressions of Jerusalem changed as a result of seeing this video?

2. Why was the temple in Jerusalem so important to the Jews during Jesus' time?

3. Why is it so significant that the temple even had a court for lepers?

4. Imagine yourself as one of the Sadducean priests who operated the temple and consider what you might have thought and how you might have responded when Jesus forced the buyers and sellers out of the temple.

Assign each group a topic.

I'll signal you when one minute is left.

After nine minutes, let participants know that they have one minute remaining. Then reassemble the entire group. After everyone is back together, begin asking one person from each small group to briefly share a key idea with the larger group. In some cases, you may not have time for every group to share their discoveries.

As time allows, let's briefly share the key ideas that your group discussed.

Topic A: The Importance of Mount Moriah

1. For what reason did Abraham travel to the region of Moriah? What happened there? (See Genesis 22:1–14.)

    Suggested Responses: God told him to sacrifice Isaac—his only beloved son, the heir God had promised—in the region of Moriah. As Abraham was about to sacrifice Isaac, God intervened and provided a ram for the sacrifice.

2. Describe how David, after receiving a prophetic word from Gad—his prophet—selected the future site of the temple on Mount Moriah. How did God confirm His approval of the site? (See 1 Chronicles 21:18–26; 22:1.)

    Suggested Responses: An angel told Gad to tell David to build an altar on the threshing floor of Araunah the Jebusite. Both men met each other, and David

Jerusalem of David and Solomon

small Group Bible Discovery

Topic A: The Importance of Mount Moriah

1. For what reason did Abraham travel to the region of Moriah? What happened there? (See Genesis 22:1–14.)

2. Describe how David, after receiving a prophetic word from Gad—his prophet—selected the future site of the temple on Mount Moriah. How did God confirm His approval of the site? (See 1 Chronicles 21:18–26; 22:1.)

3. What did David bring into his city on Mount Moriah? (See 2 Samuel 6:1–5.)

Jerusalem of David and Soloman

PLANNING NOTES:

asked Araunah to sell him the site. After David purchased it for 600 shekels (about 15 pounds) of gold, he built an altar to God and sacrificed offerings on it. Then, confirming His approval, God sent down fire on the altar.

✏ 3. What did David bring into his city on Mount Moriah? (See 2 Samuel 6:1–5.)

Suggested Response: The Ark of the Covenant.

✏ 4. Whom did God select to build the temple? What kind of a temple did he build, and where did he begin building it? (See 1 Chronicles 28:2–7; 2 Chronicles 2:5; 3:1.)

Suggested Responses: God chose Solomon, David's son. Solomon determined to build a great temple to honor God, who is greater than all gods. Solomon began building the temple on the threshing floor of Araunah the Jebusite, the site David had purchased.

✏ 5. Which other important historical event took place near Jerusalem and Mount Moriah? (See Matthew 27:32–35.)

Suggested Response: Jesus was crucified there.

✏ 6. What common thread links Abraham's experience on Mount Moriah, the Israelites' offering of sacrifices there, and Jesus' crucifixion?

Suggested Responses: On this one mountain site He had chosen, God provided a substitute for sacrificing Isaac, the Jews offered sacrifices to God as a substitutionary way to receive forgiveness of sins, and Jesus took our sins upon Himself and died as our sacrificial lamb.

The Temple Mount: A.D. 70

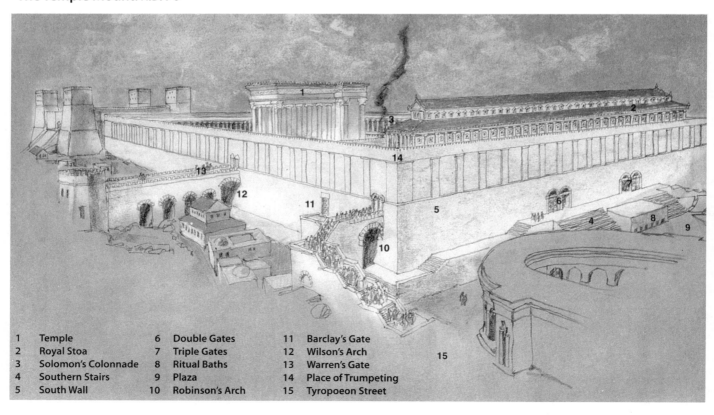

1	Temple	6	Double Gates	11	Barclay's Gate
2	Royal Stoa	7	Triple Gates	12	Wilson's Arch
3	Solomon's Colonnade	8	Ritual Baths	13	Warren's Gate
4	Southern Stairs	9	Plaza	14	Place of Trumpeting
5	South Wall	10	Robinson's Arch	15	Tyropoeon Street

4. Whom did God select to build the temple? What kind of a temple did he build, and where did he begin building it? (See 1 Chronicles 28:2–7; 2 Chronicles 2:5; 3:1.)

5. Which other important historical event took place near Jerusalem and Mount Moriah? (See Matthew 27:32–35.)

6. What common thread links Abraham's experience on Mount Moriah, the Israelites' offering of sacrifices there, and Jesus' crucifixion?

PROFILES IN CONTRAST	
Herod the Great	**Jesus**
Built spectacular buildings: the temple in Jerusalem; Masada, a fortress in the Judea Wilderness; Jericho; and the seaport in Caesarea.	Built with people—living stones (Matthew 16:18; 1 Peter 2:4–8).
Built to honor himself.	Built for the honor of God.
His works lie in ruins today.	His projects will last forever.

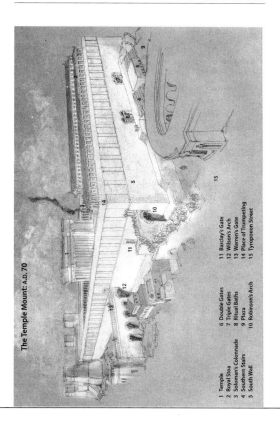

The Temple Mount: A.D. 70

1 Temple
2 Royal Stoa
3 Solomon's Colonnade
4 Southern Stairs
5 South Wall
6 Double Gates
7 Triple Gates
8 Ritual Baths
9 Plaza
10 Robinson's Arch
11 Barclay's Gate
12 Wilson's Arch
13 Warren's Gate
14 Place of Trumpeting
15 Tyropoeon Street

PROFILES IN CONTRAST	
Herod the Great	**Jesus**
Built spectacular buildings: the temple in Jerusalem; Masada, a fortress in the Judea Wilderness; Jericho; and the seaport in Caesarea.	Built with people—living stones (Matthew 16:18; 1 Peter 2:4–8).
Built to honor himself.	Built for the honor of God.
His works lie in ruins today.	His projects will last forever.

Topic B: God's Presence Among His People

1. What did God promise Solomon regarding the temple? (See 1 Kings 6:11–13.)

    Suggested Response: that He would live among the Israelites if they continued to follow His commands.

2. At the dedication of the temple, what did the priests place in the temple? How did God reveal His presence in the temple? (See 1 Kings 8:6, 10–11; 2 Chronicles 5:11–6:2; 7:1–3.)

    Suggested Responses: The priests placed the Ark of the Covenant in the temple. After that, God's cloud of glory filled the temple, and He sent fire from heaven to consume the offering and sacrifices.

3. In which other situations has God revealed His presence through fire? (See Exodus 19:17–18; 24:15–18; 1 Kings 18:22–24, 36–38; 1 Chronicles 21:25–26; Revelation 1:9–15.)

    Suggested Responses: when Moses received the Ten Commandments on Mount Sinai; when Elijah tested the prophets of Baal; after David had purchased the threshing floor, which would become the site of the future temple; when Jesus' angel appeared to John.

4. Jewish people consistently came into the temple to be in the presence of God. Read the following passages of Scripture and note the sentiment expressed:

Scripture	Sentiment
Psalm 15	Those who are holy and righteous may dwell in the sanctuary of the Lord.
Psalm 27:4	Desire to dwell in the house of the Lord for all of life and to gaze on the Lord's beauty in His temple.
Psalm 99:1–3	The Lord is enthroned in His temple, He is holy, He is exalted over all the nations, His name is worthy of praise.
Psalm 122:1, 9	Rejoicing by those who go into the house of the Lord to praise Him, to pray for peace, to seek prosperity.
Isaiah 6	The Lord is enthroned and lifted up in His holy temple, when Isaiah saw Him, he realized the filth of his own sin.
Isaiah 37:14–20	Hezekiah went to the temple to pray and ask God for deliverance.

4. Whom did God select to build the temple? What kind of a temple did he build, and where did he begin building it? (See 1 Chronicles 28:2–7; 2 Chronicles 2:5; 3:1.)

5. Which other important historical event took place near Jerusalem and Mount Moriah? (See Matthew 27:32–35.)

6. What common thread links Abraham's experience on Mount Moriah, the Israelites' offering of sacrifices there, and Jesus' crucifixion?

PROFILES IN CONTRAST

Herod the Great	Jesus
Built spectacular buildings: the temple in Jerusalem; Masada, a fortress in the Judea Wilderness; Jericho; and the seaport in Caesarea.	Built with people—living stones (Matthew 16:18; 1 Peter 2:4–8).
Built to honor himself.	Built for the honor of God.
His works lie in ruins today.	His projects will last forever.

Topic B: God's Presence Among His People

1. What did God promise Solomon regarding the temple? (See 1 Kings 6:11–13.)

2. At the dedication of the temple, what did the priests place in the temple? How did God reveal His presence in the temple? (See 1 Kings 8:6,10–11; 2 Chronicles 5:11–6:2; 7:1–3.)

3. In which other situations has God revealed His presence through fire? (See Exodus 19:17–18; 24:15–18; 1 Kings 18:22–24, 36–38; 1 Chronicles 21:25–26; Revelation 1:9–15.)

4. Jewish people consistently came into the temple to be in the presence of God. Read the following passages of Scripture and note the sentiment expressed:

Scripture	Sentiment
Psalm 15	
Psalm 27:4	
Psalm 99:1–3	
Psalm 122:1, 9	
Isaiah 6	
Isaiah 37:14–20	

DATA FILE

Solomon's Temple

Construction began about 950 B.C. on the Mount Moriah site chosen by David at God's leading—on a high point of the ridge known as David's City, just north of the original city.

- Construction took seven years.
- No hammers or chisels were used on the site; the stones were prepared at the quarry.
- Made of limestone, parts of which were covered with gold and cedar.
- It was precisely and luxuriously furnished (1 Kings 7:13–51; 2 Chronicles 4).
- It held the Ark of the Covenant (1 Kings 8:1–21; 2 Chronicles 5).
- After its dedication to God (1 Kings 8:22–66; 2 Chronicles 6), the temple was filled by God's presence (2 Chronicles 5:13–14; 7:1–3).

The First Temple at Jerusalem

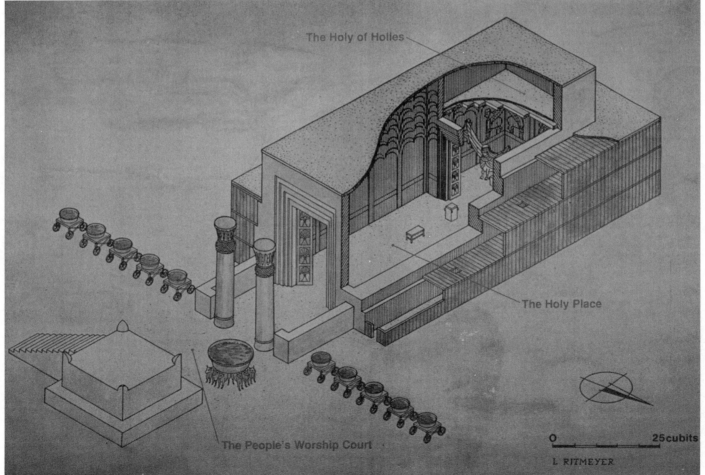

The Holy of Holies

The Holy Place

The People's Worship Court

0   25 cubits

L RITMEYER

DATA FILE

Solomon's Temple

Construction began about 950 B.C. on the Mount Moriah site chosen by David at God's leading—on a high point of the ridge known as David's City, just north of the original city.

- Construction took seven years.
- No hammers or chisels were used on the site; the stones were prepared at the quarry.
- Made of limestone, parts of which were covered with gold and cedar.
- It was precisely and luxuriously furnished (1 Kings 7:13–51; 2 Chronicles 4).
- It held the Ark of the Covenant (1 Kings 8:1–21; 2 Chronicles 5).
- After its dedication to God (1 Kings 8:22–66; 2 Chronicles 6), the temple was filled by God's presence (2 Chronicles 5:13–14; 7:1–3).

The First Temple at Jerusalem

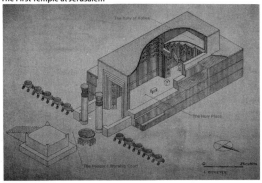

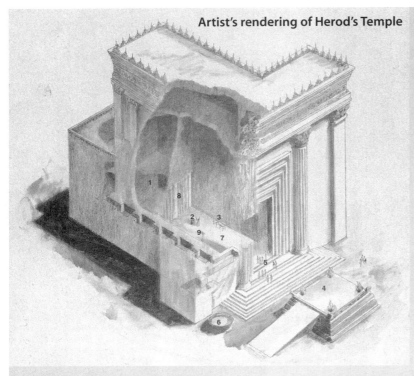

Artist's rendering of Herod's Temple

1 Holy of Holies	4 Altar	7 Holy Place
2 Altar of Incense	5 Porch	8 Veil
3 Table of Showbread	6 Bronze Sea	9 Menorah

DATA FILE

Herod's Building of the Temple

Made of marble and gold, Herod's Temple was taller than a fifteen-story building. The temple platform—the largest temple base in the ancient world—was more than 900 feet wide from east to west and more than 1,500 feet long from north to south. Built on the exact location of Solomon's temple and the temple Nehemiah reconstructed, it could accommodate hundreds of thousands of pilgrims at a time and was twice as large as the largest temple enclosure in Rome.

A thousand priests trained as masons by Herod worked on the temple, as did ten thousand highly skilled laborers using a thousand wagons. Some limestone blocks of the supporting platform weigh more than five hundred tons.

The Eastern Wall followed the original line dating from Solomon's days. The main feature in the wall, the Eastern Gate, was the original eastern entrance to Temple Mount.

At one point, the walls of the temple rose more than 225 feet above the bottom of the Kidron Valley.

The South Wall was more than 900 feet long and more than 150 feet high. Pilgrims entered the temple primarily through this entrance—the Double Gates—after climbing the Southern Stairs—a broad staircase more than 200 feet wide.

The Western Wall was a common gathering place during Jesus' time and featured various architectural wonders and gates, such as:

- *Robinson's Arch*—one of the largest masonry arches (75 feet tall, more than 45 feet across) in the ancient world; supported a massive staircase that ran from the Tyropoeon Valley and the Lower City to the Royal Stoa (the place of buying and selling, the location of the temple treasury, and the Sanhedrin's meeting place); destroyed in A.D. 70 by the Romans.
- *Barclay's Gate*—provided access to the Gentile Court from Tyropoeon Street.
- *Wilson's Arch*—supported a bridge that extended from the Upper City, where the Sadducees and other influential Jews lived, across the Tyropoeon Valley to the Temple Mount; extended 75 feet above the valley floor and spanned 45 feet.
- *Warren's Gate*—provided direct access to the temple courts.
- *Massive Ashlars*—hand-shaped stones brought from a quarry nearly a mile away. One 45-foot-long stone weighs nearly 600 tons. (See Mark 13:1–2; Luke 21:5.)

The North Wall is where the Antonia fortress was located. Built by Herod the Great, this fortress guarded the northern side of Jerusalem and held Roman troops during Jesus' time who watched the temple activities. Paul was probably brought to the Antonia after his arrest and defended himself on the stairs that apparently led to the fortress (Acts 21:27–40; 22:22–25).

The temple platform's extension to the west required enormous retaining walls on the south and west. Some of the rocks used in the wall weighed more than five hundred tons each. The finished platform was divided into courts, which became increasingly more sacred the closer they were to the temple.

The South Wall was more than 900 feet long and more than 150 feet high. Pilgrims entered the temple primarily through this entrance—the Double Gates—after climbing the Southern Stairs—a broad staircase more than 200 feet wide.

The Western Wall was a common gathering place during Jesus' time and featured various architectural wonders and gates, such as:

- *Robinson's Arch*—one of the largest masonry arches (75 feet tall, more than 45 feet across) in the ancient world; supported a massive staircase that ran from the Tyropoeon Valley and the Lower City to the Royal Stoa (the place of buying and selling, the location of the temple treasury, and the Sanhedrin's meeting place); destroyed in A.D. 70 by the Romans.
- *Barclay's Gate*—provided access to the Gentile Court from Tyropoeon Street.
- *Wilson's Arch*—supported a bridge that extended from the Upper City, where the Sadducees and other influential Jews lived, across the Tyropoeon Valley to the Temple Mount; extended 75 feet above the valley floor and spanned 45 feet.
- *Warren's Gate*—provided direct access to the temple courts.
- *Massive Ashlars*—hand-shaped stones brought from a quarry nearly a mile away. One 45-foot-long stone weighs nearly 600 tons. (See Mark 13:1–2; Luke 21:5.)

The North Wall is where the Antonia fortress was located. Built by Herod the Great, this fortress guarded the northern side of Jerusalem and held Roman troops during Jesus' time who watched the temple activities. Paul was probably brought to the Antonia after his arrest and defended himself on the stairs that apparently led to the fortress (Acts 21:27–40; 22:22–25).

The temple platform's extension to the west required enormous retaining walls on the south and west. Some of the rocks used in the wall weighed more than five hundred tons each. The finished platform was divided into courts, which became increasingly more sacred the closer they were to the temple.

Artist's rendering of Herod's Temple

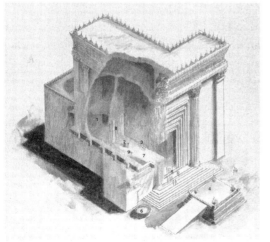

1 Holy of Holies	4 Altar	7 Holy Place
2 Altar of Incense	5 Porch	8 Veil
3 Table of Showbread	6 Bronze Sea	9 Menorah

✏ 5. After Jesus' death and resurrection, during the Jewish feast of Pentecost, what represented God's presence as it moved from the temple building into the new temple—the disciples? (See Acts 2:1–3).

Suggested Response: fire, which divided into "tongues" of fire.

✏ 6. At one time, God's presence resided in the Holy of Holies in the temple (2 Chronicles 5:7). Where does God's presence dwell today? (See 1 Corinthians 3:16–17; 6:19.)

Suggested Response: in the people who have accepted Jesus the Messiah as their personal Lord and Savior.

Topic C: Events That Occurred in the Temple Courts

✏ 1. How often did Jesus teach in the temple courts? How was His message received?

Reference	Teaching/Reception
Matthew 26:55	When the Jews came to arrest Jesus in the Garden of Gethsemane, He asked them why they didn't arrest Him when He was teaching in the temple, which He did daily.
Mark 11:27–28	The teachers of the law, elders, and chief priests questioned His authority to teach.
Mark 12:35–37	When Jesus taught about His identity, the people were delighted.
Luke 2:41–47	When Jesus went to the temple as a child, the people were amazed by His questions.
John 7:14–16	Jesus taught, and the people were amazed. They wanted to know how He knew so much, and He said His teaching came "from him who sent me."
John 8:2–11	Jesus entered the courts at dawn, and the people gathered around to hear Him teach. The religious leaders tested Him by bringing in a woman caught in adultery. Jesus asked those who were without sin to punish her, and they all left, and Jesus told her not to continue in sin.
John 10:22–33	The Jews asked if He was the Christ, He said He had told them He was, and they threatened to stone Him.

✏ 2. Why do you think Jesus spent so much time teaching in the temple courts?

Suggested Responses: there were large crowds there; people came to the temple to seek God; the temple was the house of God; etc.

✏ 3. Where did the early Christians meet and teach? What can we learn from the fact that they met and taught there? (See Acts 2:44–46; 5:17–21.)

5. After Jesus' death and resurrection, during the Jewish feast of Pentecost, what represented God's presence as it moved from the temple building into the new temple—the disciples? (See Acts 2:1–3.)

6. At one time, God's presence resided in the Holy of Holies in the temple (2 Chronicles 5:7). Where does God's presence dwell today? (See 1 Corinthians 3:16–17; 6:19.)

DATA FILE

Herod's Building of the Temple
Made of marble and gold, Herod's Temple was taller than a fifteen-story building. The temple platform—the largest temple base in the ancient world—was more than 900 feet wide from east to west and more than 1,500 feet long from north to south. Built on the exact location of Solomon's temple and the temple Nehemiah reconstructed, it could accommodate hundreds of thousands of pilgrims at a time and was twice as large as the largest temple enclosure in Rome.

A thousand priests trained as masons by Herod worked on the temple, as did ten thousand highly skilled laborers using a thousand wagons. Some limestone blocks of the supporting platform weigh more than five hundred tons.

The Eastern Wall followed the original line dating from Solomon's days. The main feature in the wall, the Eastern Gate, was the original eastern entrance to Temple Mount. At one point, the walls of the temple rose more than 225 feet above the bottom of the Kidron Valley.

Topic C: Events That Occurred in the Temple Courts

1. How often did Jesus teach in the temple courts? How was His message received?

Reference	Teaching/Reception
Matthew 26:55	
Mark 11:27–28	
Mark 12:35–37	
Luke 2:41–47	
John 7:14–16	
John 8:2–11	
John 10:22–33	

2. Why do you think Jesus spent so much time teaching in the temple courts?

3. Where did the early Christians meet and teach? What can we learn from the fact that they met and taught there? (See Acts 2:44–46; 5:17–21.)

BACKGROUND NOTES

The Pharisees

- Derived their name from the word *perushim*, which meant "separated" or "separatists."
- Tried to be devoted to God without resorting to violence against the Romans.
- Devoted themselves to obeying every detail of Jewish law and separating themselves from all influences or people who might interfere with that devotion.
- Believed that Moses had given a two-part law— the written law of the Torah and additional oral commandments that had been passed through generations to help the faithful understand and apply the written law.
- The Pharisees interpreted and greatly expanded the oral law, which became a complex guide to everyday life. Their intent was to help people understand the Torah, in much the same way that Christians use a creed or catechism to help summarize and interpret the Bible.
- Believed in the physical resurrection of the dead, a coming day of judgment, the coming of the Messiah, angels, and a loving God who desired a life of obedience.
- Recognized a combination of free choice and divine control in human life.
- Had some people within their ranks who were hypocritical or became so focused on obedience that they did not notice or care about the needs of other people. Jesus never criticized anyone for being a Pharisee and instructed His followers to obey what the Pharisees taught (Matthew 23:2–3). Jesus only criticized "hypocritical" ones (Matthew 23) and those who spoiled the whole group (Matthew 16:6, 11). In fact, many Pharisees supported Jesus, tried to protect Him (Luke 13:31), and became Jesus' followers (Acts 15:5).
- Obtained their authority by knowledge and piety.

The Sadducees

- After Israel returned from the Babylonian captivity, it was the tradition that the high priest must be from the tribe of Levi, the family of Aaron, and the family of Zadok—Solomon's high priest (1 Kings 2:35; Ezekiel 40:46). Descendants of this family, *Zedukim* (or "Sadducee" in English) were the temple authorities throughout the time before Jesus was born. Descendants of Zadok and their supporters were also called "Sadducees."
- Although there may have been fewer than a thousand of them, they wielded great power.
- Were wealthy, politically active, and had a majority in the Sanhedrin—the religious council used by the Romans and Herods as the instrument to govern the Jewish people.
- Controlled the economy of the temple, often using their position for personal gain (Mark 11:15–18). In A.D. 15, they allowed the business of buying and selling to extend beyond the Royal Stoa and into the Gentile Court, a move to which the Pharisees were opposed.
- Many were Hellenistic but faithful to temple rituals.
- Believed the written Torah alone was authoritative, rejected oral law, hated the Pharisees, denied bodily resurrection and most Pharisaic doctrines of angels and spirits, and believed that the synagogue and study of the Torah as a form of worship undermined temple ritual.
- Obtained their authority by position and birth.
- Frequently dealt brutally with anyone who undermined the temple, its economy (their income), and its ritual.
- Had the most to lose because of Jesus. Any popular movement jeopardized their place as the majority in the Sanhedrin and the support of the Romans who ruled through it (John 11:49–53).
- Ceased to exist as a group after the temple in Jerusalem was destroyed.

4. Where did Peter heal a man who had been crippled since birth? (See Acts 3:1–16, refer to diagram of the Temple Courts on page 74.)

   a. Whose example did Peter follow? (See John 5:1–14.)

BACKGROUND NOTES

The Pharisees

- Derived their name from the word *perushim*, which meant "separated" or "separatists."
- Tried to be devoted to God without resorting to violence against the Romans.
- Devoted themselves to obeying every detail of Jewish law and separating themselves from all influences or people who might interfere with that devotion.
- Believed that Moses had given a two-part law—the written law of the Torah and additional oral commandments that had been passed through generations to help the faithful understand and apply the written law.
- The Pharisees interpreted and greatly expanded the oral law, which became a complex guide to everyday life. Their intent was to help people understand the Torah, in much the same way that Christians use a creed or catechism to help summarize and interpret the Bible.
- Believed in the physical resurrection of the dead, a coming day of judgment, the coming of the Messiah, angels, and a loving God who desired a life of obedience.
- Recognized a combination of free choice and divine control in human life.
- Had some people within their ranks who were hypocritical or became so focused on obedience that they did not notice or care about the needs of other people. Jesus never criticized anyone for being a Pharisee and instructed His followers to obey what the Pharisees taught

(Matthew 23:2–3). Jesus only criticized "hypocritical" ones (Matthew 23) and those who spoiled the whole group (Matthew 16:6,11). In fact, many Pharisees supported Jesus, tried to protect Him (Luke 13:31), and became Jesus' followers (Acts 15:5).
- Obtained their authority by knowledge and piety.

The Sadducees

- After Israel returned from the Babylonian captivity, it was the tradition that the high priest must be from the tribe of Levi, the family of Aaron, and the family of Zadok—Solomon's high priest (1 Kings 2:35; Ezekiel 40:46). Descendants of this family, *Zedukim* (or "Sadducee" in English), were the temple authorities throughout the time before Jesus was born. Descendants of Zadok and their supporters were also called "Sadducees."
- Although there may have been fewer than a thousand of them, they wielded great power.
- Were wealthy, politically active, and had a majority in the Sanhedrin—the religious council used by the Romans and Herods as the instrument to govern the Jewish people.
- Controlled the economy of the temple, often using their position for personal gain (Mark 11:15–18). In A.D. 15, they allowed the business of buying and selling to extend beyond the Royal Stoa and into the Gentile Court, a move which the Pharisees opposed.
- Many were Hellenistic but faithful to temple rituals.
- Believed the written Torah alone was authoritative, rejected oral law, hated the Pharisees, denied bodily resurrection and most Pharisaic doctrines of angels and spirits, and believed that the synagogue and study of the Torah as a form of worship undermined temple ritual.
- Obtained their authority by position and birth.
- Frequently dealt brutally with anyone who undermined the temple, its economy (their income), and its ritual.
- Had the most to lose because of Jesus. Any popular movement jeopardized their place as the majority in the Sanhedrin and the support of the Romans who ruled through it (John 11:49–53).
- Ceased to exist as a group after the temple in Jerusalem was destroyed.

PLANNING NOTES:

Suggested Responses: in the temple courts. Christianity is deeply rooted in its Jewish heritage, a fact that is often overlooked today.

4. Where did Peter heal a man who had been crippled since birth? (See Acts 3:1–16, refer to diagram of the Temple Courts on page 74.)

Suggested Response: At the Beautiful Gate (near the entrance to the Women's Court).

a. Whose example did Peter follow? (See John 5:1–14.)

Suggested Response: the example of Jesus, who healed a crippled man near the Sheep Gate.

Topic D: The Temple—a House of Prayer for All Nations

At the southern end of the temple platform was a beautiful colonnade named the Royal Stoa (see diagram of The Temple Mount A.D. 70 on page 79). It had a central hall, 162 large columns, and by Jesus' time had become the area where transactions for temple sacrifices took place. However, the booths for buying and selling sacrifices, the inspection of animals, and the changing of foreign currencies—all of which were operated by Sadducean priests—overflowed into the Gentile Court, which was the large, open area around the sacred temple courts where Gentiles were allowed to worship (see diagram of the Temple Courts on page 74). These activities apparently interfered with the Gentiles' worship of the one true God.

1. Describe what Jesus did in the Royal Stoa after His triumphant entry into Jerusalem (Matthew 21:12–13; Luke 19:45; John 2:13–17).

Suggested Responses: Using a whip, He drove out the merchants and sellers of cattle, sheep, and doves; overturned the moneychangers' tables; accused the merchants of making His house a den of robbers. The people He drove out were Sadducean priests.

2. According to Isaiah 56:7, the Scripture Jesus quoted when He drove out the vendors and moneychangers, what was God's "house" to be called?

Suggested Response: A house of prayer for all nations. (In context, "nations" referred to Gentiles who would serve the Lord in Jerusalem.)

3. Why did Jesus drive the vendors and moneychangers out of the temple? (See Matthew 21:13.)

Suggested Responses: They were cheating people and using the area set aside for Gentile worship as a marketplace. Jesus refused to allow temple authorities to prevent Gentiles from having a place to worship God.

4. What truth did Jesus demonstrate by clearing out the Gentile Court?

Suggested Response: He made it clear that God wants all people to have opportunities to know Him and to worship Him.

5. What can we learn from the fact that Jesus expressed great anger toward religious leaders who didn't care about hurting, sinful, broken people and "unclean" Gentiles? What might we be doing today that would kindle Jesus' anger in a similar way?

Topic D: The Temple—a House of Prayer for All Nations

At the southern end of the temple platform was a beautiful colonnade named the Royal Stoa (see diagram of the Temple Mount A.D. 70 on page 79). It had a central hall, 162 large columns, and by Jesus' time had become the area where transactions for temple sacrifices took place. However, the booths for buying and selling sacrifices, the inspection of animals, and the changing of foreign currencies—all of which were operated by Sadducean priests—overflowed into the Gentile Court, which was the large, open area around the sacred temple courts where Gentiles were allowed to worship (see diagram of the Temple Courts on page 74). These activities apparently interfered with the Gentiles' worship of the one true God.

1. Describe what Jesus did in the Royal Stoa after His triumphant entry into Jerusalem (Matthew 21:12–13; Luke 19:45; John 2:13–17).

2. According to Isaiah 56:7, the Scripture Jesus quoted when He drove out the vendors and money changers, what was God's "house" to be called?

3. Why did Jesus drive the vendors and money changers out of the temple? (See Matthew 21:13.)

4. What truth did Jesus demonstrate by clearing out the Gentile Court?

5. What can we learn from the fact that Jesus expressed great anger toward religious leaders who didn't care about hurting, sinful, broken people and "unclean" Gentiles? What might we be doing today that would kindle Jesus' anger in a similar way?

Topic E: The Soreq—and Other Dividing Walls Within the Temple

The *Soreq* was a five-foot-tall stone wall that surrounded the inner courts of the consecrated temple area and was designed to keep Gentiles and other "unacceptable" people out of the inner courts. Gentiles could not pass the Soreq on pain of death.

1. What was Paul accused of doing? (See Acts 21:27–35.)

2. Later, in Ephesians 2:14, what did Paul say had been destroyed? When he used that phrase, what others kinds of "walls" might he have been describing?

Suggested Responses: Jesus had no tolerance for religious people who hindered other people's relationship with God or did not care to meet the needs of hurting people. He died on the cross for sinful, hurting, broken people. It's often easy for us to avoid people who have deep needs. We may feel uncomfortable around them, think we don't have anything significant to contribute to them, or simply be too busy or hard-hearted to reach out to them, etc. But God calls us to reach out to them with His love.

Topic E: The Soreq—and Other Dividing Walls Within the Temple

The *Soreq* was a five-foot-tall stone wall that surrounded the inner courts of the consecrated temple area and was designed to keep Gentiles and other "unacceptable" people out of the inner courts. Gentiles could not pass the Soreq on pain of death.

1. What was Paul accused of doing? (See Acts 21:27–35.)

   Suggested Response: bringing a Gentile into the inner court, past the Soreq, a charge which Paul denied.

2. Later, in Ephesians 2:14, what did Paul say had been destroyed? When he used that phrase, what others kinds of "walls" might he have been describing?

   Suggested Response: the "dividing wall of hostility." Paul was possibly referring to all dividing walls, which the Soreq symbolized, that had to come down between Jew and Gentile so that people could experience God's peace. In other words, the Gentiles were to be allowed to experience the blessings the Jews always had.

The Temple Courts

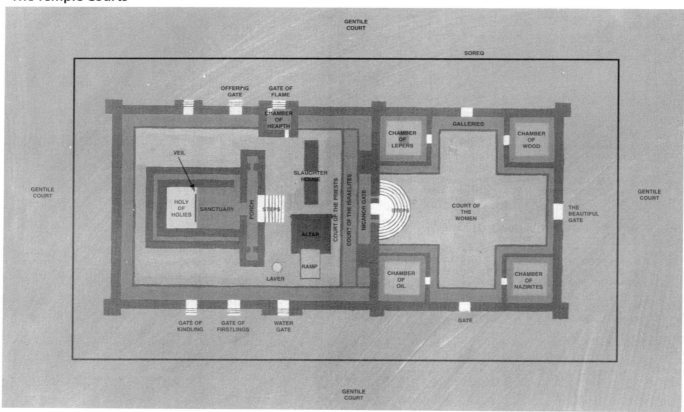

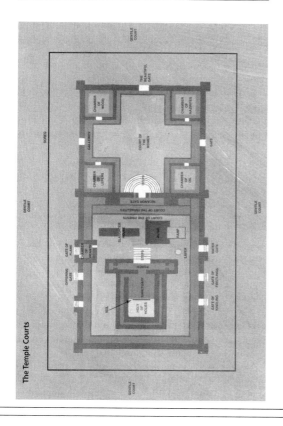

The Temple Courts

---

4. What truth did Jesus demonstrate by clearing out the Gentile Court?

5. What can we learn from the fact that Jesus expressed great anger toward religious leaders who didn't care about hurting, sinful, broken people and "unclean" Gentiles? What might we be doing today that would kindle Jesus' anger in a similar way?

Topic E: The Soreq—and Other Dividing Walls Within the Temple

The *Soreq* was a five-foot-tall stone wall that surrounded the inner courts of the consecrated temple area and was designed to keep Gentiles and other "unacceptable" people out of the inner courts. Gentiles could not pass the Soreq on pain of death.

1. What was Paul accused of doing? (See Acts 21:27–35.)

2. Later, in Ephesians 2:14, what did Paul say had been destroyed? When he used that phrase, what others kinds of "walls" might he have been describing?

These walls include walls between races and the walls between men and women. Jesus broke down the symbolic wall between Jew and Gentile through His death and resurrection, but it is important for us to identify and embrace our religious heritage. By reclaiming our Jewish roots, we can become more intimately acquainted with the character of God.

3. In light of the previous question, if Paul were alive today which walls might he point out to us that divide us from other people?

Suggested Responses: walls of pride, economic status, race, social status, bitterness, etc.

4. What can you do to break down walls that divide you from other people?

Suggested Responses will vary greatly: ask God to make me aware of the walls and to help me break them down, reach out to other people, get to know Christians from other races in my city, help out at a food pantry, become a volunteer in a local nonprofit organization that helps people in need, etc.

5. In addition to the Soreq, there were a number of other walls and divisions within the temple. Identify the separation indicated by each of the following (Refer to the diagram of the Temple Courts on page 74):

Area of the Temple	Type of Separation
The Court of the Women	Area outside the temple building, which was as close as women were allowed to the temple.
Chamber of Nazirites	Nazirites had been set apart for service to God.
Chamber of Lepers	Had to be separate because they were unclean.
Court of the Israelites	Were separate because they were God's people.
Court of the Priests	Were separated by their calling, which was to be set apart to represent the people to God.
Sanctuary of the Temple	Separated the people from the presence of God.
The Holy of Holies	The holiest part of the temple, where the Ark of the Covenant was. The veil separated the presence of God from the priests.

faith Lesson

10 minutes

Time for Reflection (6 minutes)

It's time for each of us to think quietly about how we can apply what we've learned today. On pages 77–78 of the Participant's Guide, you'll find a passage of Scripture. Let's each read this passage silently and take the next few minutes to consider some of the questions that follow the Scripture passage.

Please do not talk during this time. It's a time when we all can reflect on God's temple and how the message of the temple applies to our lives.

The Scripture passage and questions are reproduced in their entirety in the Participant's Guide on pages 77–78.

3. In light of the previous question, if Paul were alive today which walls might he point out to us that divide us from other people?

4. What can you do to break down walls that divide you from other people?

5. In addition to the Soreq, there were a number of other walls and divisions within the temple. Identify the separation indicated by each of the following (refer to the diagram of the Temple Courts on page 74):

Area of the Temple	Type of Separation
The Court of the Women	
Chamber of Nazirites	
Chamber of Lepers	
Court of the Israelites	
Court of the Priests	
Sanctuary of the Temple	
The Holy of Holies	

faith Lesson

Time for Reflection

The following passages of Scripture provide a glimpse of how God viewed His temple. Read these passages silently and consider the importance of God's temple and how the message of the temple applies to your life.

"And foreigners who bind themselves to the LORD to serve him, to love the name of the LORD, and to worship him, all who keep the Sabbath without desecrating it and who hold fast to my covenant— these I will bring to my holy mountain and give them joy in my house of prayer. Their burnt offerings and sacrifices will be accepted on my altar; for my house will be called a house of prayer for all nations."

ISAIAH 56:6–7

On reaching Jerusalem, Jesus entered the temple area and began driving out those who were buying and selling there. He overturned the tables of the money changers and the benches of those selling doves, and would not allow anyone to carry merchandise through the temple courts. And as he taught them, he said, "Is it not written: "'My house will be called a house of prayer for all nations'? But you have made it 'a den of robbers.'" The chief priests and the teachers of the law heard this and began looking for a way to kill him, for they feared him, because the whole crowd was amazed at his teaching.

MARK 11:15–18

Meanwhile, the high priest questioned Jesus about his disciples and his teaching. "I have spoken openly to the world," Jesus replied. "I always taught in synagogues or at the temple, where all the Jews come together. I said nothing in secret. Why question me? Ask those who heard me. Surely they know what I said." When Jesus said this,

PLANNING NOTES:

"And foreigners who bind themselves to the LORD to serve him, to love the name of the LORD, and to worship him, all who keep the Sabbath without desecrating it and who hold fast to my covenant—these I will bring to my holy mountain and give them joy in my house of prayer. Their burnt offerings and sacrifices will be accepted on my altar; for my house will be called a house of prayer for all nations."

ISAIAH 56:6–7

On reaching Jerusalem, Jesus entered the temple area and began driving out those who were buying and selling there. He overturned the tables of the money changers and the benches of those selling doves, and would not allow anyone to carry merchandise through the temple courts. And as he taught them, he said, "Is it not written: "'My house will be called a house of prayer for all nations'? But you have made it 'a den of robbers.'" The chief priests and the teachers of the law heard this and began looking for a way to kill him, for they feared him, because the whole crowd was amazed at his teaching.

MARK 11:15–18

Meanwhile, the high priest questioned Jesus about his disciples and his teaching. "I have spoken openly to the world," Jesus replied. "I always taught in synagogues or at the temple, where all the Jews come together. I said nothing in secret. Why question me? Ask those who heard me. Surely they know what I said." When Jesus said this, one of the officials nearby struck him in the face. "Is this the way you answer the high priest?" he demanded. "If I said something wrong," Jesus replied, "testify as to what is wrong. But if I spoke the truth, why did you strike me?" Then Annas sent him, still bound, to Caiaphas the high priest.

JOHN 18:19–24

1. In light of what the temple symbolized for the Jews, what have you learned about the character of God and the relationship He desires to have with us?

2. Now that you've learned more about the ancient temple, what insights have you gained into why Jesus drove out the moneychangers? Into why the Sadducees wanted to kill Him?

3. In what ways has understanding the power of the temple leaders and the might of the Roman empire helped you understand the commitment Jesus had to communicating God's truth—no matter what the cost?

As soon as participants have spent six minutes reflecting on the above questions, get the entire group's attention and move to the next section.

faith lesson

Time for Reflection

The following passages of Scripture provide a glimpse of how God viewed His temple. Read these passages silently and consider the importance of God's temple and how the message of the temple applies to your life.

> "And foreigners who bind themselves to the LORD to serve him, to love the name of the LORD, and to worship him, all who keep the Sabbath without desecrating it and who hold fast to my covenant— these I will bring to my holy mountain and give them joy in my house of prayer. Their burnt offerings and sacrifices will be accepted on my altar; for my house will be called a house of prayer for all nations."
>
> ISAIAH 56:6–7

> On reaching Jerusalem, Jesus entered the temple area and began driving out those who were buying and selling there. He overturned the tables of the money changers and the benches of those selling doves, and would not allow anyone to carry merchandise through the temple courts. And as he taught them, he said, "Is it not written: "'My house will be called a house of prayer for all nations'? But you have made it 'a den of robbers.'" The chief priests and the teachers of the law heard this and began looking for a way to kill him, for they feared him, because the whole crowd was amazed at his teaching.
>
> MARK 11:15–18

> Meanwhile, the high priest questioned Jesus about his disciples and his teaching. "I have spoken openly to the world," Jesus replied. "I always taught in synagogues or at the temple, where all the Jews come together. I said nothing in secret. Why question me? Ask those who heard me. Surely they know what I said." When Jesus said this,

> one of the officials nearby struck him in the face. "Is this the way you answer the high priest?" he demanded. "If I said something wrong," Jesus replied, "testify as to what is wrong. But if I spoke the truth, why did you strike me?" Then Annas sent him, still bound, to Caiaphas the high priest.
>
> JOHN 18:19–24

1. In light of what the temple symbolized for the Jews, what have you learned about the character of God and the relationship He desires to have with us?

2. Now that you've learned more about the ancient temple, what insights have you gained into why Jesus drove out the money changers? Into why the Sadducees wanted to kill Him?

3. In what ways has understanding the power of the temple leaders and the might of the Roman empire helped you understand the commitment Jesus had to communicating God's truth—no matter what the cost?

PLANNING NOTES:

A CHRONOLOGY OF TEMPLE EVENTS

Approx. 2,000 B.C. Abraham was sent to the Moriah area to sacrifice Isaac. Jerusalem was later built on the mountain named Moriah.

Approx. 1,000 B.C. David captured the Canaanite city of Jebus (2 Samuel 5:6–7) and named it the City of David, which he made his capital (1 Chronicles 11:7). He selected the temple site on the threshing floor of Araunah on Mount Moriah, where he built an altar.

Approx. 950 B.C. Solomon built the temple on the Mount Moriah site chosen by David at God's leading. After the Ark of the Covenant—the resting place of God's glorious presence—was moved into the temple—God's earthly home—the people prayed for God's presence (2 Chronicles 6) and God sent fire to consume their sacrifices (2 Chronicles 7:1–3).

586 B.C. The Babylonians destroyed the temple and took many Israelites captive.

Approx. 500 B.C. Cyrus, king of Persia, decreed that the Israelites could return to Jerusalem. Under Ezra and Nehemiah's leadership, the temple was rebuilt (Ezra 1:1–4; 3:7–13; 6:15). Since there was no Ark of the Covenant, the Holy of Holies was left empty. The Jews rejoiced when the Torah was read (Nehemiah 8:17).

Continued on page 128

Development of the Temple Mount

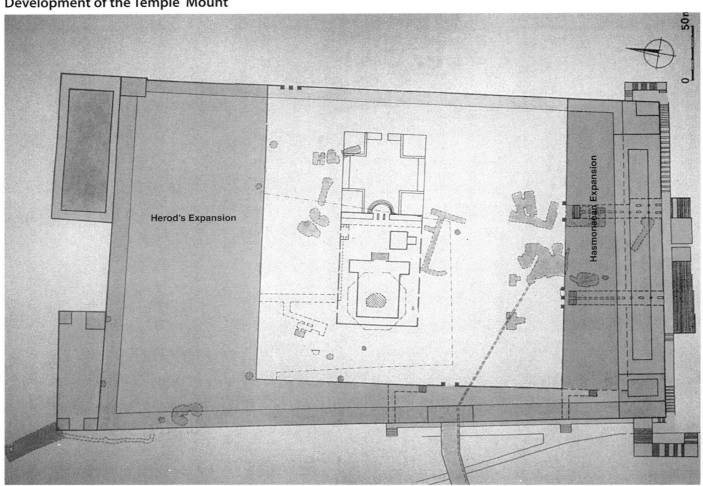

PLANNING NOTES:

Development of the Temple Mount

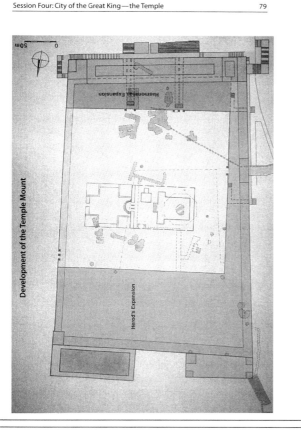

Hasmonean Expansion

Herod's Expansion

50m
0

80 The Death and Resurrection of the Messiah

A Chronology of Temple Events

Approx. 2,000 B.C.   Abraham was sent to the Moriah area to sacrifice Isaac. Jerusalem was later built on the mountain named Moriah.

Approx. 1,000 B.C.   David captured the Canaanite city of Jebus (2 Samuel 5:6–7) and named it the City of David, which he made his capital (1 Chronicles 11:7). He selected the temple site on the threshing floor of Araunah on Mount Moriah, where he built an altar.

Approx. 950 B.C.   Solomon built the temple on the Mount Moriah site chosen by David at God's leading. After the Ark of the Covenant—the resting place of God's glorious presence—was moved into the temple—God's earthly home—the people prayed for God's presence (2 Chronicles 6) and God sent fire to consume their sacrifices (2 Chronicles 7:1–3).

586 B.C.   The Babylonians destroyed the temple and took many Israelites captive.

Approx. 500 B.C.   Cyrus, king of Persia, decreed that the Israelites could return to Jerusalem. Under Ezra and Nehemiah's leadership, the temple was rebuilt (Ezra 1:1–4; 3:7–13; 6:15). Since there was no Ark of the Covenant, the Holy of Holies was left empty. The Jews rejoiced when the Torah was read (Nehemiah 8:17).

322 B.C.   Jerusalem, rebuilt during Ezra's time, became part of Alexander the Great's empire. The city suffered more than a century of conflict at the hands of Alexander's Hellenistic successors. Antiochus, the king of the Syrians, outlawed the Sabbath, circumcision, the study of Torah, and even defiled the great altar by sacrificing pigs on it.

165 B.C.   The Maccabean revolt against the Greek army brought Jerusalem back under Jewish control. The menorah—the symbol of eternal light in the Holy of

A Chronology of Temple Events—continued from page 126

322 B.C.	Jerusalem, rebuilt during Ezra's time, became part of Alexander the Great's empire. The city suffered more than a century of conflict at the hands of Alexander's Hellenistic successors. Antiochus, the king of the Syrians, outlawed the Sabbath, circumcision, the study of Torah, and even defiled the great altar by sacrificing pigs on it.
165 B.C.	The Maccabean revolt against the Greek army brought Jerusalem back under Jewish control. The menorah—the symbol of eternal light in the Holy of Holies—was relit. Descendants of the Maccabees expanded the Temple Mount. The city now covered 175 acres and had more than 30,000 inhabitants.
63 B.C.	The Romans take control of Judea.
37–4 B.C.	Herod, the king of Israel appointed by Rome, lavishly expanded Temple Mount, embellished the temple, fortified the city, and built many spectacular buildings. A wonder of the ancient world, the city was now ready for the ministry of Jesus, the Messiah. But Herod also conducted a reign of terror designed to keep the Jewish people in line. To keep his position, Herod needed the might of Rome, the support of the Sadducees (the temple authorities), and the favor of Hellenistic Jews. Afraid of losing his throne to the Messiah, Herod killed the male babies in Bethlehem (Matthew 2:16).
Approx. A.D. 30	The Sadducees had Jesus crucified. The Holy Spirit came upon the disciples in the temple courts; the veil separating the inner chamber of the temple (the Holy of Holies) split from top to bottom, symbolizing the access all believers now had to God's presence through Jesus. On the Christian fulfillment of Pentecost, God took up residence in a new temple—His community of believers (1 Corinthians 3:16–17).
A.D. 44	Herod Agrippa I, grandson of Herod the Great, died. Rebel Jews began killing Romans and Jews who cooperated with them, and Roman governors became increasingly cruel. The temple priesthood became more dependent on the Romans for security and support and became more corrupt.
A.D. 66	A Gentile offered a "pagan" sacrifice next to the synagogue's entrance in Caesarea. The Jerusalem authorities decided to end all foreign sacrifices. The Rome-appointed governor, Florus, authorized Roman troops to raid the temple treasury. When the Jews protested, Florus's troops killed many innocent civilians. In turn, Jewish mobs drove out the Roman troops, stormed the Antonia (the Roman fort), and occupied the fortress of Masada. When the Romans in Caesarea learned what had happened, they killed 20,000 Jews within a day's time.
A.D. 68	Ultra-nationalistic Jews (the Zealots) appointed their own temple priest and slaughtered the Sadducee priests who resisted.
A.D. 70	Under Titus, at least 80,000 Roman troops destroyed Jerusalem, slaughtering hundreds of thousands of Jews. The streets ran with Jewish blood. On August 9, the temple was burned and destroyed. All the citizens of Jerusalem (more than one million) were executed, sold into slavery, or captured for games in the arena.
A.D. 131	A second Jewish revolt started, driving Christianity to the ends of the earth, where it soon became a largely Gentile faith. Only today are the Jewish roots of Christianity being fully appreciated.
A.D. 135	Rome squashed the second revolt, outlawed the Jewish religion, and Judea became Palestine. Rabbinic Judaism became the Orthodox faith of Jewish people today. The Jews became a people without a country.

	Holies—was relit. Descendants of the Maccabees expanded the Temple Mount. The city now covered 175 acres and had more than 30,000 inhabitants.
63 B.C.	The Romans take control of Judea.
37–4 B.C.	Herod, the king of Israel appointed by Rome, lavishly expanded the Temple Mount, embellished the temple, fortified the city, and built many spectacular buildings. A wonder of the ancient world, the city was now ready for the ministry of Jesus, the Messiah. But Herod also conducted a reign of terror designed to keep the Jewish people in line. To keep his position, Herod needed the might of Rome, the support of the Sadducees (the temple authorities), and the favor of Hellenistic Jews. Afraid of losing his throne to the Messiah, Herod killed the male babies in Bethlehem (Matthew 2:16).
Approx. A.D. 30	The Sadducees had Jesus crucified. The Holy Spirit came upon the disciples in the temple courts; the veil separating the inner chamber of the temple (the Holy of Holies) split from top to bottom, symbolizing the access all believers now had to God's presence through Jesus. On the Christian fulfillment of Pentecost, God took up residence in a new temple—His community of believers (1 Corinthians 3:16–17).
A.D. 44	Herod Agrippa I, grandson of Herod the Great, died. Rebel Jews began killing Romans and Jews who cooperated with them, and Roman governors became increasingly cruel. The temple priesthood became more dependent on the Romans for security and support and became more corrupt.
A.D. 66	A Gentile offered a "pagan" sacrifice next to the synagogue's entrance in Caesarea. The Jerusalem authorities decided to end all foreign sacrifices. The Rome-appointed governor, Florus, authorized Roman troops to raid the temple treasury. When the Jews protested, Florus's troops killed many innocent civilians.

	In turn, Jewish mobs drove out the Roman troops, stormed the Antonia (the Roman fort), and occupied the fortress of Masada. When the Romans in Caesarea learned what had happened, they killed 20,000 Jews within a day's time.
A.D. 68	Ultra-nationalistic Jews (the Zealots) appointed their own temple priest and slaughtered the Sadducee priests who resisted.
A.D. 70	Under Titus, at least 80,000 Roman troops destroyed Jerusalem, slaughtering hundreds of thousands of Jews. The streets ran with Jewish blood. On August 9, the temple was burned and destroyed. All the citizens of Jerusalem (more than one million) were executed, sold into slavery, or captured for games in the arena.
A.D. 131	A second Jewish revolt started, driving Christianity to the ends of the earth, where it soon became a largely Gentile faith. Only today are the Jewish roots of Christianity being fully appreciated.
A.D. 135	Rome squashed the second revolt, outlawed the Jewish religion, and Judea became Palestine. Rabbinic Judaism became the Orthodox faith of Jewish people today. The Jews became a people without a country.

Action Points (4 minutes)

The following points are reproduced on page 83 of the Participant's Guide:

Now it's time to wrap up our session.

Give participants a moment to transition from their thoughtfulness to giving you their full attention.

I'd like to take a moment to summarize the key points we explored. After I have reviewed each point, I will give you a moment to jot down an action step (or steps) that you will commit to this week as a result of what you have learned today.

Read each point and pause after each so that participants can consider and write out their commitment.

1. *Learning about the temple in Jerusalem—its structures, practices, history—gives us insight into the heart of God and His desire to bring salvation to His people.* It also helps us visualize biblical events that occurred in Jerusalem.

   What will you do to continue to learn the ways in which the Christian faith is rooted in Jewish culture?

2. *God wanted His temple—the symbol of His presence on earth—to be available to everyone.* He designated it to be a house of prayer for all nations—Jews, Gentiles, even lepers. Ray Vander Laan believes that's why Jesus became so angry when the temple authorities allowed vendors to carry on their trade in the Court of the Gentiles, which would disrupt the Gentiles who had come to worship God.

   In what ways might you be insensitive to the spiritual needs of other people around you, just as the temple authorities were insensitive to the Gentiles by allowing merchandise to be bought and sold in the area set aside for their worship?

   What steps will you take to broaden your horizons and invite people who are presently outside the church, outside the community of believers, to come in and discover and worship God?

closing prayer

1 minute

Dear God, thank You for giving us the opportunity to learn more about Jerusalem and Your temple today. You wanted to be accessible to everyone during Jesus' day—You still are accessible to anyone today who seeks You. Help us to reach out and share Your desire for all people to worship You. Make us aware of the spiritual needs of people around us—in our families, our neighborhoods, and our cities. Just as You guided people and events in Jesus' day to fulfill Your plans, You are working in our lives today. Please make us sensitive to Your leading. Amen.

Action Points

Take a moment to review the key points you explored today. Then write down the action step (or steps) you will commit to this week as a result of what you have discovered.

1. *Learning about the temple in Jerusalem—its structures, practices, history—gives us insight into the heart of God and His desire to bring salvation to His people.* It also helps us visualize biblical events that occurred in Jerusalem.

    What will you do to continue to learn the ways in which the Christian faith is rooted in Jewish culture?

2. *God wanted His temple—the symbol of His presence on earth—to be available to everyone.* He designated it to be a house of prayer for all nations—Jews, Gentiles, even lepers. Ray Vander Laan believes that's why Jesus became so angry when the temple authorities allowed vendors to carry on their trade in the Court of the Gentiles, which would disrupt the Gentiles who had come to worship God.

    In what ways might you be insensitive to the spiritual needs of other people around you, just as the temple authorities were insensitive to the Gentiles by allowing merchandise to be bought and sold in the area set aside for their worship?

What steps will you take to broaden your horizons and invite people who are presently outside the church, outside the community of believers, to come in and discover and worship God?

PLANNING NOTES:

city of the great king— Jerusalem

before you lead

Synopsis

To the Jewish people, such places as the Mount of Olives, Kidron Valley, Mount Zion, and the temple had deep cultural and religious significance. Many soul-stirring events had occurred in and around their city. Many influential people—King David, Hezekiah, Nehemiah, King Solomon, and others—had made significant marks on their culture and even the world while living in Jerusalem, and their deeds have been recorded for generations to remember. In the region of the Gentile Court, God had spoken to Abraham and Isaac. He had allowed David to prepare for the temple, commissioned Solomon to build it, and for more than a thousand years had exhibited His presence in that temple. But few Jews living during Jesus' time realized the plan that God was still accomplishing in their bustling city.

Here, as a young man, Jesus worshiped His heavenly Father. Here, the King of the universe celebrated Passover, Pentecost, Hanukkah, and the Feast of Tabernacles. Here, the chosen Lamb of God participated in temple ceremonies and taught Scripture. And just outside the city walls, God had chosen to demonstrate the greatest act of love and redemption the world would ever know. There, by a hill outside the city, Jesus ascended His throne by way of a cross—and the world forever changed for both Jews and Gentiles. Thus Jerusalem—the city of great kings—will always be remembered as the city of the eternal King of Kings—our Messiah, Jesus.

As we learn about Jerusalem, we understand more about God's power and love—and how He has worked throughout history to bring His plans to fruition. For Christians, understanding Jerusalem's rich heritage provides an opportunity to visualize more fully God's great redemptive work. With this purpose in mind, Ray Vander Laan shares insights into:

- Herod's marvelous construction of Robinson's Arch.
- What Herod the Great's palace looked like. (At this palace, the wise men seeking Jesus probably met with Herod the Great, and years later Herod Antipas probably interrogated Jesus after His arrest.)
- The lifestyle of influential religious leaders. The ruins of an opulent mansion reveal what Jesus may have seen when the Jewish leaders interrogated Him in Caiaphas's home.

- The city walls within which Jesus conducted a portion of His ministry and the areas of the city that Jesus likely passed through on market day as He carried His cross.
- The horror of the Romans' destruction of Jerusalem in A.D. 70, which caused Jesus to weep when He foresaw it.
- The huge fortress—the Antonia—that Herod the Great built to protect the city and house the Roman garrison.

Key Points of this Session

1. *To understand more about Jerusalem—its structures, its people, its activity—is to understand the Jewish heritage on which the Christian faith is built.* As we see (through a scale model and actual ruins) what the city and its structures looked like during Jesus' time—and learn about significant events in His life that took place in or near those structures—the great work God accomplished in that city becomes more real to us.

2. *Just as God used the temple to represent His kingdom and invite the world to know Him, God is using us today—His temples—to represent His kingdom to the world.* As God's Spirit fills us and lives within us, we are called to take His kingdom to all the people of God's world.

Session Outline (53 minutes)

I. Introduction (4 minutes)
Welcome
What's to Come
Questions to Think About

II. Video Presentation "City of the Great King—Jerusalem" (20 minutes)

III. Group Discovery (20 minutes)
Video Highlights
Small Group Bible Discovery

IV. Faith Lesson (8 minutes)
Time for Reflection
Action Points

V. Closing Prayer (1 minute)

Materials

No additional materials are needed for this session. Simply view the video prior to leading the session so you are familiar with its main points.

city of the great king— Jerusalem

introduction

4 minutes

Welcome

Assemble the participants together. Welcome them to session five of *Faith Lessons on the Death and Resurrection of the Messiah*.

What's to Come

In today's session—part two of the video series on Jerusalem—Ray Vander Laan focuses on historical sites within the various districts of the city. We'll see the interior of a mansion that was probably owned by a Jewish religious leader— maybe even the house in which Jesus was interrogated after His arrest. We'll also explore other historical sites related to Jesus' ministry and catch a glimpse of what daily life was like for the people of Jerusalem during the time Jesus lived there.

Questions to Think About

Participant's Guide page 85.

Turn to page 85 of your Participant's Guide. Let's consider several questions that will help us begin thinking about the impact the city of Jerusalem has on our Christian faith.

Ask each question and solicit a few responses from group members.

1. Think for a moment about the times you have explored great historical sites—perhaps the U.S. capitol building, or White House, the site of the Battle of Gettysburg, the Great Wall of China, the great castles of Europe, the pyramids of Egypt, etc.—or viewed a reenactment of a great event. Consider for a moment what life was like for people who lived through the significant events of those places. Consider what life would have been like for you in those places.

Suggested Responses will vary widely: Encourage several people to share what they have seen and felt and possibly the impact that exploring a great historical site has had on their lives. This will help participants prepare their hearts to understand what life was like during Jesus' day.

SESSION FIVE

city of the great king—
jerusalem

questions to think about

1. Think for a moment about the times you have explored great historical sites—perhaps the U.S. capitol building, or White House, the site of the Battle of Gettysburg, the Great Wall of China, the great castles of Europe, the pyramids of Egypt, etc.—or viewed a reenactment of a great event. Consider for a moment what life was like for people who lived through the significant events of those places. Consider what life would have been like for you in those places.

2. Consider what you know about the sights, sounds, fears, hopes, joys, and heartaches of the people of Jerusalem in Jesus' day.

2. Consider what you know about the sights, sounds, fears, hopes, joys, and heartaches of the people of Jerusalem in Jesus' day.

Suggested Responses: Again, these will vary widely. Most likely everyone greatly feared the Romans; the Sadducees and high priests were allowed to live a comfortable life by the Romans, but it could end abruptly if the people got out of hand; it was a bustling center of commerce and cultures that could have been very exciting and stimulating—rich with the sounds of many languages, ripe with the aroma of spices from the known world; as the center for Jewish worship, there was probably great hope for the coming of the Messiah; the ordinary people, dominated by the Romans, Herods, and temple leaders, probably were oppressed with many heartaches—no wonder they wanted a messiah; etc.

Let's keep these thoughts in mind as we view the video.

video presentation

20 minutes

Participant's Guide page 86.

On page 86 of your Participant's Guide, you will find a space in which to take notes on key points as we watch this video.

Leader's Video Observations

Features of the City Districts

Herod's Palace

The Jewish Mansion

The Antonia

Jesus: Our Scapegoat

SESSION FIVE

city of the great king— Jerusalem

questions to think about

1. Think for a moment about the times you have explored great historical sites—perhaps the U.S. capitol building, or White House, the site of the Battle of Gettysburg, the Great Wall of China, the great castles of Europe, the pyramids of Egypt, etc.—or viewed a reenactment of a great event. Consider for a moment what life was like for people who lived through the significant events of those places. Consider what life would have been like for you in those places.

2. Consider what you know about the sights, sounds, fears, hopes, joys, and heartaches of the people of Jerusalem in Jesus' day.

86   The Death and Resurrection of the Messiah

video notes

Features of the City Districts

Herod's Palace

The Jewish Mansion

The Antonia

Jesus: Our Scapegoat

Group Discovery

If your group has seven or more members, use the **Video Highlights** with the entire group (5 minutes), then break into small groups of three to five to discuss the **Small Group Bible Discovery** (10 minutes). Then reassemble the group to discuss the key points discovered (5 minutes).

If your group has fewer than seven members, begin with the **Video Highlights** (5 minutes), then do one or more of the topics found in the **Small Group Bible Discovery** as a group (10 minutes). Finally, spend five minutes at the end discussing points that had an impact on participants.

Video Highlights (5 minutes)

Here you'll ask one or more of the following questions that directly relate to the video the participants have just seen.

Turn to the map of Jerusalem on page 88 of your Participant's Guide. Note the various districts of the city, and the locations of the Mount of Olives, the Temple Mount, the Eastern Gate, Herod's Palace, the Jewish mansions, the Antonia, and the Garden Gate.

1. In our previous session, we explored the ancient temple and learned quite a bit about the Jews' religious practices, temple history, and Jesus' ministry in the temple. Today, we looked at other historical sites in Jerusalem. In what ways have you gained a better understanding of what life was like during Jesus' day?

   Suggested Responses: Allow several participants to share their perspectives with the group.

2. Explain what you think it would have been like to have been an ordinary Jewish person who lived in a city ruled by the temple authorities, Herod, and the Romans.

   Suggested Responses: It probably would have been a fearful place in which to live. The temple authorities were quick to deal with anyone who didn't follow their rules; Herod executed his favorite wife, then built a tower in her honor; the Romans apparently needed little excuse to slaughter Jews; etc. It also would have been exciting to live in the place God had chosen as a dwelling place for His presence, to participate in the feasts and ceremonies, to live in expectation of the Messiah, etc.

3. What did you feel as you saw what Herod's palace looked like—and realized that the wise men and Jesus had probably been there?

   Suggested Response: thoughtful as I began to realize what the palace was like and the events that really happened there; felt as if the biblical events were more real to me, etc.

video Highlights

On the map of Jerusalem (page 88) note the various districts of the city and the locations of the Mount of Olives, the Temple Mount, the Eastern Gate, Herod's Palace, the Jewish mansions, the Antonia, and the Garden Gate.

1. In our previous session, we explored the ancient temple and learned quite a bit about the Jews' religious practices, temple history, and Jesus' ministry in the temple. Today, we looked at other historical sites in Jerusalem. In what ways have you gained a better understanding of what life was like during Jesus' day?

2. Explain what you think it would have been like to have been an ordinary Jewish person who lived in a city ruled by the temple authorities, Herod, and the Romans.

3. What did you feel as you saw what Herod's palace looked like—and realized that the wise men and Jesus had probably been there?

☞ 4. What surprised you as you learned about the mansion that was probably owned by one of the Jewish high priests?

Suggested Responses: how beautiful and elaborate it was, that the Jewish leaders even had stone tables and jars instead of clay ones to maintain ceremonial cleanliness, that the mansion had bathrooms, etc.

☞ 5. In what ways does Jerusalem, which has experienced more than 3,000 years of history, inspire you?

Suggested Responses: Allow several participants to share their thoughts.

Jerusalem's Districts

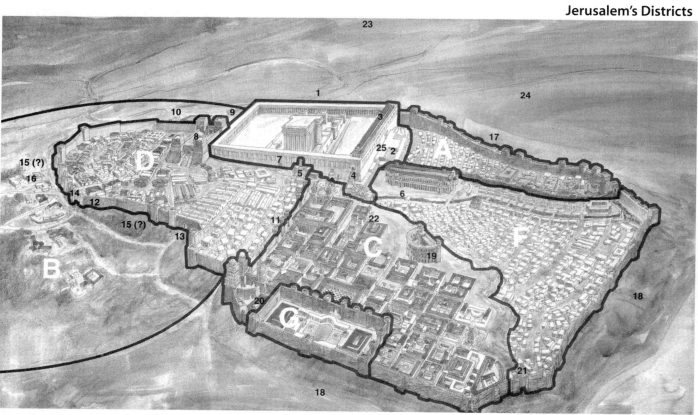

A	David's City	1	Eastern Gate	8	Antonia	15	Golgotha (?)
B	New City	2	Southern Gate	9	Tadi Gate	16	Garden Tomb
C	Upper City	3	Royal Stoa	10	Pool of Bethesda	17	Spring of Gihon
D	Business District	4	Robinson's Arch	11	First Wall	18	Hinnom Valley
E	Temple Mount	5	Wilson's Arch	12	Second Wall	19	Theatre
F	Lower City	6	Tyropoeon Street	13	Garden Gate	20	Citadel and Herod's palace
G	Herod's Palace	7	Warren's Gate	14	Towers (Damascus) Gate	21	Essence Quarter
						22	Mansions
						23	Mount of Olives
						24	Kidron Valley
						25	Huldah Gates

88   The Death and Resurrection of the Messiah

4. What surprised you as you learned about the mansion that was probably owned by one of the Jewish high priests?

5. In what ways does Jerusalem, which has experienced more than three thousand years of history, inspire you?

Jerusalem's Districts

A	David's City	1	Eastern Gate	8	Antonia	15	Golgotha (?)
B	New City	2	Southern Gate	9	Tadi Gate	16	Garden Tomb
C	Upper City	3	Royal Stoa	10	Pool of Bethesda	17	Spring of Gihon
D	Business District	4	Robinson's Arch	11	First Wall	18	Hinnom Valley
E	Temple Mount	5	Wilson's Arch	12	Second Wall	19	Theatre
F	Lower City	6	Tyropoeon Street	13	Garden Gate	20	Citadel and
G	Herod's Palace	7	Warren's Gate	14	Towers		Herod's palace
					(Damascus) Gate		

21 Essence Quarter
22 Mansions
23 Mount of Olives
24 Kidron Valley
25 Huldah Gates

DATA FILE

The Geographic Features and Events of Jerusalem

Hinnom Valley formed the western boundary of the Western Hill and the Upper City of Jesus' time; began along the Western Hill and ended where the Tyropoeon and Kidron Valleys met.

Location where the kings and people of Judah sacrificed their children to Baal (2 Kings 23:10; 2 Chronicles 28:3–4; 33:1, 6; Jeremiah 7:31; 19:5–6; 32:35) and where Jerusalem's garbage was burned; became a synonym for hell itself (Matthew 5:22, 29; 10:28; 18:9; 23:33; Mark 9:43–48; James 3:6).

Kidron Valley, a deep wadi about three miles long, east of the city between David's city and the Mount of Olives.

David crossed here when fleeing Absalom (2 Samuel 15:13–24); various kings destroyed idols and pagan objects here (1 Kings 15:11–12; 2 Kings 23:4–7, 12–14; 2 Chronicles 15:16); Jesus crossed here on his way to Gethsemane just before His arrest (John 18:1); Joel prophesied concerning the judgment of nations in the Valley of Johoshaphat—believed to be part or all of this valley (Joel 3:2, 12); and Solomon refused to allow Shimei to cross here (1 Kings 2:36–38). Hezekiah's tunnel brought fresh water from the Spring of Gihon, which was in the valley, to the Pool of Siloam.

Mount of Olives, the highest peak in the area.

David went here to escape Absalom's revolt (2 Samuel 15:13–37); Jesus entered Jerusalem from here (Matthew 21:1–11; Luke 19:1, 28–44), gave His final teaching here (Matthew 24:3–46), and ascended to heaven from here (Luke 24:50–52; Acts 1:6–12). May be the location for Jesus' return (Zechariah 14:4; Acts 1:11).

Tyropoeon Valley, between David's City and the Western Hill where the Upper City was located.

Hezekiah expanded the city into this valley; the western wall of Herod's Gentile Court was located here, as was the Pool of Siloam where Jesus sent a blind man to wash (John 9:1–12); Nehemiah repaired the wall near the Pool of Siloam (Nehemiah 3:15).

Western Hill, now called Mount Zion, was called the "Upper City" during Jesus' time.

The site of Herod's palace; probably where the wise men talked with Herod the Great (Matthew 2:1–7), Herod Antipas met Jesus (Luke 23:6–7), and where the Upper Room was located (Luke 22:7–13; Acts 1:12–13).

Topography of Jerusalem

DATA FILE

The Geographic Features and Events of Jerusalem

Hinnom Valley formed the western boundary of the Western Hill and the Upper City of Jesus' time; began along the Western Hill and ended where the Tyropoeon and Kidron Valleys met.

Location where the kings and people of Judah sacrificed their children to Baal (2 Kings 23:10; 2 Chronicles 28:3–4; 33:1, 6; Jeremiah 7:31; 19:5–6; 32:35) and where Jerusalem's garbage was burned; became a synonym for hell itself (Matthew 5:22, 29; 10:28; 18:9; 23:33; Mark 9:43–48; James 3:6).

Kidron Valley, a deep wadi about three miles long, east of the city between David's city and the Mount of Olives.

David crossed here when fleeing Absalom (2 Samuel 15:13–24); various kings destroyed idols and pagan objects here (1 Kings 15:11–12; 2 Kings 23:4–7, 12–14; 2 Chronicles 15:16); Jesus crossed here on his way

Topography of Jerusalem

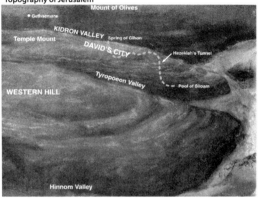

to Gethsemane just before His arrest (John 18:1); Joel prophesied concerning the judgment of nations in the Valley of Jehoshaphat—believed to be part or all of this valley (Joel 3:2, 12); and Solomon refused to allow Shimei to cross here (1 Kings 2:36–38). Hezekiah's tunnel brought fresh water from the Spring of Gihon, which was in the valley, to the Pool of Siloam.

Mount of Olives, the highest peak in the area.

David went here to escape Absalom's revolt (2 Samuel 15:13–37); Jesus entered Jerusalem from here (Matthew 21:1–11; Luke 19:1, 28–44), gave His final teaching here (Matthew 24:3–46), and ascended to heaven from here (Luke 24:50–52; Acts 1:6–12). May be the location for Jesus' return (Zechariah 14:4; Acts 1:11).

Tyropoeon Valley, between David's City and the Western Hill where the Upper City was located.

Hezekiah expanded the city into this valley; the western wall of Herod's Gentile Court was located here, as was the Pool of Siloam where Jesus sent a blind man to wash (John 9:1–12); Nehemiah repaired the wall near the Pool of Siloam (Nehemiah 3:15).

Western Hill, now called Mount Zion, was called the "Upper City" during Jesus' time.

The site of Herod's palace; probably where the wise men talked with Herod the Great (Matthew 2:1–7), Herod Antipas met Jesus (Luke 23:6–7), and where the Upper Room was located (Luke 22:7–13; Acts 1:12–13).

Small Group Bible Discovery (15 minutes)

> *Participant's Guide pages 91–99.*
>
> During this time, a group with fewer than seven participants will stay together. A group larger than seven participants will break into small groups and reassemble as a large group during the final five minutes. Assign each group one of the following topics. If you have more than five small groups, assign some topics to more than one group.

Let's break into groups of three to five—people sitting near you—and study some of the Bible passages and truths mentioned in the video.

Turn to pages 91–99 in your Participant's Guide. There you'll find a list of five topics. You'll have ten minutes to read and discuss the topic I'll assign to you. Choose one person in your group to be a spokesperson for your group when we discuss these topics later.

> Assign each group a topic.

I'll signal you when one minute is left.

> After nine minutes, let participants know that they have one minute remaining. Then reassemble the entire group. After everyone is back together, begin asking one person from each small group to briefly share a key idea with the larger group. In some cases, you may not have time for every group to share their discoveries.

As time allows, let's briefly share the key ideas that your group discussed.

Topic A: God Preserves His Holy City

During King Hezekiah's reign over Judah, he prepared for attack by Assyria, a pagan nation that in 722 B.C. destroyed the northern kingdom of Israel.

✏ 1. What kind of a king was Hezekiah? (See 2 Chronicles 29:1–3, 35–36; 31:1, 20–21.)

Suggested Responses: Hezekiah was God fearing; brought Israel back to God; repaired the temple; resumed the practice of sacrificing to God in the temple; ordered that pagan altars, idols, and sacred stones be destroyed; sought God; etc.

✏ 2. What did Assyria do during the fourteenth year of King Hezekiah's reign? (See Isaiah 36:1; 2 Kings 18:13.)

Suggested Response: attacked and captured all the fortified cities of Judah, threatening the existence of God's people.

✏ 3. What had Hezekiah done to prepare for the Assyrian attack against Jerusalem? (See 1 Kings 20:20; 2 Chronicles 32:1–5.)

Suggested Responses: everything he could—fixed walls, blocked up water sources, dug a tunnel to bring water into the city, built walls and towers, made vast quantities of weapons, etc.

small Group Bible Discovery

Topic A: God Preserves His Holy City

During King Hezekiah's reign over Judah, he prepared for attack by Assyria, a pagan nation that in 722 B.C. destroyed the northern kingdom of Israel.

1. What kind of a king was Hezekiah? (See 2 Chronicles 29:1–3, 35–36; 31:1, 20–21.)

2. What did Assyria do during the fourteenth year of King Hezekiah's reign? (See Isaiah 36:1; 2 Kings 18:13.)

3. What had Hezekiah done to prepare for the Assyrian attack against Jerusalem? (See 1 Kings 20:20; 2 Chronicles 32:1–5.)

4. How did Hezekiah respond upon receiving the Assyrians' ultimatum? (See Isaiah 37:14–20.)

✏ 4. How did Hezekiah respond upon receiving the Assyrians' ultimatum? (See Isaiah 37:14–20.)

Suggested Responses: Hezekiah immediately laid the letter before God, prayed, and trusted God for deliverance. He also, like David before him, asked for God's deliverance "so that all kingdoms on earth may know that you alone, O Lord, are God."

✏ 5. How did God deliver His people? (See 2 Chronicles 32:20–23.)

Suggested Response: His angel killed all the Assyrian fighting men, leaders, and officers in the enemy camp.

✏ 6. As we consider how God saved Jerusalem, what lessons can we learn about God and the problems we face today?

Suggested Responses: to trust God with our problems, that God is faithful, that He hears our prayers, that no problem is too great for Him, that God will act to reveal Himself, etc.

Topic B: Jesus Heals at the Pool of Bethesda

Refer to the map of Jerusalem on page 88 in your Participant's Guide and locate the Sheep Gate (also called Tadi Gate) on Jerusalem's northern wall. Just north of the gate is the Pool of Bethesda, which was believed to have healing powers.

✏ 1. Who would come to the pool and why? (See John 5:1–7.)

Suggested Response: disabled people such as the blind, lame, and paralyzed came because when the waters were stirred the first person into the water would be healed.

✏ 2. When Jesus came to the pool, what was His response? What did He do? (See John 5:6–9.)

Suggested Responses: When Jesus learned that the man had been waiting to be healed for thirty-eight years, Jesus had compassion on him and asked him if he wanted to be well. When the man answered by complaining about his situation, Jesus told him to get up and walk, and the man was immediately cured.

✏ 3. What did the man do? How do we know that he didn't know who Jesus was? (See John 5:11–13.)

Suggested Responses: He did exactly what Jesus told him to do. When he was questioned by the Jews, he replied that he didn't know who had healed him.

✏ 4. After being healed, where did the man go? Why do you think he went there? (See John 5:8–9, 14.)

Suggested Responses: He went to the temple. He went to praise and thank God for his healing.

small Group Bible Discovery

Topic A: God Preserves His Holy City
During King Hezekiah's reign over Judah, he prepared for attack by
Assyria, a pagan nation that in 722 B.C. destroyed the northern king-
dom of Israel.

1. What kind of a king was Hezekiah? (See 2 Chronicles
   29:1–3, 35–36; 31:1, 20–21.)

2. What did Assyria do during the fourteenth year of King
   Hezekiah's reign? (See Isaiah 36:1; 2 Kings 18:13.)

3. What had Hezekiah done to prepare for the Assyrian attack
   against Jerusalem? (See 1 Kings 20:20; 2 Chronicles 32:1–5.)

4. How did Hezekiah respond upon receiving the Assyrians'
   ultimatum? (See Isaiah 37:14–20.)

5. How did God deliver His people? (See 2 Chronicles 32:20–23.)

6. As we consider how God saved Jerusalem, what lessons
   can we learn about God and the problems we face today?

Topic B: Jesus Heals at the Pool of Bethesda
Refer to the map of Jerusalem on page 88 and locate the Sheep Gate
(also called Tadi Gate) on Jerusalem's northern wall. Just north of the
gate is the Pool of Bethesda, which was believed to have healing powers.

1. Who would come to the pool and why? (See John 5:1–7.)

2. When Jesus came to the pool, what was his response?
   What did He do? (See John 5:6–9.)

3. What did the man do? How do we know that He didn't
   know who Jesus was? (See John 5:11–13.)

148   Session Five

DATA FILE

THE DEVELOPMENT OF JERUSALEM

2,000 B.C. (circa) — God sends Abraham to the area of Mount Moriah to sacrifice Isaac. (The temple and part of Jerusalem is built on the mountain ridge named Moriah.)

1,000 B.C. (circa) — David captures Jerusalem (then the Canaanite city of Jebus), names it the City of David, and makes it his capital (2 Samuel 5:6–7; 1 Chronicles 11:4–7). The city is about ten acres in size and is home to 1,500 people.

950 B.C. (circa) — Solomon spends seven years building the temple, then spends thirteen years building his lavish palace (1 Kings 6:37–7:12), apparently between the temple and David's City. The city has about 4,500 people and covers approximately thirty acres.

700 B.C. (circa) — Hezekiah expands Jerusalem—west across the Tyropoeon Valley onto the Western Hill—and fortifies the city against the Babylonian threat by building walls and tearing down houses in order to expand the walls (2 Chronicles 32:1–5; Isaiah 22:10). The city at that time covered about 100 acres and housed 24,000 people.

500 B.C. (circa) — The Babylonians capture Jerusalem, destroy the temple, and take many Israelites captive.

430 B.C. (circa) — Cyrus, king of Persia, allows the Israelites to return to Jerusalem. They rebuild the temple, and restore and dedicate the city walls (Nehemiah 2:1–8; 3; 12:27–47).

322 B.C. — Jerusalem becomes part of Alexander the Great's empire. The city suffers more than a century of conflict at the hands of Alexander's successors.

165 B.C. — The Maccabean revolt brings Jerusalem back under Jewish control. Descendants of the Maccabees enclose the Western Hill, build the fortress Baris (later the Antonia), and expand the Gentile Court. The city now covers 175 acres and has more than 30,000 inhabitants.

63 B.C. — The Romans under Pompey capture Jerusalem from the Hasmonaeans (Maccabean descendants) and eventually place the city and country under Herod's control.

37–4 B.C. — Herod the Great expands the Gentile Court, lavishly embellishes the temple, fortifies the city, and builds many structures. A wonder of the ancient world, the city has expanded to nearly 250 acres and has a population of 45,000.

A.D. 70 — Under Titus, at least 80,000 Roman troops destroy Jerusalem, slaughtering hundreds of thousands of Jews. The streets run with Jewish blood. On August 9, the temple is burned and destroyed. All the citizens of Jerusalem (more than one million) are executed, sold into slavery, or captured for games in the arena.

DATA FILE

The Development of Jerusalem

2,000 B.C.
(circa)
God sends Abraham to the area of Mount Moriah to sacrifice Isaac. (The temple and part of Jerusalem is built on the mountain ridge named Moriah.)

1,000 B.C.
(circa)
David captures Jerusalem (then the Canaanite city of Jebus), names it the City of David, and makes it his capital (2 Samuel 5:6–7; 1 Chronicles 11:4–7). The city is about ten acres in size and is home to 1,500 people.

950 B.C.
(circa)
Solomon spends seven years building the temple, then spends thirteen years building his lavish palace (1 Kings 6:37–7:12), apparently between the temple and David's City. The city has about 4,500 people and covers approximately thirty acres.

700 B.C.
(circa)
Hezekiah expands Jerusalem—west across the Tyropoeon Valley onto the Western Hill—and fortifies the city against the Babylonian threat by building walls and tearing down houses in order to expand the walls (2 Chronicles 32:1–5; Isaiah 22:10). The city at that time covered about 100 acres and housed 24,000 people.

500 B.C.
(circa)
The Babylonians capture Jerusalem, destroy the temple, and take many Israelites captive.

430 B.C.
(circa)
Cyrus, king of Persia, allows the Israelites to return to Jerusalem. They rebuild the temple and restore and dedicate the city walls (Nehemiah 2:1–8; 3; 12:27–47).

322 B.C.
Jerusalem becomes part of Alexander the Great's empire. The city suffers more than a century of conflict at the hands of Alexander's successors.

165 B.C.
The Maccabean revolt brings Jerusalem back under Jewish control. Descendants of the Maccabees enclose the Western Hill, build the fortress Baris (later the Antonia), and expand the Gentile Court. The city now covers 175 acres and has more than 30,000 inhabitants.

63 B.C.
The Romans under Pompey capture Jerusalem from the Hasmonaeans (Maccabean descendants) and eventually place the city and country under Herod's control.

37–4 B.C.
Herod the Great expands the Gentile Court, lavishly embellishes the temple, fortifies the city, and builds many structures. A wonder of the ancient world, the city has expanded to nearly 250 acres and has a population of 45,000.

A.D. 70
Under Titus, at least 80,000 Roman troops destroy Jerusalem, slaughtering hundreds of thousands of Jews. The streets run with Jewish blood. On August 9, the temple is burned and destroyed. All the citizens of Jerusalem (more than one million) are executed, sold into slavery, or captured for games in the arena.

4. After being healed, where did the man go? Why do you think he went there? (See John 5:8–9, 14.)

5. If you feel comfortable doing so, share a time when you experienced an unusual blessing from God that at first you did not realize came from Him.

6. When God provides for us in miraculous ways, what messages do you think He is trying to convey? (See John 5:6, 8–9, 14.)

5.   If you feel comfortable doing so, share a time when you experienced an unusual blessing from God that at first you did not realize came from Him.

Suggested Responses: will vary widely.

6.   When God provides for us in miraculous ways, what messages do you think He is trying to convey? (See John 5:6, 8–9, 14.)

Suggested Responses: His love and concern for us, how we can be healed, how important it is to live as He commands, etc.

Topic C: Jesus Heals in the Lower City

Refer to the map of Jerusalem on page 88 in your Participant's Guide and locate the Lower City.

1.   During Jesus' day, the Lower City was home to most of the common people. What had King Hezekiah done years earlier to bring fresh water into this part of the city? (See 2 Kings 20:20; 2 Chronicles 32:30.)

Suggested Response: He dug a tunnel from the Spring of Gihon in the City of David to channel water to the Tyropoeon Valley and the Lower City.

2.   What happened at the Pool of Siloam, which was located in the Lower City and filled by the water flowing through Hezekiah's tunnel? (See John 9:1–12.)

Suggested Response: Jesus, who had left the temple, saw a blind man and made a mud pack, which He put on the blind man's eyes. Jesus then sent the man to wash in the Pool of Siloam. In faith, the man walked there, and when he washed the mud off his eyes he could see.

3.   Apparently the blind man mentioned in the previous question was near the temple when Jesus saw him (John 8:58–9:1). In order to reach the Pool of Siloam, he would have had to work his way down many steps. Why do you think Jesus put mud on the man's eyes and then asked him to walk down such a long, difficult path?

Suggested Responses: to demonstrate his faith, to give him the opportunity to think about what Jesus would do for him, to avoid drawing any more attention to Himself near the temple (since the Jews had been ready to stone Him), etc.

4.   Jesus required the blind man to demonstrate faith and obedience, which resulted in his healing. In what way(s) does God ask us to demonstrate our faith and obedience when He accomplishes His work in our lives?

Suggested Responses: will vary, but might include to keep trusting in Him during difficult times, to keep doing what He wants us to do even though we may not see any results, to obey Him even if what He seems to want us to do seems silly at the time, etc.

5.   Why is it important for us, like the blind man mentioned in John 9:1–12, to step out in faith when we ask God to work in and through us?

Suggested Responses: God wants us to rely solely on Him, not on our own abilities; God wants to receive honor for what He does in our lives; as we step out in faith, our faith grows as we know God more fully; etc.

94 The Death and Resurrection of the Messiah

63 B.C.	The Romans under Pompey capture Jerusalem from the Hasmonaeans (Maccabean descendants) and eventually place the city and country under Herod's control.
37–4 B.C.	Herod the Great expands the Gentile Court, lavishly embellishes the temple, fortifies the city, and builds many structures. A wonder of the ancient world, the city has expanded to nearly 250 acres and has a population of 45,000.
A.D. 70	Under Titus, at least 80,000 Roman troops destroy Jerusalem, slaughtering hundreds of thousands of Jews. The streets run with Jewish blood. On August 9, the temple is burned and destroyed. All the citizens of Jerusalem (more than one million) are executed, sold into slavery, or captured for games in the arena.

4. After being healed, where did the man go? Why do you think he went there? (See John 5:8–9, 14.)

5. If you feel comfortable doing so, share a time when you experienced an unusual blessing from God that at first you did not realize came from Him.

6. When God provides for us in miraculous ways, what messages do you think He is trying to convey? (See John 5:6, 8–9, 14.)

Session Five: City of the Great King—Jerusalem 95

Topic C: Jesus Heals in the Lower City
Refer to the map of Jerusalem on page 88 and locate the Lower City.

1. During Jesus' day, the Lower City was home to most of the common people. What had King Hezekiah done years earlier to bring fresh water into this part of the city? (See 2 Kings 20:20; 2 Chronicles 32:30.)

2. What happened at the Pool of Siloam, which was located in the Lower City and filled by the water flowing through Hezekiah's tunnel? (See John 9:1–12.)

3. Apparently the blind man mentioned in the previous question was near the temple when Jesus saw him (John 8:58–9:1). In order to reach the Pool of Siloam, he would have had to work his way down many steps. Why do you think Jesus put mud on the man's eyes and then asked him to walk down such a long, difficult path?

4. Jesus required the blind man to demonstrate faith and obedience, which resulted in his healing. In what way(s) does God ask us to demonstrate our faith and obedience when He accomplishes His work in our lives?

PLANNING NOTES:

Topic D: Jesus Creates a Stir in the Upper City

Herod built his palace in the Upper City, which was located on the Western Hill (today called Mount Zion) in the highest section of Jerusalem. The palace, which covered nearly five acres, had beautiful gardens, fountains, and accommodations for hundreds of guests. In the vicinity of the palace are several mansions that are believed to have been the homes of priestly families and wealthy nobility. Although the Romans burned these houses in A.D. 70, evidence of their splendor remains. They help us picture the wealth of the Jewish religious leaders, who were so threatened by Jesus that they wanted to have Him killed.

1. When was the news of the arrival of Jesus, King of the Jews, first heard in the Upper City? How did the people of that district respond? (See Matthew 2:1–12, 16–18.)

   Suggested Responses: The wise men from the East, who had seen His star and sought to worship Him, came to the palace of Herod and asked where the King of the Jews was. Herod was quite disturbed and consulted all the chief priests and teachers of the law about what this meant. The result was that Herod, in an effort to secure his throne, had all the baby boys in Bethlehem killed.

DATA FILE

The Districts of Jerusalem
To locate these districts, please refer to the map of Jerusalem on page 88 .

David's City: The Jerusalem of David's time, located on a narrow strip of land (Mount Moriah) about ten acres in size, populated by about 1,500 people, naturally defended by the Kidron Valley to the east and the Tyropoeon Valley to the west, originally named Zion, received fresh water from the Spring of Gihon.

Events that happened here: Abraham brought Isaac to Mount Moriah to sacrifice him (Genesis 22:1–2,14); the Philistines returned the Ark of the Covenant (1 Samuel 6:1–2, 12–16); and David purchased the threshing floor of Araunah, which became the site of the temple (2 Samuel 24:18–25); Solomon built the temple on Mount Moriah (2 Chronicles 3:1–2); David was tempted and committed adultery with Bathsheba (2 Samuel 11:2–5); Michal, David's wife, saw him dancing joyfully before the Lord and "despised him" (1 Chronicles 15:27–29).

Lower City: Home to most of the common people during Jesus' day; built on the slope of the Western Hill, reaching into the Tyropoeon Valley; where Jesus sent the blind man to wash the mud from his eyes in the Pool of Siloam.

Upper City: Highest area in Jerusalem (located on the Western Hill now named Mount Zion), site of Herod's palace, home to wealthy Jews, probably more Hellenists lived here than lived in the Lower City.

Business District: Although not named by ancient sources, this district inside the Second Wall held many shops and markets. The area Jesus walked through on market day on His way to the cross.

New City: During and after Jesus' time, the city expanded north. Many wealthy people lived here. Herod Agrippa walled it about thirty or more years after Jesus' crucifixion.

5. Why is it important for us, like the blind man mentioned in John 9:1–12, to step out in faith when we ask God to work in and through us?

Topic D: Jesus Creates a Stir in the Upper City

Herod built his palace in the Upper City, which was located on the Western Hill (today called Mount Zion) in the highest section of Jerusalem. The palace, which covered nearly five acres, had beautiful gardens, fountains, and accommodations for hundreds of guests. In the vicinity of the palace are several mansions that are believed to have been the homes of priestly families and wealthy nobility. Although the Romans burned these houses in A.D. 70, evidence of their splendor remains. They help us picture the wealth of the Jewish religious leaders, who were so threatened by Jesus that they wanted to have Him killed.

1. When was the news of the arrival of Jesus, King of the Jews, first heard in the Upper City? How did the people of that district respond? (See Matthew 2:1–12, 16–18.)

2. After Jesus raised Lazarus from the dead (John 11:38–44), what did the chief priests and religious leaders who lived in the mansions in the Upper City do? (See John 11:45–53.)

DATA FILE

The Districts of Jerusalem
To locate these districts, please refer to the map of Jerusalem on page 88.

David's City: The Jerusalem of David's time, located on a narrow strip of land (Mount Moriah) about ten acres in size, populated by about 1,500 people, naturally defended by the Kidron Valley to the east and the Tyropoeon Valley to the west, originally named Zion, received fresh water from the Spring of Gihon.

Events that happened here: Abraham brought Isaac to Mount Moriah to sacrifice him (Genesis 22:1–2, 14); the Philistines returned the Ark of the Covenant (1 Samuel 6:1–2, 12–16); and David purchased the threshing floor of Araunah, which became the site of the temple (2 Samuel 24:18–25); Solomon built the temple on Mount Moriah (2 Chronicles 3:1–2); David was tempted and committed adultery with Bathsheba (2 Samuel 11:2–5); Michal, David's wife, saw him dancing joyfully before the Lord and "despised him" (1 Chronicles 15:27–29).

Lower City: Home to most of the common people during Jesus' day; built on the slope of the Western Hill, reaching into the Tyropoeon Valley; where Jesus sent the blind man to wash the mud from his eyes in the Pool of Siloam.

Upper City: Highest area in Jerusalem (located on the Western Hill now named Mount Zion), site of Herod's palace, home to wealthy Jews, probably more Hellenists lived here than lived in the Lower City.

Business District: Although not named by ancient sources, this district inside the Second Wall held many shops and markets. The area Jesus walked through on market day on His way to the cross.

New City: During and after Jesus' time, the city expanded north. Many wealthy people lived here. Herod Agrippa walled it about thirty or more years after Jesus' crucifixion.

✏ 2.   After Jesus raised Lazarus from the dead (John 11:38–44), what did the chief priests and religious leaders who lived in the mansions in the Upper City do? (See John 11:45–53.)

Suggested Response: They met together and decided to kill Jesus.

✏ 3.   The Sadducees gained wealth and power by controlling the temple's functions. Why do you think they felt so threatened by Jesus? (See John 11:47–48.)

Suggested Response: They saw Jesus doing miracles. If they allowed Him to keep doing that, the Sadducees believed, the local people would believe in Him and lose faith in the rituals and rules of the temple. Then the Romans would take away the Sadducees' power and crush the nation.

✏ 4.   Where did Peter go after Jesus was taken prisoner? (See Luke 22:54–56; John 18:12–24.)

Suggested Response: Peter went to the high priest's house, where Jesus had been taken for questioning before Annas, Caiaphas, and the Sanhedrin. It is likely that this house was one of the mansions located in the Upper City.

✏ 5.   Think about the differences between the members of the Sanhedrin (John 11:45–53) and Jesus—a poor Galilean rabbi. Why do you think wealth and power were able to corrupt the Sanhedrin?

Suggested Responses: Wealth and power draw out the worst in people; wealth and power are highly prized in most cultures; wealth and power tend to be addictive, motivating people to strive for more; people are drawn to what's available here and now, and it becomes easy to rationalize behavior that provides tangible benefits; etc.

Topic E: Jesus Takes His Ministry Outside the City Walls

By going through the Garden Gate, people leaving Jerusalem during Jesus' time could reach the area called the New City—the area where the city was expanding to the north. Just outside the gate was an old quarry, where people were taken to be stoned.

✏ 1.   After the Jewish leaders decided to have Jesus put to death, where was He taken? (See Matthew 27:1–2, 11–31.)

Suggested Responses: He was "led away" and turned over to Pilate, the Roman governor, who was probably staying in Herod's palace. Later, he was led out of the city (through the business district) to be crucified.

✏ 2.   Where did the soldiers take Jesus to be crucified? (See Matthew 27:32–33, 39–40; John 19:17–18, 41–42; refer to the map of Jerusalem on page 88 of your Participant's Guide.)

Suggested Response: To a place outside the city located near a garden and a well-traveled route. Note there are two possible locations for the crucifixion.

98   The Death and Resurrection of the Messiah

3. The Sadducees gained wealth and power by controlling the temple's functions. Why do you think they felt so threatened by Jesus? (See John 11:47–48.)

4. Where did Peter go after Jesus was taken prisoner? (See Luke 22:54–56; John 18:12–24.)

5. Think about the differences between the members of the Sanhedrin (John 11:45–53) and Jesus—a poor Galilean rabbi. Why do you think wealth and power were able to corrupt the Sanhedrin?

Topic E: Jesus Takes His Ministry Outside the City Walls
By going through the Garden Gate, people leaving Jerusalem during Jesus' time could reach the area called the New City—the area where the city was expanding to the north. Just outside the gate was an old quarry, where people were taken to be stoned.

1. After the Jewish leaders decided to have Jesus put to death, where was He taken? (See Matthew 27:1–2, 11–31.)

Session Five: City of the Great King—Jerusalem   99

2. Where did the soldiers take Jesus to be crucified? (See Matthew 27:32–33, 39–40; John 19:17–18, 41–42; refer to the map of Jerusalem on page 88.)

3. What routinely happened outside the city walls? What does "going outside the camp" seem to mean? (See Numbers 5:1–4; Hebrews 13:11.)

4. What does it mean to you that Jesus went "outside the city" and faced total rejection in order to die for our sins? (See Leviticus 20:20–22; Hebrews 13:11–12.)

PLANNING NOTES:

✏ 3.   What routinely happened outside the city walls? What does "going outside the camp" seem to mean? (See Numbers 5:1–4; Hebrews 13:11.)

Suggested Responses: The high priest used the blood of animals as a sin offering, but the animals' bodies were burned outside the city. Going "outside the camp" was required by the law of Moses in order to maintain purity within the community. Going "outside the camp" seems to mean disgrace, public rejection, and uncleanness.

✏ 4.   What does it mean to you that Jesus went "outside the city" and faced total rejection in order to die for our sins? (See Leviticus 20:20–22; Hebrews 13:11–12.)

Suggested Responses: Just as the sins of the Israelites were placed on a scapegoat which was then sent out into the wilderness, Jesus became our scapegoat. Our sins were placed on Him so we don't have to "go outside the camp." He bore the burden of our sins for us, but we can choose to "go outside the camp" to be identified with Him.

ꜰɑith ʟesson

8 minutes   **Time for Reflection (5 minutes)**

It's time for each of us to think quietly about how we can apply what we've learned today. On page 100 of the Participant's Guide, you'll find a passage of Scripture. Let's each read this passage silently and take the next few minutes to consider some of the questions that follow the Scripture passage.

Please do not talk during this time. It's a time when we all can reflect on God's great work of redemption that took place in the city of Jerusalem and consider what it means to our lives.

> *The Scripture passage and questions are reproduced in their entirety in the Participant's Guide on pages 100–101.*

Then the governor's soldiers took Jesus into the Praetorium and gathered the whole company of soldiers around him. They stripped him and put a scarlet robe on him, and then twisted together a crown of thorns and set it on his head. They put a staff in his right hand and knelt in front of him and mocked him. "Hail, king of the Jews!" they said. They spit on him, and took the staff and struck him on the head again and again. After they had mocked him, they took off the robe and put his own clothes on him. Then they led him away to crucify him. As they were going out, they met a man from Cyrene, named Simon, and they forced him to carry the cross. They came to a place called Golgotha (which means The Place of the Skull). . . . Those who passed by hurled insults at him, shaking their heads and saying, "You who are going to destroy the temple and build it in three days, save yourself! Come down from the cross, if you are the Son of God!" In the same way the chief priests, the teachers of the law and the elders mocked him.

MATTHEW 27:27–33, 39–41

Session Five: City of the Great King—Jerusalem   99

2. Where did the soldiers take Jesus to be crucified? (See Matthew 27:32–33, 39–40; John 19:17–18, 41–42; refer to the map of Jerusalem on page 88.)

3. What routinely happened outside the city walls? What does "going outside the camp" seem to mean? (See Numbers 5:1–4; Hebrews 13:11.)

4. What does it mean to you that Jesus went "outside the city" and faced total rejection in order to die for our sins? (See Leviticus 20:20–22; Hebrews 13:11–12.)

---

100   The Death and Resurrection of the Messiah

faith Lesson

Time for Reflection

Read the following passage of Scripture silently and take the next few minutes to reflect on God's great work of redemption that took place in the city of Jerusalem and consider what it means to your life.

Then the governor's soldiers took Jesus into the Praetorium and gathered the whole company of soldiers around him. They stripped him and put a scarlet robe on him, and then twisted together a crown of thorns and set it on his head. They put a staff in his right hand and knelt in front of him and mocked him. "Hail, king of the Jews!" they said. They spit on him, and took the staff and struck him on the head again and again. After they had mocked him, they took off the robe and put his own clothes on him. Then they led him away to crucify him. As they were going out, they met a man from Cyrene, named Simon, and they forced him to carry the cross. They came to a place called Golgotha (which means The Place of the Skull). . . . Those who passed by hurled insults at him, shaking their heads and saying, "You who are going to destroy the temple and build it in three days, save yourself! Come down from the cross, if you are the Son of God!" In the same way the chief priests, the teachers of the law and the elders mocked him.

MATTHEW 27:27–33, 39–41

1. What do you feel when you realize that Jesus was willing to be your "scapegoat," to go outside the city and symbolically carry your sins into the wilderness in order to enable you to come into His kingdom—His holy city?

✏ 1.   What do you feel when you realize that Jesus was willing to be your "scape-goat," to go outside the city and symbolically carry your sins into the wilderness in order to enable you to come into His kingdom—His holy city?

✏ 2.   How will what you've seen and discussed today impact your view of Jerusalem and Jesus?

> As soon as participants have spent five minutes reflecting on the above questions, get the entire group's attention and move to the next section.

Action Points (3 minutes)

> *The following points are reproduced on pages 100–101 of the Participant's Guide:*

Now it's time to wrap up our session.

> Give participants a moment to transition from their thoughtfulness to giving you their full attention.

I'd like to take a moment to summarize what we have discovered in this session. After this brief review, I will give you a moment to jot down an action step (or steps) that you will commit to this week as a result of what you have learned today.

> Read the following and pause for a few moments so that participants can consider and write out their commitment.

✏ 1.   *To understand more about Jerusalem—its structures, its people, its activity—is to understand the Jewish heritage on which our faith is built.* And as we saw (through the scale model and some actual ruins) what actual structures looked like during Jesus' time—and learned about significant events in His life that took place in or near those structures—the reality of what God did in that city became more real to us.

Learning about Jewish history and culture—especially Jerusalem—adds greatly to our understanding of Jesus' life and God's redemptive work on earth. The city also gives us a picture of a greater city to come—the heavenly Jerusalem. There, God's faithful will live forever in His presence.

Until then, His followers are called to bring His love to a broken world, much as God did to Jerusalem throughout history. Just as God initially used the temple to extend His kingdom to the Jews, today God is using us—His temples, His "Jerusalems"—to extend His kingdom throughout the world, to touch the lives of people with God's presence, power, and forgiveness. As His Spirit fills us and lives within us, we are called to take His kingdom to all the people of God's world.

To whom can you take the message of the Messiah during the coming days? Who can you touch with God's presence, power, and the forgiveness brought about through Jesus' death and resurrection?

100   The Death and Resurrection of the Messiah

ꜰaith ᴌesson

Time for Reflection

Read the following passage of Scripture silently and take the next few minutes to reflect on God's great work of redemption that took place in the city of Jerusalem and consider what it means to your life.

> Then the governor's soldiers took Jesus into the Praetorium and gathered the whole company of soldiers around him. They stripped him and put a scarlet robe on him, and then twisted together a crown of thorns and set it on his head. They put a staff in his right hand and knelt in front of him and mocked him. "Hail, king of the Jews!" they said. They spit on him, and took the staff and struck him on the head again and again. After they had mocked him, they took off the robe and put his own clothes on him. Then they led him away to crucify him. As they were going out, they met a man from Cyrene, named Simon, and they forced him to carry the cross. They came to a place called Golgotha (which means The Place of the Skull). . . . Those who passed by hurled insults at him, shaking their heads and saying, "You who are going to destroy the temple and build it in three days, save yourself! Come down from the cross, if you are the Son of God!" In the same way the chief priests, the teachers of the law and the elders mocked him.
>
> MATTHEW 27:27–33, 39–41

1. What do you feel when you realize that Jesus was willing to be your "scapegoat," to go outside the city and symbolically carry your sins into the wilderness in order to enable you to come into His kingdom—His holy city?

Session Five: City of the Great King—Jerusalem   101

2. How will what you've seen and discussed today impact your view of Jerusalem and Jesus?

Action Points

Take a moment to review the key points you explored today. Then write down the action step (or steps) that you will commit to this week as a result of what you have discovered.

1. *To understand more about Jerusalem—its structures, its people, its activity—is to understand the Jewish heritage on which our faith is built.* And as we saw (through the scale model and some actual ruins) what actual structures looked like during Jesus' time—and learned about significant events in His life that took place in or near those structures—the reality of what God did in that city became more real to us.

   Learning about Jewish history and culture—especially Jerusalem—adds greatly to our understanding of Jesus' life and God's redemptive work on earth. The city also gives us a picture of a greater city to come—the heavenly Jerusalem. There, God's faithful will live forever in His presence.

   Until then, His followers are called to bring His love to a broken world, much as God did to Jerusalem throughout history. Just as God initially used the temple to extend His kingdom to the Jews, today God is using us—His temples, His "Jerusalems"—to extend His kingdom throughout the world, to touch the lives of people with God's presence, power, and forgiveness. As His Spirit fills us and lives within us, we are called to take His kingdom to all the people of God's world.

> **DATA FILE**
>
> **Where Jerusalem Is Located:**
> - On a high plateau in the Judea Mountains, about 2,400 feet above sea level. (This location fulfilled Isaiah's prophecy in Isaiah 2:2–3, that people would go up to the mountain of the Lord's house.)
> - Thirty miles east of the Mediterranean Sea, twenty miles from the Dead Sea.
> - Six miles from Bethlehem where Jesus was born; sixty miles from Nazareth where He grew up; and seventy-five miles from Capernaum where He focused His ministry.

closing prayer

1 minute

I hope this session has given you, as it has me, a new appreciation of Jerusalem and the amazing events that God has orchestrated there through the centuries—and also what Jesus the Messiah did for us. I'll close our time together in prayer now.

Dear God, You are holy and powerful, all knowing and loving. We thank You for revealing who You are through biblical events. For many years, long before Jesus was born, You arranged the timing of so many events in Jerusalem in preparation for His birth, death, and resurrection. Thank You for loving us so much that You sent Jesus to be born in the little town of Bethlehem and then allowed Him to be crucified outside Jerusalem's walls. May we be even more mindful of Your presence during the days ahead. Amen.

102   The Death and Resurrection of the Messiah

To whom can you take the message of the Messiah during the coming days? Who can you touch with God's presence, power, and forgiveness brought about through Jesus' death and resurrection?

DATA FILE

Where Jerusalem Is Located:

- On a high plateau in the Judea Mountains, about 2,400 feet above sea level. (This location fulfilled Isaiah's prophecy in Isaiah 2:2–3, that people would go up to the mountain of the Lord's house.)
- Thirty miles east of the Mediterranean Sea, twenty miles from the Dead Sea.
- Six miles from Bethlehem where Jesus was born; sixty miles from Nazareth where He grew up; and seventy-five miles from Capernaum where He focused His ministry.

The Lamb of God

Before You Lead

Synopsis

When Jesus took His disciples to Caesarea Philippi, He explained and dramatically illustrated their mission—which is also the mission of the church—to actively confront "the gates of Hades." Jesus then turned His attention to fulfilling His mission, His ultimate confrontation against evil. From that point on, He resolutely focused on the journey toward Jerusalem—and the cross that awaited Him.

On the way, between Jericho and Jerusalem, He passed through the rugged Judea wilderness. He knew the wilderness well. There He had fasted for forty days and forty nights, and Satan had tempted Him to abandon God's plan of redemption. The wilderness could have provided an easy refuge, a welcome escape from the horrible death He would otherwise face. But His love for the human race was so great that He didn't disappear into the wilderness. Instead, He chose to stay on the path that led to the cross.

That path led Him directly into Jerusalem and the dramatic events of what Christians now call "Palm Sunday." Ray Vander Laan shares historical, cultural, religious, and political insights that provide a profound understanding of what really took place in the minds of the Jewish people on "Palm Sunday." This understanding makes it evident that Jesus—God's Anointed (Messiah in the Hebrew translation)—never proclaimed His Messianic identity more clearly, nor displayed the method He would use to bring about His kingdom more pointedly, than during His entry into Jerusalem just five days before His death.

For the Jewish people, Passover was more than a religious observance. It was the time of year when they celebrated their liberation from Egyptian bondage. During Jesus' time, they also used this opportunity to express their longing for political freedom from Rome. Jews who claimed to be "messiahs" had so often caused riots during Passover that the Romans brought extra troops into Jerusalem during Passover season. And the Roman soldiers did not hesitate to shed blood to keep the peace.

So what really happened as Jesus rode the donkey toward Jerusalem? On that day, the Sunday before Passover, Jesus came out of the wilderness on the eastern side of the Mount of Olives (just as prophecy said the Messiah would come). People spread cloaks and branches on the road before Him. Then, near where the road went down the Mount of Olives, the disciples "began, joyfully, to praise God in loud voices for all the miracles they had seen" (Luke 19:37). Prior to this point, the crowd seemingly remained silent—probably to avoid giving Roman troops a reason to become brutal. But then the crowd began shouting "Hosanna," which meant, "Please save us! Give us freedom! We're sick of these Romans!" The people also waved palm branches, a symbol that had once been placed on Jewish coins when the Jewish nation was free. Thus the palm branches were not a symbol of peace and love, as Christians usually assume; they were a symbol of Jewish nationalism, an expression of the people's desire for political freedom.

Yet Jesus came to the people as the Lamb of God. He presented Himself in Jerusalem on the day when each Jewish family selected a "perfect lamb" that would be sacrificed the following Friday. Jesus—the sinless Messiah who would die on humankind's behalf—appeared on the day the people chose their sacrificial lambs! As Ray Vander Laan points out in the video, "It's almost as if God said to the world, 'Here's My Lamb. Will you choose Him?'" But instead of turning to Jesus as the Lamb of God, the crowds misunderstood His proclamation that He was the Messiah. They wanted Him to be their political-military deliverer.

In response, Jesus wept. His tears were not the sorrowful tears of one who feels the pain of a loved one's death. Recently, Jesus had shed those tears at the home of Lazarus, whom He then raised from the dead (John 11:33–35). The tears Jesus shed as the people cried out their political "Hosannas" were tears of grief for the hearts of His people. Jesus foresaw the terrible devastation of Jerusalem that would result because the people did not recognize Him as God's Messiah. The people were looking for a Messiah who offered political deliverance and a political kingdom. They would have nothing to do with the Messiah who offered forgiveness and deliverance from sin and ushered in the kingdom of God by sacrificing His own life. That is why He wept aloud.

Key Points of This Session

1. *On lamb selection day, Jesus came into Jerusalem as the Lamb of God, but the people—despite their praises—didn't recognize who He was.* He did not fit their idea of what the Messiah would be. They wanted a Messiah who would provide political-military liberation. The vision of a suffering Messiah who would give His life to defeat the "gates of Hades" and to provide freedom from the spiritual bondage of sin was foreign to them. And the idea of following Jesus' example by giving themselves as servants to others was shocking. Consequently, many people (including His disciples) either did not understand His teaching or rejected Him completely.

2. *Jesus weeps for us.* He grieves when we suffer loss and pain, just as He grieved at the tomb of Lazarus. He also longs for us to recognize and accept Him for who He is. The Messiah, who came on "lamb selection day" to establish His kingdom by being a servant and giving up His life as the Lamb of God, wept for the people of Jerusalem when they didn't receive Him as God's Messiah and rejected the deliverance He offered. His heart breaks for us today, just as it did that day in Jerusalem, when we miss Him and His message.

Session Outline (53 minutes)

    I. Introduction (5 minutes)

        Welcome

        What's to Come

        Questions to Think About

    II. Video Presentation "The Lamb of God" (20 minutes)

    III. Group Discovery (20 minutes)

        Video Highlights

        Small Group Bible Discovery

    IV. Faith Lesson (7 minutes)

        Time for Reflection

        Action Points

    V. Closing Prayer (1 minute)

Materials

You may want to use a marker board, chalkboard, or overhead projector to record the responses of participants to the **Questions to Think About.** No additional materials are needed for this session. Simply view the video prior to leading the session so you are familiar with its main points.

The Lamb of God

Introduction

5 minutes

Welcome

Assemble the participants together. Welcome them to session six of *Faith Lessons on the Death and Resurrection of the Messiah*.

What's to Come

During this session, we will consider who Jesus presented Himself to be on "Palm Sunday," the day He entered Jerusalem to the sound of the crowd's "Hosannas." We'll learn fascinating details about Passover, the people's expectations for their Messiah, and the crowd's response to Him as He rode the colt into the city. We will discover how deeply He feels when we experience hurt and grief. We will see how His heart breaks when we don't recognize and accept Him for who He is.

Questions to Think About

Participant's Guide page 103.

Turn to page 103 of the Participant's Guide. To help set the stage for the video we'll see in a few minutes, let's consider who Jesus is in the minds of people today.

Ask each question and solicit a few responses from group members. If desired, write responses to questions one and three on a marker board, chalkboard, or overhead projector so that participants may keep them in view as the session progresses.

1. Which words or phrases have you heard people use to describe Jesus?

   Suggested Responses: a revolutionary, prophet, great man, teacher, peasant, good man, miracle worker, healer, Son of God, Redeemer, fraud, helper, etc.

2. Why do you think people create their own pictures of who Jesus is instead of discovering who the Bible says He is?

   Suggested Responses: they don't know what the Bible says, they don't want to investigate the Bible, they don't want to deal with the consequences of Jesus being God's Son, they don't think they need a Savior, they don't believe that sin exists, they don't believe that Jesus came to earth to be their Messiah, they want

SESSION SIX

the Lamb of god

questions to think about

1. Which words or phrases have you heard people use to describe Jesus?

2. Why do you think people create their own pictures of who Jesus is instead of discovering who the Bible says He is?

3. Which words would *you* use to describe who Jesus is?

103

a Jesus who meets the needs that are most important to them, they allow others to define Jesus for them, they are afraid of knowing Him, etc.

✏ 3.   Which words would *you* use to describe who Jesus is?

Suggested Responses: Allow participants to share their images of Jesus, which may include Son of God, prophet, Redeemer, Lamb of God, Messiah, teacher, etc.

Let's keep in mind these images of Jesus as we view the video.

video presentation

20 minutes   *Participant's Guide page 104.*

On page 104 of your Participant's Guide, you will find a space in which to take notes on key points as we watch this video.

Leader's Video Observations

Jesus' Journey Toward Jerusalem

Jesus' Entry into Jerusalem

"Lamb Day"

Passover Politics

Jesus' Tears

SESSION SIX

the Lamb of God

questions to think about

1. Which words or phrases have you heard people use to describe Jesus?

2. Why do you think people create their own pictures of who Jesus is instead of discovering who the Bible says He is?

3. Which words would *you* use to describe who Jesus is?

---

104   The Death and Resurrection of the Messiah

video notes

Jesus' Journey Toward Jerusalem

Jesus' Entry into Jerusalem

"Lamb Day"

Passover Politics

Jesus' Tears

Group Discovery

20 minutes

If your group has seven or more members, use the **Video Highlights** with the entire group (5 minutes), then break into small groups of three to five to discuss the **Small Group Bible Discovery** (10 minutes). Then reassemble the group to discuss the key points discovered (5 minutes).

If your group has fewer than seven members, begin with the **Video Highlights** (5 minutes), then do one or more of the topics found in the **Small Group Bible Discovery** as a group (10 minutes). Finally, spend five minutes at the end discussing points that had an impact on participants.

Video Highlights (5 minutes)

Here you'll ask one or more of the following questions that directly relate to the video the participants have just seen.

Please turn to the map of the land of Jesus' ministry on page 106 of your Participant's Guide. Trace the route Jesus took from Caesarea Philippi through the Decapolis, Perea, across the Jordan, to Jericho, and through the Judea Wilderness to Jerusalem.

1. Which aspects of Jesus' entrance into Jerusalem surprised you or were new to you?

   Suggested Responses may include: what the "Hosannas" meant, the political significance of the palm branches, the crowd's initial silence in relation to previous unrest during Passover seasons, the emphasis on political-military deliverance, that it was lamb selection day, etc.

The Land of Jesus' Ministry

video нighlights

Look at the map (on page 106) of the land of Jesus' ministry and note the route Jesus took from Caesarea Philippi to Jerusalem. He stayed on the east side of the Jordan River and traveled through the Decapolis and Peria. Then he crossed the Jordan River north of the Dead Sea at Jericho. From Jericho he went through the Judea Wilderness to Jerusalem.

1. Which aspects of Jesus' entrance into Jerusalem surprised you or were new to you?

2. Imagine that you were in the crowd as Jesus entered Jerusalem. What do you think you'd have felt and thought?

3. In the video, Ray Vander Laan asked us to think about the Jesus who cared so deeply about people that He cried on their behalf. Is this the Jesus you know? Is that a side of Jesus to which you are attracted? Why or why not?

✏ 2.   Imagine that you were in the crowd as Jesus entered Jerusalem. What do you think you'd have felt and thought?

Suggested Responses may include: hopeful, eager to be delivered from Roman rule, wondering what Jesus would do, skeptical that He'd be just another false messiah, etc.

✏ 3.   In the video, Ray Vander Laan asked us to think about the Jesus who cared so deeply about people that He cried on their behalf. Is this the Jesus you know? Is that a side of Jesus to which you are attracted? Why or why not?

Suggested Responses may vary widely: If people choose not to open up, share your view of Jesus with them.

Small Group Bible Discovery (15 minutes)

Participant's Guide page 107.

During this time, a group with fewer than seven participants will stay together. A group larger than seven participants will break into small groups and reassemble as a large group during the final five minutes. Assign each group one of the following topics. If you have more than four small groups, assign some topics to more than one group.

Let's break into groups of three to five—people sitting near you—and study some of the Bible passages and truths mentioned in the video.

Turn to pages 107–13 in your Participant's Guide. There you'll find a list of four topics. You'll have ten minutes to read and discuss the topic I'll assign to you. Choose one person in your group to be a spokesperson for your group when we discuss these topics later.

Assign each group a topic.

I'll signal you when one minute is left.

After nine minutes, let participants know that they have one minute remaining. Then reassemble the entire group. After everyone is back together, begin asking one person from each small group to briefly share a key idea with the larger group. In some cases, you may not have time for every group to share their discoveries.

As time allows, let's briefly share the key ideas that your group discussed.

Topic A: Jesus Presents Himself as the Messiah—the Lamb of God

✏ 1.   After Peter confessed, on behalf of the disciples, that Jesus was the Messiah (Matthew 16:13–16), Jesus immediately began to teach them about the way in which He would carry out His divine mission. How did the disciples respond to His teaching about His imminent suffering and death? What did their response reveal about their expectations of Jesus? (See Matthew 16:21–25; 17:22–23.)

Suggested Responses: The disciples didn't believe Him; Peter tried to argue with Him; they were filled with grief; they didn't understand the kind of Messiah He

video highlights

Look at the map (on page 106) of the land of Jesus' ministry and note the route Jesus took from Caesarea Philippi to Jerusalem. He stayed on the east side of the Jordan River and traveled through the Decapolis and Peria. Then he crossed the Jordan River north of the Dead Sea at Jericho. From Jericho he went through the Judea Wilderness to Jerusalem.

1. Which aspects of Jesus' entrance into Jerusalem surprised you or were new to you?

2. Imagine that you were in the crowd as Jesus entered Jerusalem. What do you think you'd have felt and thought?

3. In the video, Ray Vander Laan asked us to think about the Jesus who cared so deeply about people that He cried on their behalf. Is this the Jesus you know? Is that a side of Jesus to which you are attracted? Why or why not?

small Group Bible Discovery

Topic A: Jesus Presents Himself as the Messiah—the Lamb of God

1. After Peter confessed, on behalf of the disciples, that Jesus was the Messiah (Matthew 16:13–16), Jesus immediately began to teach them about the way in which He would carry out His divine mission. How did the disciples respond to His teaching about His imminent suffering and death? What did their response reveal about their expectations of Jesus? (See Matthew 16:21–25; 17:22–23.)

2. Which principles did Jesus repeatedly seek to communicate to His disciples during this time? (See Matthew 16:24–26; 20:17–27.)

3. What does the Bible say about the disciples' understanding of the kind of Messiah Jesus was? (See John 12:16; Acts 1:4–6.)

was; they didn't understand how He would accomplish His mission by suffering, serving others, and even dying. The disciples didn't understand what Jesus' mission was all about. They seemed to expect Jesus to remain on earth, perhaps to keep teaching and healing as He had during His public ministry.

2. Which principles did Jesus repeatedly seek to communicate to His disciples during this time? (See Matthew 16:24–26; 20:17–27.)

    Suggested Responses: that His followers were to "take up their crosses" and follow Him, that He did not come to be served but to serve and give His life, that His followers should also be servants who were willing to die, that He would carry out His mission to bring in God's kingdom and that it would lead to His death and resurrection, etc.

3. What does the Bible say about the disciples' understanding of the kind of Messiah Jesus was? (See John 12:16; Acts 1:4–6.)

    Suggested Response: The disciples didn't understand the kind of Messiah Jesus was, nor did they understand the meaning of His triumphant entry into Jerusalem.

4. After walking through the Judea Wilderness, Jesus reached the Mount of Olives and proceeded into Jerusalem, where the people triumphantly acclaimed Him as their king. The following questions will help you to understand the messages Jesus was sending through the manner, timing, and location of His entrance into Jerusalem.

    a. What was the significance of the direction from which Jesus came, in light of Old Testament prophecy? (See Isaiah 40:3.)

        Suggested Responses: Isaiah had foretold that the Messiah would come from the wilderness, east of Jerusalem. So when He appeared from the east, they were excited and hopeful that He would be their deliverer.

    b. Jesus entered the city as Messiah on the tenth day of the month when Jewish families picked Passover lambs for sacrifice. What was He asking the people to recognize? (See Exodus 12:1–6, 12–15; Matthew 17:22–23; John 1:29; John 12:1, 12–18.)

        Suggested Responses: During Passover, the Jews celebrated the time when God's judgment passed over their homes in Egypt. Just as the Jews would sacrifice lambs in Jerusalem, Jesus—the sacrificial Lamb of God—would be sacrificed for all humankind in Jerusalem. He was giving them a final opportunity to recognize who He was and choose Him—the Messiah—to be the sacrificial Lamb who would take away their sins.

    c. What did Jesus communicate by getting on the donkey as soon as He arrived at Bethphage—the town the rabbis had decided was the city limit of Jerusalem? (See Zechariah 9:9–10; Matthew 21:1–6.)

        Suggested Response: He communicated that He was the Messiah, God's King, who was coming to fulfill Zechariah's prophecy.

small group bible discovery

Topic A: Jesus Presents Himself as the Messiah—the Lamb of God

1. After Peter confessed, on behalf of the disciples, that Jesus was the Messiah (Matthew 16:13–16), Jesus immediately began to teach them about the way in which He would carry out His divine mission. How did the disciples respond to His teaching about His imminent suffering and death? What did their response reveal about their expectations of Jesus? (See Matthew 16:21–25; 17:22–23.)

2. Which principles did Jesus repeatedly seek to communicate to His disciples during this time? (See Matthew 16:24–26; 20:17–27.)

3. What does the Bible say about the disciples' understanding of the kind of Messiah Jesus was? (See John 12:16; Acts 1:4–6.)

4. After walking through the Judea Wilderness, Jesus reached the Mount of Olives and proceeded into Jerusalem, where the people triumphantly acclaimed Him as their king. The following questions will help you to understand the messages Jesus was sending through the manner, timing, and location of His entrance into Jerusalem.

   a. What was the significance of the direction from which Jesus came, in light of Old Testament prophecy? (See Isaiah 40:3.)

   b. Jesus entered the city as Messiah on the tenth day of the month when Jewish families picked Passover lambs for sacrifice. What was He asking the people to recognize? (See Exodus 12:1–6, 12–15; Matthew 17:22–23; John 1:29; John 12:1, 12–18.)

   c. What did Jesus communicate by getting on the donkey as soon as He arrived at Bethphage—the town the rabbis had decided was the city limit of Jerusalem? (See Zechariah 9:9–10; Matthew 21:1–6.)

5. Describe the difference between the way the people responded to Jesus and the way He responded to them (John 12:12–13; Luke 19:38–44).

> **COMPELLING EVIDENCE**
>
> **The Messiah From the East**
>
> A number of significant events in the history of the Jewish people, particularly events that relate to God's presence, have been recorded as occurring "from the east":
>
> - The children of Israel, with the ark symbolizing God's presence, entered the Promised Land from the east (Joshua 3:1, 15–17).
> - In Ezekiel's visions, the glory (presence) of the Lord left the corrupted temple and departed to the east (Ezekiel 10:4, 18–19; 11:22–24).
> - Ezekiel also saw the glory of the Lord return to the temple from the east (Ezekiel 43:1–5).
> - Jesus' birth was announced in the east (Matthew 2:1–2, 9).
> - The prophet Isaiah said that the Messiah would come from the wilderness east of Jerusalem (Isaiah 40:3).
> - Jesus ascended into heaven from the Mount of Olives, east of Jerusalem (Acts 1:6–12).
> - The Mount of Olives, east of Jerusalem, represents Jesus' Second Coming (Zechariah 14:4; Joel 3:2, 12).

✎ 5.   Describe the difference between the way the people responded to Jesus and the way He responded to them (John 12:12–13; Luke 19:38–44).

Suggested Responses: The people were elated and waved palm branches and shouted, "Blessed is the king who comes in the name of the Lord!" Jesus wept because He foresaw the devastation Jerusalem would experience because the people refused to recognize Him—the Messiah, the Lamb of God—and rejected the redemption He came to offer. Instead, they sought deliverance through political-military power rather than through spiritual means.

Topic B: Jesus—Our Model for Selfless Sacrifice

✎ 1.   Look up each of the following verses and consider what Jesus wanted His disciples to be.

Matthew 5:14

Suggested Response: to be "the light of the world."

Matthew 5:43–47

Suggested Response: to love their enemies and pray for those who persecute them.

Matthew 18:1–6

Suggested Response: to be humble, like a little child.

Matthew 18:21–35

Suggested Response: to have mercy and be forgiving.

---

108   The Death and Resurrection of the Messiah

4. After walking through the Judea Wilderness, Jesus reached the Mount of Olives and proceeded into Jerusalem, where the people triumphantly acclaimed Him as their king. The following questions will help you to understand the messages Jesus was sending through the manner, timing, and location of His entrance into Jerusalem.

     a. What was the significance of the direction from which Jesus came, in light of Old Testament prophecy? (See Isaiah 40:3.)

     b. Jesus entered the city as Messiah on the tenth day of the month when Jewish families picked Passover lambs for sacrifice. What was He asking the people to recognize? (See Exodus 12:1–6, 12–15; Matthew 17:22–23; John 1:29; John 12:1, 12–18.)

     c. What did Jesus communicate by getting on the donkey as soon as He arrived at Bethphage—the town the rabbis had decided was the city limit of Jerusalem? (See Zechariah 9:9–10; Matthew 21:1–6.)

5. Describe the difference between the way the people responded to Jesus and the way He responded to them (John 12:12–13; Luke 19:38–44).

Session Six: The Lamb of God   109

COMPELLING EVIDENCE

The Messiah from the East

A number of significant events in the history of the Jewish people, particularly events that relate to God's presence, have been recorded as occurring "from the east":

- The children of Israel, with the ark symbolizing God's presence, entered the Promised Land from the east (Joshua 3:1, 15–17).
- In Ezekiel's visions, the glory (presence) of the Lord left the corrupted temple and departed to the east (Ezekiel 10:4, 18–19; 11:22–24).
- Ezekiel also saw the glory of the Lord return to the temple from the east (Ezekiel 43:1–5).
- Jesus' birth was announced in the east (Matthew 2:1–2, 9).
- The prophet Isaiah said that the Messiah would come from the wilderness east of Jerusalem (Isaiah 40:3).
- Jesus ascended into heaven from the Mount of Olives, east of Jerusalem (Acts 1:6–12).
- The Mount of Olives, east of Jerusalem, represents Jesus' Second Coming (Zechariah 14:4; Joel 3:2, 12).

Topic B: Jesus—Our Model for Selfless Sacrifice

1. Look up each of the following verses and consider what Jesus wanted His disciples to be.

Matthew 5:14

Matthew 5:43–47

Matthew 18:1–6

Matthew 18:21–35

Matthew 19:13–14

Matthew 20:20–28

FAITH PROFILE

The "Doubting Thomas" Most of Us Never Knew

Most Christians remember Thomas as the disciple who:

- didn't believe the other disciples when they told him they'd seen the risen Jesus (John 20:19–25).
- said that he'd only believe if he touched Jesus' scarred hands and side (John 20:25).

But Thomas was also the disciple who demonstrated great faith and dedication to Jesus during the walk to Jerusalem. When Jesus told His disciples that they were returning to Judea, they protested, recalling that the Jews had tried to stone Him there (John 11:8–9). But Thomas courageously agreed with Jesus, saying, "Let us also go, that we may die with him" (John 11:16). And the disciples remained with Jesus and headed toward Jerusalem.

Matthew 19:13–14

Suggested Response: to be like little children.

Matthew 20:20–28

Suggested Response: to be servants.

2. Which unusual method did Jesus use to carry out His mission as Messiah? (See Matthew 20:25–28.)

Suggested Response: He came to be a servant and to sacrifice Himself for others.

3. In contrast to the example Jesus lived out, what did the disciples want for themselves? (See Matthew 20:20–22.)

Suggested Responses: They wanted recognition, power, authority, and control.

4. When Jesus heard what the disciples desired, what did He say to them? (See Matthew 20:25–28.)

Suggested Responses: that whoever wants to be great must be a servant; whoever wants to be first must be a slave; that they were to serve other people in the way that He—the Son of Man—had come to serve.

Topic C: Jesus Turns His Focus on Jerusalem

As Jesus set His course for Jerusalem, He knew He'd face jeering crowds, betrayal by friends, a Roman cross, and finally the rejection of His own Father while He bore the agony of hell for the very people who despised Him. Yet He refused to escape into the Judea Wilderness along the more than ten miles of road from Jericho to Jerusalem.

1. The following verses are in chronological order. Look up each passage and write out what you discover concerning Jesus' goal and His determination to complete His work.

110   The Death and Resurrection of the Messiah

2. Which unusual method did Jesus use to carry out His mission as Messiah? (See Matthew 20:25–28.)

3. In contrast to the example Jesus lived out, what did the disciples want for themselves? (See Matthew 20:20–22.)

4. When Jesus heard what the disciples desired, what did He say to them? (See Matthew 20:25–28.)

FAITH PROFILE

The "Doubting Thomas" Most of Us Never Knew

Most Christians remember Thomas as the disciple who:

- didn't believe the other disciples when they told him they'd seen the risen Jesus (John 20:19–25).
- said that he'd only believe if he touched Jesus' scarred hands and side (John 20:25).

But Thomas was also the disciple who demonstrated great faith and dedication to Jesus during the walk to Jerusalem. When Jesus told His disciples that they were returning to Judea, they protested, recalling that the Jews had tried to stone Him there (John 11:8–9). But Thomas courageously agreed with Jesus, saying, "Let us also go, that we may die with him" (John 11:16). And the disciples remained with Jesus and headed toward Jerusalem.

Session Six: The Lamb of God   111

Topic C: Jesus Turns His Focus on Jerusalem

As Jesus set His course for Jerusalem, He knew He'd face jeering crowds, betrayal by friends, a Roman cross, and finally the rejection of His own Father while He bore the agony of hell for the very people who despised Him. Yet He refused to escape into the Judea Wilderness along the more than ten miles of road from Jericho to Jerusalem.

1. The following verses are in chronological order. Look up each passage and write out what you discover concerning Jesus' goal and His determination to complete His work.

   Matthew 17:22

   Luke 9:51

   Matthew 19:1

   Matthew 20:17–19

   Luke 10:5–7

   Luke 13:22

   Luke 18:31–33

   Matthew 20:29–30

   Matthew 21:1

   Matthew 21:12–16, 23–24

   Matthew 26:1

   Matthew 26:10–12

   Matthew 26:31–32

2. Why was Jesus so determined to go to Jerusalem to die? (See John 12:27–28.)

Matthew 17:22

Suggested Response: Jesus explained that He had to go to Jerusalem to die.

Luke 9:51

Suggested Response: Jesus was absolutely determined to go to Jerusalem. (The Greek literally says, "He strengthened His face for Jerusalem.")

Matthew 19:1

Suggested Response: Jesus set out for Jerusalem by way of Perea (Caesarea Philippi).

Matthew 20:17–19

Suggested Response: Jesus again explained His coming death and resurrection.

Luke 10:5–7

Suggested Response: Jesus described the strategy the disciples were to follow after He was gone.

Luke 13:22

Suggested Response: Jesus continued to teach the disciples.

Luke 18:31–33

Suggested Response: Jesus privately stressed His future suffering and death in Jerusalem.

Matthew 20:29–30

Suggested Response: Jesus continued toward Jerusalem by way of Jericho.

Matthew 21:1

Suggested Response: Jesus arrived in Jerusalem.

Matthew 21:12–16, 23–24

Suggested Response: Jesus drove out the buyers and sellers in the temple, healed people, and taught in the temple courts. He stayed in Jerusalem, confronting His opponents.

Matthew 26:1

Suggested Response: Again, Jesus taught about His death and resurrection.

Matthew 26:10–12

Suggested Response: Jesus prepared His disciples for His death.

Matthew 26:31–32

Suggested Response: On the night He would be arrested, Jesus explained His coming death and resurrection.

Topic C: Jesus Turns His Focus on Jerusalem

As Jesus set His course for Jerusalem, He knew He'd face jeering crowds, betrayal by friends, a Roman cross, and finally the rejection of His own Father while He bore the agony of hell for the very people who despised Him. Yet He refused to escape into the Judea Wilderness along the more than ten miles of road from Jericho to Jerusalem.

1. The following verses are in chronological order. Look up each passage and write out what you discover concerning Jesus' goal and His determination to complete His work.

    Matthew 17:22

    Luke 9:51

    Matthew 19:1

    Matthew 20:17–19

    Luke 10:5–7

    Luke 13:22

    Luke 18:31–33

    Matthew 20:29–30

    Matthew 21:1

    Matthew 21:12–16, 23–24

    Matthew 26:1

    Matthew 26:10–12

    Matthew 26:31–32

2. Why was Jesus so determined to go to Jerusalem to die? (See John 12:27–28.)

✏ 2. Why was Jesus so determined to go to Jerusalem to die? (See John 12:27–28.)

    Suggested Response: He had come to earth for that purpose and would glorify His Father's name.

DATA FILE

The Judea Wilderness

Provided a place to hide:
- David hid from Saul (1 Samuel 23:14).
- Elijah hid from evil Ahab and Jezebel (1 Kings 19:1–5).
- An Egyptian hid from the Roman authorities (Acts 21:8).

Perceived as a place of temptation and evil:
- The name of the scapegoat, who symbolically carried the Israelites' sins into the wilderness, was derived from the Hebrew word *Azazel*. This word apparently came from the name of the goat-demon who was thought to live in the wilderness.
- Goat-gods (satyrs) were believed to live in the wilderness (Leviticus 17:7; 2 Chronicles 11:15; Isaiah 13:21).
- Jewish tradition taught that demons, including a fallen angel, lived there (1 Enoch 6–13).
- Satan tempted Jesus in the wilderness for forty days (Luke 4:1–13).
- Jesus used the wilderness walk between Jerusalem and Jericho as the setting for His parable about the man who was beaten by robbers and left for dead (Luke 10:30–37).

Topic D: Praised as Messiah, But Not as the Lamb of God

✏ 1. What did the crowd do as Jesus rode into Jerusalem? (See Matthew 21:6–9; John 12:13.)

    Suggested Responses: They went ahead of Him and followed behind Him. They spread their cloaks and tree branches on the road. They shouted, "Hosanna to the Son of David, blessed is he who comes in the name of the Lord, blessed is the King of Israel, and hosanna in the highest!"

✏ 2. The word *Hosanna* means "Please save!" (derived from two Hebrew words, *hosha* and *na* found in Psalm 118:25–26). But *save* can mean many different things. What did it mean in the minds of the people?

    Suggested Responses: They wanted salvation, or deliverance, from Roman rule, and they expected the Messiah to accomplish that for them.

✏ 3. Picture what happened next. The crowd shouted, but Jesus wept! Why did Jesus weep when so many people recognized Him as Messiah? (See Luke 19:41–44.)

    Suggested Responses: He wept because they didn't know the kind of peace the Messiah would bring. They were looking for the Messiah to usher in a political peace that would free them from Rome's tyranny. Jesus foresaw that Jerusalem would be destroyed because the people were looking for the wrong kind of peace and as a result would not recognize who He really was, nor would they accept the peace He offered.

112   The Death and Resurrection of the Messiah

DATA FILE

The Judea Wilderness

Provided a place to hide:
- David hid from Saul (1 Samuel 23:14).
- Elijah hid from evil Ahab and Jezebel (1 Kings 19:1–5).
- An Egyptian hid from the Roman authorities (Acts 21:8).

Perceived as a place of temptation and evil:
- The name of the scapegoat, who symbolically carried the Israelites' sins into the wilderness, was derived from the Hebrew word *Azazel*. This word apparently came from the name of the goat-demon who was thought to live in the wilderness.
- Goat-gods (satyrs) were believed to live in the wilderness (Leviticus 17:7; 2 Chronicles 11:15; Isaiah 13:21).
- Jewish tradition taught that demons, including a fallen angel, lived there (1 Enoch 6–13).
- Satan tempted Jesus in the wilderness for forty days (Luke 4:1–13).
- Jesus used the wilderness walk between Jerusalem and Jericho as the setting for His parable about the man who was beaten by robbers and left for dead (Luke 10:30–37).

Topic D: Praised as Messiah, But Not as the Lamb of God

1. What did the crowd do as Jesus rode into Jerusalem? (See Matthew 21:6–9; John 12:13.)

Session Six: The Lamb of God   113

2. The word *Hosanna* means "Please save!" (derived from two Hebrew words, *hosha* and *na* found in Psalm 118:25–26). But *save* can mean many different things. What did it mean in the minds of the people?

3. Picture what happened next. The crowd shouted, but Jesus wept! Why did Jesus weep when so many people recognized Him as Messiah? (See Luke 19:41–44.)

4. What is the significance of Jesus coming into Jerusalem on selection day for the Passover lamb? (See John 1:29–36; 1 Corinthians 5:7.)

   a. What is the significance of Jesus choosing to ride the donkey into Jerusalem on lamb selection day? (See Matthew 21:1–7.)

5. Why, as the video has communicated, is it so important for us to recognize Jesus for who He is, not who we want Him to be?

✏ 4. What is the significance of Jesus coming into Jerusalem on selection day for the Passover lamb? (See John 1:29–36; 1 Corinthians 5:7.)

Suggested Responses: Jesus was the Lamb of God and His blood would be shed as the sacrifice for sins on Passover; it was important that His identity as the Lamb of God be clearly revealed to Israel.

   a. What is the significance of Jesus choosing to ride the donkey into Jerusalem on lamb selection day? (See Matthew 21:1–7.)

   Suggested Responses: Jesus wanted to be seen as the fulfillment of Old Testament prophecy concerning the Messiah and wanted the people to profess faith in Him as their Messiah.

✏ 5. Why, as the video has communicated, is it so important for us to recognize Jesus for who He is, not who we want Him to be?

Suggested Responses: People have considered Jesus to be a revolutionary, a good man, a prophet, and the like, but what's important is to grasp who God says He is. Jesus is God's Lamb, whose blood was shed to save us from our sins. When we look for Him to be someone else, we will not recognize who He is and will miss the salvation He has provided for us.

faith Lesson

7 minutes

Time for Reflection (4 minutes)

It's time for each of us to think quietly about how we can apply what we've learned today. On page 114 of the Participant's Guide, you'll find a passage of Scripture. Let's each read this passage silently and take the next few minutes to reflect on the questions that follow the Scripture passage.

Please do not talk during this time. It's a time when we all can reflect on today's lesson and how it applies to our lives.

The Scripture passage and questions are reproduced in their entirety in the Participant's Guide on pages 114–15.

The tears of Jesus at Lazarus' tomb:

> On his arrival, Jesus found that Lazarus had already been in the tomb for four days. . . . When Mary reached the place where Jesus was and saw him, she fell at his feet and said, "Lord, if you had been here, my brother would not have died." When Jesus saw her weeping, and the Jews who had come along with her also weeping, he was deeply moved in spirit and troubled. "Where have you laid him?" he asked. "Come and see, Lord," they replied. Jesus wept. Then the Jews said, "See how he loved him!"
>
> JOHN 11:17, 32–36

The tears of Jesus at Jerusalem:

> After Jesus had said this, he went on ahead, going up to Jerusalem. . . . When he came near the place where the road goes down the Mount of

2. The word *Hosanna* means "Please save!" (derived from two Hebrew words, *hosha* and *na* found in Psalm 118:25–26). But *save* can mean many different things. What did it mean in the minds of the people?

3. Picture what happened next. The crowd shouted, but Jesus wept! Why did Jesus weep when so many people recognized Him as Messiah? (See Luke 19:41–44.)

4. What is the significance of Jesus coming into Jerusalem on selection day for the Passover lamb? (See John 1:29–36; 1 Corinthians 5:7.)

   a. What is the significance of Jesus choosing to ride the donkey into Jerusalem on lamb selection day? (See Matthew 21:1–7.)

5. Why, as the video has communicated, is it so important for us to recognize Jesus for who He is, not who we want Him to be?

ꜰᴀɪᴛʜ ʟᴇꜱꜱᴏɴ

Time for Reflection

The following Scripture passages reveal the depth of Jesus' love for us. Read these passages silently and consider how greatly Jesus loves you.
   The tears of Jesus at Lazarus' tomb:

> On his arrival, Jesus found that Lazarus had already been in the tomb for four days.... When Mary reached the place where Jesus was and saw him, she fell at his feet and said, "Lord, if you had been here, my brother would not have died." When Jesus saw her weeping, and the Jews who had come along with her also weeping, he was deeply moved in spirit and troubled. "Where have you laid him?" he asked. "Come and see, Lord," they replied. Jesus wept. Then the Jews said, "See how he loved him!"
>
> JOHN 11:17, 32–36

The tears of Jesus at Jerusalem:

> After Jesus had said this, he went on ahead, going up to Jerusalem.... When he came near the place where the road goes down the Mount of Olives, the whole crowd of disciples began joyfully to praise God in loud voices for all the miracles they had seen: "Blessed is the king who comes in the name of the Lord!" "Peace in heaven and glory in the highest!" Some of the Pharisees in the crowd said to Jesus, "Teacher, rebuke your disciples!" "I tell you," he replied, "if they keep quiet, the stones will cry out." As he approached Jerusalem and saw the city, he wept over it and said, "If you, even you, had only known on this day what would bring you peace—but now it is hidden from your eyes. The days will come upon you when your enemies will build an embankment against you and encircle you and hem you in on every side. They will dash you to the ground, you and the children within your walls. They will not leave one stone on another, because you did not recognize the time of God's coming to you."
>
> LUKE 19:28, 37–44

Olives, the whole crowd of disciples began joyfully to praise God in loud voices for all the miracles they had seen: "Blessed is the king who comes in the name of the Lord!" "Peace in heaven and glory in the highest!" Some of the Pharisees in the crowd said to Jesus, "Teacher, rebuke your disciples!" "I tell you," he replied, "if they keep quiet, the stones will cry out." As he approached Jerusalem and saw the city, he wept over it and said, "If you, even you, had only known on this day what would bring you peace—but now it is hidden from your eyes. The days will come upon you when your enemies will build an embankment against you and encircle you and hem you in on every side. They will dash you to the ground, you and the children within your walls. They will not leave one stone on another, because you did not recognize the time of God's coming to you."

LUKE 19:28, 37–44

1. What was Jesus mourning in each of these instances?

2. What do the tears Jesus shed for the family and friends of Lazarus and the people of Jerusalem reveal about His great love and compassion for people?

3. How does Jesus' determination to travel through the barren wilderness to Jerusalem and die a horrible death for your sins add to your understanding of His great love for you?

4. How has the love of Jesus the Messiah touched your heart and life?

5. How can you help people better understand the loving heart of Jesus the Messiah? How can you help them correctly interpret His message?

As soon as participants have spent four minutes reflecting on the above questions, get the entire group's attention and move to the next section.

Action Points (3 minutes)

The following points are reproduced on pages 116–17 of the Participant's Guide:

Now it's time to wrap up our session.

Give participants a moment to transition from their thoughtfulness to giving you their full attention.

I'd like to take a moment to summarize the key points we explored. After I have reviewed each point, I will give you a moment to jot down an action step (or steps) that you will commit to this week as a result of what you have learned about Jesus—the Messiah, God's chosen Passover Lamb—today.

Read each point and pause after each point so that participants can consider and write out their commitment.

1. *On lamb selection day, Jesus came into Jerusalem as the Lamb of God, but the people—despite their praises—didn't recognize who He was.* He did not fit

1. What was Jesus mourning in each of these instances?

2. What do the tears Jesus shed for the family and friends of Lazarus and the people of Jerusalem reveal about His great love and compassion for people?

3. How does Jesus' determination to travel through the barren wilderness to Jerusalem and die a horrible death for your sins add to your understanding of His great love for you?

4. How has the love of Jesus the Messiah touched your heart and life?

5. How can you help people better understand the loving heart of Jesus the Messiah? How can you help them correctly interpret His message?

Action Points

Take a moment to review the key points you explored today. Then write down an action step (or steps) that you will commit to this week as a result of what you have discovered about Jesus—the Messiah, God's chosen Passover Lamb.

1. *On lamb selection day, Jesus came into Jerusalem as the Lamb of God, but the people—despite their praises—didn't recognize who He was.* He did not fit their idea of what the Messiah would be. They wanted a Messiah who would provide political-military liberation. The vision of a suffering Messiah who would give His life to defeat the "gates of Hades" and to provide freedom from the spiritual bondage of sin was foreign to them. And the idea of following Jesus' example by giving themselves as servants to others was shocking.

   Consequently, many people (including His disciples) did not understand His mission. Most of them wanted political liberation rather than spiritual liberation from sin and the peace of a personal relationship with Him. Because Jesus did not offer what they wanted, many people rejected Him completely.

   In what ways have you misunderstood Jesus and His message?

   In what ways have you reinterpreted Jesus to be what you want Him to be and missed out on what He had to offer?

   What is your commitment to Jesus the Messiah? Will you choose Him as the perfect Lamb of God, the sacrifice for your sins?

PLANNING NOTES:

their idea of what the Messiah would be. They wanted a Messiah who would provide political-military liberation. The vision of a suffering Messiah who would give His life to defeat the "gates of Hades" and to provide freedom from the spiritual bondage of sin was foreign to them. And the idea of following Jesus' example by giving themselves as servants to others was shocking.

Consequently, many people (including His disciples) did not understand His mission. Most of them wanted political liberation rather than spiritual liberation from sin and the peace of a personal relationship with Him. Because Jesus did not offer what they wanted, many people rejected Him completely.

In what ways have you misunderstood Jesus and His message?

In what ways have you reinterpreted Jesus to be what you want Him to be and missed out on what He had to offer?

What is your commitment to Jesus the Messiah? Will you choose Him as the perfect Lamb of God, the sacrifice for your sins?

✏ 2.   *Jesus weeps for us. He grieves when we suffer loss and pain, just as He grieved at the tomb of Lazarus.* He also longs for us to recognize and accept Him for who He is. The Messiah, who came on "lamb selection day" to establish His kingdom by being a servant and giving up His life as the Lamb of God, wept for the people of Jerusalem when they didn't receive Him as God's Messiah and rejected the deliverance He offered. His heart breaks for us today, just as it did that day in Jerusalem, when we miss Him and His message.

Why does Jesus weep for you?

closing prayer

I minute

I hope that this lesson has given you, as it has me, a new appreciation of Jesus the Messiah, the Lamb of God who came to sacrifice Himself for us as an offering of forgiveness for our sins. Let's close in prayer.

Dear Jesus, thank You for staying on that wilderness road to Jerusalem and for being committed to Your mission as Messiah. Please help us understand areas in our lives in which we've misunderstood Your teachings and believed You to be someone You aren't. You are truly our Lamb, who died on the cross and rose again as the ultimate sacrifice for our sins. Please help us to live for You and to serve others, as You did throughout Your life. Amen.

Action Points

Take a moment to review the key points you explored today. Then write down an action step (or steps) that you will commit to this week as a result of what you have discovered about Jesus—the Messiah, God's chosen Passover Lamb.

1. *On lamb selection day, Jesus came into Jerusalem as the Lamb of God, but the people—despite their praises—didn't recognize who He was.* He did not fit their idea of what the Messiah would be. They wanted a Messiah who would provide political-military liberation. The vision of a suffering Messiah who would give His life to defeat the "gates of Hades" and to provide freedom from the spiritual bondage of sin was foreign to them. And the idea of following Jesus' example by giving themselves as servants to others was shocking.

   Consequently, many people (including His disciples) did not understand His mission. Most of them wanted political liberation rather than spiritual liberation from sin and the peace of a personal relationship with Him. Because Jesus did not offer what they wanted, many people rejected Him completely.

   In what ways have you misunderstood Jesus and His message?

   In what ways have you reinterpreted Jesus to be what you want Him to be and missed out on what He had to offer?

   What is your commitment to Jesus the Messiah? Will you choose Him as the perfect Lamb of God, the sacrifice for your sins?

2. *Jesus weeps for us. He grieves when we suffer loss and pain, just as He grieved at the tomb of Lazarus.* He also longs for us to recognize and accept Him for who He is. The Messiah who came on "lamb selection day" to establish His kingdom by being a servant and giving up His life as the Lamb of God, wept for the people of Jerusalem when they didn't receive Him as God's Messiah and rejected the deliverance He offered. His heart breaks for us today, just as it did that day in Jerusalem, when we miss Him and His message.

   Why does Jesus weep for you?

The weight of the world

Before you Lead

Synopsis

During Jesus' time, olives were the most significant crop in Israel. Olives and the oil they produced were used for such everyday purposes as food, lighting, and lubrication. They were also used for ceremonial purposes such as offerings and the anointing of leaders. Images of the olive tree, its fruit, and its oil are frequently used in the Bible to portray God, His blessing, and His Messiah.

In order to extract the olive oil, the Jews used an olive press—a *gethsemane*. They lowered heavy stone slabs onto baskets of olives that had already been crushed in an olive crusher. Gradually the enormous pressure of the slabs' weight squeezed the oil out of the olive pulp, and the oil ran into a pit. There the oil was collected in clay jars.

After the Last Supper, when He washed His disciples' feet, Jesus went to Gethsemane—to an olive press located in or near an olive grove on the Mount of Olives (see Mark 14:32; John 18:1), where His betrayer would be certain to find Him.

The image of the Gethsemane where Jesus went the night before His crucifixion provides a vivid image of the suffering He experienced that night. The weight of the world's sin pressed down upon Him in the same way a heavy stone slab pressed down upon olives in an olive press.

Greatly distressed over His imminent suffering, Jesus fell on His face and sought to find strength in prayer—through His own prayers to His Father and through the prayers of His friends. When He was abandoned by His sleeping friends, Jesus expressed Himself openly to His Father—sharing the deep emotions He felt as He anticipated the dreadful day ahead. Jesus agonized under the pressing weight of all humanity's sin.

Jesus knew He would have to face the weight of:

- Abandonment by His friends.
- A trial by His religious leaders.
- Torture at the Romans' hands.
- Crucifixion and physical death.
- The rejection of His Father as He suffered the agonies of hell to pay for the sins of those He loved—the sins of you and me.

As Jesus prayed, the emotional weight of what would be laid on Him was so heavy that it literally squeezed His own blood out of Him. His sweat, "like drops of blood falling to the ground" (Luke 22:44), flowed from Him like olive oil as it was squeezed out and flowed into the pit of the olive press. His flowing blood was His "anointing" for us (2 Corinthians 1:21).

The agony Jesus faced the night before His trial and execution provides a profound picture of God's love, Jesus' humanity, and the awful price that had to be paid for our sin.

Key Points of This Lesson

Using the imagery of the olive tree, olives, olive oil, and the olive press, this lesson will help participants understand the weight of sin that Jesus carried for each of us so that we can have a personal relationship with God and receive eternal life. The following key points are emphasized through this lesson:

1. *The olive press—the gethsemane—symbolizes the agonizing weight of our sin that Jesus willingly carried when He was crucified.*
2. *We each must choose how we will respond to Jesus' incredible love and sacrifice for us.*
3. *The choice we make concerning what Jesus has done for us has serious consequences.*

Session Outline (55 minutes total)

I. Introduction (5 minutes)
Welcome
What's to Come
Questions to Think About

II. Video Presentation "The Weight of the World" (19 minutes)

III. Group Discovery (20 minutes)
Video Highlights
Small Group Bible Discovery

IV. Faith Lesson (10 minutes)
Time for Reflection
Action Points

V. Closing Prayer (1 minute)

Materials

You may want to use a marker board, chalkboard, or overhead projector to record the responses of participants to the introductory **Questions to Think About.** No additional materials are needed. Simply view the video prior to leading the session so you are familiar with its main points.

the weight of the world

introduction

5 minutes

Welcome

Assemble the participants together. Welcome them to session seven of *Faith Lessons on the Death and Resurrection of the Messiah*.

What's to Come

In this session, we will learn about Jesus' final night in Gethsemane on the slope of the Mount of Olives before He bore the weight of our sins on the cross. We will also look at ways in which God used the symbols of olives and olive trees to reveal truths that apply to our lives. We'll start by reflecting on what sin feels like.

Questions to Think About

Participant's Guide page 118.

Turn to page 118 of the Participant's Guide. Let's start by considering several questions that will help set the stage for the video we'll see in a few minutes.

Ask each question and solicit responses from group members. You may record the responses on a marker board, chalkboard, or overhead projector so they are visible to the group.

1. Which words would you use to describe how you felt during a time when you were under enormous pressure?

   Suggested Responses: heavy, lonely, fearful, oppressed, anguished, weary, hopeless, etc.

2. In contrast, how would you describe what it felt like when that pressure was lifted?

   Suggested Responses: relieved, happy, peaceful, free, hopeful, etc.

Let's continue to think about these ideas as we view the video.

video presentation

19 minutes

Participant's Guide page 119.

On page 119 of your Participant's Guide, you will find a space in which to take notes on key points as we watch this video.

SESSION SEVEN

the weight of the world

questions to think about

1. Which words would you use to describe how you felt during a time when you were under enormous pressure?

2. In contrast, how would you describe what it felt like when that pressure was lifted?

118

PLANNING NOTES:

Leader's Video Observations

Symbolism of the Olives

Gethsemane (Olive Press)

The Curse

The Importance of Producing Fruit

Group Discovery

20 minutes

> If your group has seven or more members, use the **Video Highlights** with the entire group (5 minutes), then break into small groups of three to five to discuss the **Small Group Bible Discovery** (15 minutes). Then reassemble the larger group to discuss the key points discovered (5 minutes).
>
> If your group has fewer than seven members, begin with the **Video Highlights** (5 minutes), then do one or more of the topics found in the **Small Group Bible Discovery** as a group (10 minutes). Finally, spend five minutes at the end discussing points that had an impact on participants.

Video Highlights (5 minutes)

> Here you'll ask one or more of the following questions that directly relate to the video the participants have just seen.

1. Which images presented in the video stood out to you? Why?

2. What was Jesus' state of mind that night in Gethsemane? What was the "weight" on Him? Why was He so sorrowful? (See Luke 22:44.)

   Suggested Responses: He felt the crushing weight of our sin; He felt the loneliness of his friends abandoning Him; He was aware of the pain of His upcoming trial, torture, and physical death; He anticipated His Father's rejection because of the sin He bore.

video notes

Symbolism of the Olives

Gethsemane (Olive Press)

The Curse

The Importance of Producing Fruit

video highlights

1. Which images presented in the video stood out to you? Why?

2. What was Jesus' state of mind that night in Gethsemane? What was the "weight" on Him? Why was He so sorrowful? (See Luke 22:44.)

3. For what did Jesus ask?

Topography of Jerusalem

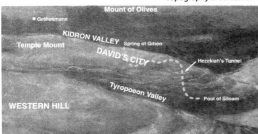

PLANNING NOTES:

3. For what did Jesus ask?

Suggested Response: He asked if there was another way for humankind's sin to be removed.

4. Describe the difference between Jesus' mindset and that of His disciples.

Suggested Responses: He was deeply troubled and asked them to support Him in prayer. They weren't overly concerned about His needs and just went to sleep.

5. Why did Jesus curse Capernaum?

Suggested Responses: The people there witnessed His miracles, experienced His love in action, and heard His Words, yet they failed to respond positively to Him.

6. Why is it important for us to bear fruit in our lives?

Suggested Responses: We are created to bear fruit for God's kingdom. We are to receive life-giving strength from Christ, our vine.

Topography of Jerusalem

Small Group Bible Discovery (15 minutes)

Participant's Guide pages 122–28.

During this time, a group with fewer than seven participants will stay together. A group larger than seven participants will break into small groups and reassemble as a large group during the final five minutes. Assign each group one of the following topics. If you have more than five small groups, assign some topics to more than one group.

Let's break into groups of three to five—people sitting near you—and study some of the Bible passages and truths mentioned in the video.

Turn to pages 122–28 in your Participant's Guide. There you'll find a list of five topics. You'll have ten minutes to read and discuss the topic I'll assign to you. Choose one person in your group to be a spokesperson for your group when we discuss these topics later.

Assign each group a topic.

120   The Death and Resurrection of the Messiah

video highlights

1. Which images presented in the video stood out to you? Why?

2. What was Jesus' state of mind that night in Gethsemane? What was the "weight" on Him? Why was He so sorrowful? (See Luke 22:44.)

3. For what did Jesus ask?

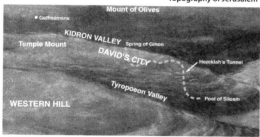

Topography of Jerusalem

Session Seven: The Weight of the World   121

4. Describe the difference between Jesus' mindset and that of His disciples.

5. Why did Jesus curse Capernaum?

6. Why is it important for us to bear fruit in our lives?

I'll signal you when one minute is left.

> After nine minutes, let participants know that they have one minute remaining. Then reassemble the entire group. After everyone is back together, begin asking one person from each small group to briefly share a key idea with the larger group. In some cases, you may not have time for every group to share their discoveries.

As time allows, let's briefly share the key ideas that your group discussed.

Topic A: Jesus' Prayer
Look up Matthew 26:39, 42, 44, 47–54; Mark 14:35–36, 39; Luke 22:42.

1. What was Jesus asking in His prayer?

   Suggested Response: He asked if God could take away the cup of His suffering.

2. What does this prayer reveal about Jesus' relationship with God the Father?

   Suggested Responses: Jesus loved Him, sought to do His will, trusted Him completely, etc.

3. What do these verses reveal about God's love for us?

   Suggested Responses: He loves us deeply, He wanted a relationship with us, He had for a long time planned to redeem us.

4. Why is it important for us to trust God during difficult times?

   Suggested Responses: God loves us, knows what's best for us, is sovereign, and is working out His plan for our lives. It is by trusting and obeying Him during difficult times that our faith is deepened.

5. Which temptations might Jesus have faced during this time?

   Suggested Responses: to call down angels to deliver Him and to destroy those who would kill Him, to walk away from His suffering, to use His power to establish His kingdom on earth and be the kind of king the people wanted, etc.

Topic B: The Disciples' Response
Look up Matthew 26:36–46; Mark 14:37–42; Luke 22:45–46.

1. What did Jesus want the disciples to do? Why do you think He asked that of them?

   Suggested Responses: to stay awake and keep watch and pray. He loved them and knew they loved Him; He wanted the support of His closest spiritual companions as He agonized over what lay ahead.

2. Why do you think the disciples acted so differently from Jesus?

   Suggested Responses: they didn't understand the depth of His need for them; they were tired and valued their own physical comfort; their relationship with God the Father wasn't strong enough to endure the night of prayer; their spirit was willing, but their flesh was weak.

small Group Bible Discovery

Topic A: Jesus' Prayer
Look up Matthew 26:39, 42, 44, 47–54; Mark 14:35–36, 39; Luke 22:42.

1. What was Jesus asking in His prayer?

2. What does this prayer reveal about Jesus' relationship with God the Father?

3. What do these verses reveal about God's love for us?

4. Why is it important for us to trust God during difficult times?

5. Which temptations might Jesus have faced during this time?

Topic B: The Disciples' Response
Look up Matthew 26:36–46; Mark 14:37–42; Luke 22:45–46.

1. What did Jesus want the disciples to do? Why do you think He asked that of them?

2. Why do you think the disciples acted so differently from Jesus?

3. Which temptation did the disciples face? How could they have resisted it?

4. If you feel comfortable sharing, describe a time when your friends or family members didn't support you during a crucial time. How did you feel?

5. In what way(s) can you relate to Jesus' loneliness as He faced His anguish alone?

PLANNING NOTES:

✏ 3.   Which temptation did the disciples face? How could they have resisted it?

Suggested Responses: they were tempted to abandon Jesus, to take their eyes off Him. They could have resisted by watching and praying.

✏ 4.   If you feel comfortable sharing, describe a time when your friends or family members didn't support you during a crucial time. How did you feel?

✏ 5.   In what way(s) can you relate to Jesus' loneliness as He faced His anguish alone?

DATA FILE

Gethsemane—The word *Gethsemane* is derived from two Hebrew words: *gat,* which means "a place for pressing oil (or wine)" and *shemanim,* which means "oils." During Jesus' time, heavy stone slabs were lowered onto olives that had already been crushed in an olive crusher. Gradually the slabs' weight squeezed the olive oil out of the pulp, and the oil ran into a pit. There the oil was collected in clay jars.

The image of the gethsemane on the slope of the Mount of Olives where Jesus went the night before His crucifixion provides a vivid picture of Jesus' suffering. The weight of the sins of the world pressed down upon Him like a heavy slab of rock pressed down on olives in their baskets. His sweat, "like drops of blood falling to the ground" (Luke 22:44), flowed from Him like olive oil as it was squeezed out and flowed into the pit of an olive press.

Olive Crusher—The stone basin used to crush olives into pulp. A donkey pushed on a horizontal beam, which in turn rolled a millstone that crushed into a pulp ripe olives placed in a large, round basin. An olive crusher was often placed in a cave, where the moderated temperature improved the efficiency of oil production.

An Olive Press

The Amazing Olive Tree

- Its roots can live for more than a thousand years.
- Rarely reaches twenty feet high.
- Must be cut down when it becomes old (often after hundreds of years) in order to become fruitful again. The next year, new shoots will grow out of the stump, and the new tree will grow and produce olives again.
- A good olive tree may produce fifty pounds of olives and four to six pounds of oil each year.
- Olive oil was used for food (1 Kings 17:12), skin care (Ecclesiastes 9:7–8), fuel, medicine, and as trade (1 Kings 5:11). It kept leather soft (Isaiah 21:5), priests mixed it with the morning burnt offerings (Exodus 29:40), and it was a symbol of God's Spirit (James 5:14).

Topic B: The Disciples' Response

Look up Matthew 26:36–46; Mark 14:37–42; Luke 22:45–46.

1. What did Jesus want the disciples to do? Why do you think He asked that of them?

2. Why do you think the disciples acted so differently from Jesus?

3. Which temptation did the disciples face? How could they have resisted it?

4. If you feel comfortable sharing, describe a time when your friends or family members didn't support you during a crucial time. How did you feel?

5. In what way(s) can you relate to Jesus' loneliness as He faced His anguish alone?

DATA FILE

"Gethsemane"—The word *Gethsemane* is derived from two Hebrew words: *gat*, which means "a place for pressing oil (or wine)" and *she-manim*, which means "oils." During Jesus' time, heavy stone slabs were lowered onto olives that had already been crushed in an olive crusher. Gradually the slabs' weight squeezed the olive oil out of the pulp, and the oil ran into a pit. There the oil was collected in clay jars.

The image of the gethsemane on the slope of the Mount of Olives where Jesus went the night before His crucifixion provides a vivid picture of Jesus' suffering. The weight of the sins of the world pressed down upon Him like a heavy slab of rock pressed down on olives in their baskets. His sweat, "like drops of blood falling to the ground" (Luke 22:44), flowed from Him like olive oil as it was squeezed out and flowed into the pit of an olive press.

Olive Crusher—The stone basin used to crush olives into pulp. A donkey pushed on a horizontal beam, which in turn rolled a millstone that crushed into a pulp ripe olives placed in a large, round basin. An olive crusher was often placed in a cave, where the moderated temperature improved the efficiency of oil production.

An Olive Press

The Amazing Olive Tree
- Its roots can live for more than a thousand years.
- Rarely reaches twenty feet high.
- Must be cut down when it becomes old (often after hundreds of years) in order to become fruitful again. The next year, new shoots will grow out of the stump, and the new olive tree will produce olives again.
- A good olive tree may produce fifty pounds of olives and four to six pounds of oil each year.
- Olive oil was used for food (1 Kings 17:12), skin care (Ecclesiastes 9:7–8), fuel, medicine, and as trade (1 Kings 5:11). It kept leather soft (Isaiah 21:5), priests mixed it with the morning burnt offerings (Exodus 29:40), and it was a symbol of God's Spirit (James 5:14).

Topic C: Christians Are to Bear Fruit

In the Bible, God's relationship to His people is represented by the olive tree, and a Christian's fruitfulness is likened to a tree that bears fruit.

1. In Psalm 52:8, Psalm 128:3, and Hosea 14:5–6, which images are used to describe God's followers?

2. What was the unfaithful nation of Israel compared to? (See Jeremiah 11:16.)

Topic C: Christians Are to Bear Fruit

In the Bible, God's relationship to His people is represented by the olive tree, and a Christian's fruitfulness is likened to a tree that bears fruit.

1. In Psalm 52:8, Psalm 128:3, and Hosea 14:5–6, which images are used to describe God's followers?

    Suggested Responses: a flourishing olive tree in the temple, olive shoots, the splendor of an olive tree.

2. What was the unfaithful nation of Israel compared to? (See Jeremiah 11:16.)

    Suggested Response: a burned olive tree with broken branches.

3. What are the consequences of not bearing good fruit? (See Matthew 3:10–12; 7:16–20.)

    Suggested Responses: the axe will cut down the tree (which represents God's people), it will be thrown into the fire, others will recognize the bad fruit for what it is.

4. What did God, through Isaiah's prophecy, promise to do with the stump of unfaithful Israel? (See Isaiah 11:1–3; Jeremiah 23:5–6; 33:15–16.)

    Suggested Responses: God would grow a shoot from the stump of Jesse, a branch would come from the roots and bear fruit, God would raise up a king who would reign wisely and do what is just and right, God would make a righteous "branch" sprout from David's line, etc.

Topic D: Jesus' Blood Shed for Us

1. What happened to Jesus in Gethsemane as the weight of what He would soon face pressed down upon Him? (See Luke 22:40–45.)

    Suggested Responses: He was in agony, He prayed fervently, His sweat was like drops of blood, He asked the Father to remove His cup of suffering if He was willing.

2. What do the following verses reveal about the impact of Jesus' shed blood on us today?

Ephesians 1:7	gave us our redemption, enabled our sins to be forgiven
Colossians 1:19–20	reconciled all things unto Himself by making peace
Hebrews 13:12	made peace for us, reconciled humankind to Him
1 John 1:7–10	purifies us from all sin, enables us to receive forgiveness for our sins
Revelation 1:4–6	freed us from our sins

The Amazing Olive Tree
- Its roots can live for more than a thousand years.
- Rarely reaches twenty feet high.
- Must be cut down when it becomes old (often after hundreds of years) in order to become fruitful again. The next year, new shoots will grow out of the stump, and the new olive tree will produce olives again.
- A good olive tree may produce fifty pounds of olives and four to six pounds of oil each year.
- Olive oil was used for food (1 Kings 17:12), skin care (Ecclesiastes 9:7–8), fuel, medicine, and as trade (1 Kings 5:11). It kept leather soft (Isaiah 21:5), priests mixed it with the morning burnt offerings (Exodus 29:40), and it was a symbol of God's Spirit (James 5:14).

Topic C: Christians Are to Bear Fruit

In the Bible, God's relationship to His people is represented by the olive tree, and a Christian's fruitfulness is likened to a tree that bears fruit.

1. In Psalm 52:8, Psalm 128:3, and Hosea 14:5–6, which images are used to describe God's followers?

2. What was the unfaithful nation of Israel compared to? (See Jeremiah 11:16.)

3. What are the consequences of not bearing good fruit? (See Matthew 3:10–12; 7:16–20.)

4. What did God, through Isaiah's prophecy, promise to do with the stump of unfaithful Israel? (See Isaiah 11:1–3; Jeremiah 23:5–6; 33:15–16.)

Topic D: Jesus' Blood Shed for Us

1. What happened to Jesus in Gethsemane as the weight of what He would soon face pressed down on Him? (See Luke 22:40–45.)

2. What do the following verses reveal about the impact of Jesus' shed blood on us today?

Ephesians 1:7

Colossians 1:19–20

Hebrews 13:12

Topic E: Caring for the "Little Ones"

Look up Matthew 18:1–6; Mark 9:33–37, 42.

1. Why do you think Jesus told the disciples to stop thinking of themselves as important?

    Suggested Responses: He wanted them to be humble, wanted to encourage servanthood, wanted them to assume God's perspective and values, knew the value of trusting God and being a servant.

2. What do you think "becoming like little children" means?

    Suggested Responses: trusting God completely, approaching Him honestly and innocently, approaching Him on the basis of a childlike faith in who He is rather than on the basis of our own merit.

3. Why is humility a less common trait in people today?

    Suggested Responses: our culture honors accomplishment and pride rather than humility, our sinful nature is inclined to desire pride over humility, people equate humility with weakness, people don't understand what humility is, etc.

4. What did Jesus say would happen to someone who causes a "little one"—someone who seems to be unimportant in society—to stumble in his or her faith?

    Suggested Response: He indicated they would face the most severe consequences because to not welcome a little one is to not welcome Jesus. To reject a little one is to reject Jesus.

5. As Ray Vander Laan points out, Jesus felt deeply for the unimportant, for the "little ones" who had no status. Why is it so easy to overlook people in our church . . . school . . . neighborhood . . . who have no status in our world's eyes?

    Suggested Responses: they usually have no resources or power to help us, they often need care or support from us, we generally don't gain earthly honor or status by reaching out to them, the world would prefer that they not be encumbered by them.

6. Which "little ones" might we tend to overlook today?

7. Which "little ones" are under your leadership or influence right now?

faith Lesson

10 minutes

Time for Reflection (5 minutes)

It's time for each of us to think quietly about how we can apply what we've learned today. On page 129 of the Participant's Guide, you'll find a Scripture passage that describes Jesus' last night in Gethsemane. Let's each read this passage silently and take the next five minutes or so to consider some questions related to the Scripture passage.

1 John 1:7–10

Revelation 1:4–6

Topic E: Caring for the "Little Ones"
Look up Matthew 18:1–6; Mark 9:33–37, 42.

1. Why do you think Jesus told the disciples to stop thinking of themselves as important?

2. What do you think "becoming like little children" means?

3. Why is humility a less common trait in people today?

4. What did Jesus say would happen to someone who causes a "little one"—someone who seems to be unimportant in society—to stumble in his or her faith?

5. As Ray Vander Laan points out, Jesus felt deeply for the unimportant, for the "little ones" who had no status. Why is it so easy to overlook people in our church . . . school . . . neighborhood . . . who have no status in our world's eyes?

6. Which "little ones" might we tend to overlook today?

7. Which "little ones" are under your leadership or influence right now?

Please do not talk during this time. It's a time when we all can reflect on today's session and how it applies to our lives.

The Scripture passage and questions are reproduced in their entirety in the Participant's Guide on pages 129–31.

Then Jesus went with his disciples to a place called Gethsemane, and he said to them, "Sit here while I go over there and pray." He took Peter and the two sons of Zebedee along with him, and he began to be sorrowful and troubled. Then he said to them, "My soul is overwhelmed with sorrow to the point of death. Stay here and keep watch with me." Going a little farther, he fell with his face to the ground and prayed, "My Father, if it is possible, may this cup be taken from me. Yet not as I will, but as you will." Then he returned to his disciples and found them sleeping. "Could you men not keep watch with me for one hour?" he asked Peter. "Watch and pray so that you will not fall into temptation. The spirit is willing, but the body is weak." He went away a second time and prayed, "My Father, if it is not possible for this cup to be taken away unless I drink it, may your will be done." When he came back he again found them sleeping because their eyes were heavy. So he left them and went away once more and prayed the third time, saying the same thing. Then he returned to the disciples and said to them, "Are you still sleeping and resting? Look, the hour is near, and the Son of Man is betrayed into the hands of sinners. Rise, let us go! Here comes my betrayer!"

MATTHEW 26:36–46

1. Jesus loves each of us with a love we cannot fully comprehend. What did you learn about Jesus' love for you today? In what ways can you express your thankfulness to God today for what He has done for you?

2. Jesus was willing to pay a terribly high price for our sin. Which particular sin in your life right now is hindering your walk with Him? Take time to confess your sin to Him now and determine to change your ways. If possible, find a person to whom you can be accountable in making those changes.

3. Why do you think Jesus didn't just disappear into the night instead of waiting to be arrested? How would your life be different if He had?

4. In which ways might you be a "Capernaum" in that you know about Jesus and perhaps have seen Him do special things in your life or others' lives, yet have not committed your life to Him? What will you do today to reestablish a closer relationship with Him?

5. How does the way in which Jesus handled His suffering in Gethsemane relate to the times you face stress, sorrow, and/or agony? What did Jesus do that you can do today during tough times at work? At home? How often do you turn honestly to God in complete devotion to His will?

As soon as participants have spent five minutes reflecting on the above questions, get the entire group's attention and move to the next section.

Session Seven: The Weight of the World 129

faith Lesson

Time for Reflection

The following Scripture passage describes Jesus' last night in Gethsemane. Read it and take some time to think about the questions that follow it. Consider how you can begin to live out what you have learned through this video.

Then Jesus went with his disciples to a place called Gethsemane, and he said to them, "Sit here while I go over there and pray." He took Peter and the two sons of Zebedee along with him, and he began to be sorrowful and troubled. Then he said to them, "My soul is overwhelmed with sorrow to the point of death. Stay here and keep watch with me." Going a little farther, he fell with his face to the ground and prayed, "My Father, if it is possible, may this cup be taken from me. Yet not as I will, but as you will." Then he returned to his disciples and found them sleeping. "Could you men not keep watch with me for one hour?" he asked Peter. "Watch and pray so that you will not fall into temptation. The spirit is willing, but the body is weak." He went away a second time and prayed, "My Father, if it is not possible for this cup to be taken away unless I drink it, may your will be done." When he came back he again found them sleeping because their eyes were heavy. So he left them and went away once more and prayed the third time, saying the same thing. Then he returned to the disciples and said to them, "Are you still sleeping and resting? Look, the hour is near, and the Son of Man is betrayed into the hands of sinners. Rise, let us go! Here comes my betrayer!"

MATTHEW 26:36–46

130 The Death and Resurrection of the Messiah

1. Jesus loves each of us with a love we cannot fully comprehend. What did you learn about Jesus' love for you today? In what ways can you express your thankfulness to God today for what He has done for you?

2. Jesus was willing to pay a terribly high price for our sin. Which particular sin in your life right now is hindering your walk with Him? Take time to confess your sin to Him now and determine to change your ways. If possible, find a person to whom you can be accountable in making those changes.

3. Why do you think Jesus didn't just disappear into the night instead of waiting to be arrested? How would your life be different if He had?

4. In which ways might you be a "Capernaum" in that you know about Jesus and perhaps have seen Him do special things in your life or others' lives, yet have not committed your life to Him? What will you do today to reestablish a closer relationship with Him?

208   Session Seven

Action Points (5 minutes)

The following three points are reproduced on page 131–33 of the Participant's Guide:

Now it's time to wrap up our session.

Give participants a moment to transition from their thoughtfulness to giving you their full attention.

Let's take a moment to summarize the key points we explored today. As I review each point, I will give you a moment to jot down the action step (or steps) you will take this week.

Read each point and pause so that participants can write out their responses.

1. *The olive press—the gethsemane—symbolizes the agonizing weight of our sin that Jesus willingly carried when He was crucified.* Our sins are like the big rock in the olive press that forced the olive oil out of the olives. We were the burden He bore. Our guilt and the required penalty for sin were great, but Jesus' love for us and His obedient devotion to His Father's will were greater. Despite the powerful emotions He felt, Jesus submitted completely to His Father's will.

   "He was pierced for our transgressions, he was crushed for our iniquities; the punishment that brought us peace was upon him, and by his wounds we are healed." (Isaiah 53:5)

   "He himself bore our sins in his body on the tree, so that we might die to sins and live for righteousness; by his wounds you have been healed." (1 Peter 2:24)

   Recognizing the weight that Jesus bore, how will you view your sins differently this week?

2. *You must choose how you will respond to what Jesus has done for you.* Because of His deep love and compassion, Jesus willingly accepted the agonizing burden of our sin and went to the cross alone. He willingly died for our sins—a miracle that only He could perform. You can respond with thanksgiving and dedicate your life to following Him, or you can fail to respond to what Jesus has done for you.

   How will you respond this week to the love Jesus demonstrated for you?

3. *How you respond to what Jesus has done for you has serious consequences.* If you know what Jesus has done for you and understand His words, yet do not respond positively to Him and what He has done for you, you will be judged accordingly.

   Jesus cursed the people in His hometown of Capernaum, saying, "If the miracles that were performed in you had been performed in Sodom, it would have remained to this day. But I tell you that it will be more bearable for Sodom on the day of judgment than for you" (Matthew 11:23–24). They saw

5. How does the way in which Jesus handled His suffering in Gethsemane relate to the times you face stress, sorrow, and/or agony? What did Jesus do that you can do today during tough times at work? At home? How often do you turn honestly to God in complete devotion to His will?

Action Points

Take a moment to review the key points you explored today. Jot down the action step or steps you will take this week.

1. *The olive press—the gethsemane—symbolizes the agonizing weight of our sin that Jesus willingly carried when He was crucified.* Our sins are like the big rock in the olive press that forced the olive oil out of the olives. We were the burden He bore. Our guilt and the required penalty for sin were great, but Jesus' love for us and His obedient devotion to His Father's will were greater. Despite the powerful emotions He felt, Jesus submitted completely to His Father's will.

   "He was pierced for our transgressions, he was crushed for our iniquities; the punishment that brought us peace was upon him, and by his wounds we are healed." (Isaiah 53:5)

   "He himself bore our sins in his body on the tree, so that we might die to sins and live for righteousness; by his wounds you have been healed." (1 Peter 2:24)

   Recognizing the weight that Jesus bore, how will you view your sins differently this week?

2. *You must choose how you will respond to what Jesus has done for you.* Because of His deep love and compassion, Jesus willingly accepted the agonizing burden of our sin and went to the cross alone. He willingly died for our sins—a miracle that only He could perform. You can respond with thanksgiving and dedicate your life to following Him, or you can fail to respond to what Jesus has done for you.

   How will you respond this week to the love Jesus demonstrated for you?

3. *How you respond to what Jesus has done for you has serious consequences.* If you know what Jesus has done for you and understand His words, yet do not respond positively to Him and what He has done for you, you will be judged accordingly.

   Jesus cursed the people in His hometown of Capernaum, saying, "If the miracles that were performed in you had

JESUS: OUR SOURCE OF LIFE

When an olive tree that is being cared for becomes too old, it stops bearing fruit and is cut down. From the stump, a new branch is cultivated into a new olive tree. Thousands of years before Jesus came to earth, the prophet Isaiah compared Jesus—the Messiah (the "anointed one")—to a new shoot that will spring out of the unbelieving nation of Israel and revitalize it. When we become Christians, we are in a sense grafted into Jesus—our life-giving branch. We gain our life and energy from Him.

PLANNING NOTES:

Jesus' love in action and knew what to do, yet didn't respond positively to Him and chose to do evil.

But if you submit completely to Jesus and allow God to live through you, you will be spiritually fruitful and derive your life from Him.

What kind of fruit will you produce this week? Will you yield yourself to Jesus daily, or will you be unresponsive to His will for your life?

> **JESUS: OUR SOURCE OF LIFE**
> When an olive tree that is being cared for becomes too old, it stops bearing fruit and is cut down. From the stump, a new branch is cultivated into a new olive tree. Thousands of years before Jesus came to earth, the prophet Isaiah compared Jesus—the Messiah (the "anointed one")—to a new shoot that will spring out of the unbelieving nation of Israel and revitalize it. When we become Christians, we are in a sense grafted into Jesus—our life-giving branch. We gain our life and energy from Him.

closing prayer

1 minute

I'm sure that God has revealed some exciting truths to you, as He has to me. Now I'd like to close in prayer, asking God to help us remember what we've learned today.

Dear Jesus, thank You so much for being our compassionate Savior. You experienced the agonizing weight of our sins so our sins can be forgiven and we can have an eternal relationship with You. Help us to look to You—our compassionate and caring Friend—for our strength when times get tough and to seek Your will as You sought Your Father's will in Gethsemane. We want to be fruitful for You. Please help us to be the people You want us to be. And give us the strength and courage to continue to wrestle with some of the issues we've looked at today. Amen.

2. *You must choose how you will respond to what Jesus has done for you.* Because of His deep love and compassion, Jesus willingly accepted the agonizing burden of our sin and went to the cross alone. He willingly died for our sins—a miracle that only He could perform. You can respond with thanksgiving and dedicate your life to following Him, or you can fail to respond to what Jesus has done for you.

How will you respond this week to the love Jesus demonstrated for you?

3. *How you respond to what Jesus has done for you has serious consequences.* If you know what Jesus has done for you and understand His words, yet do not respond positively to Him and what He has done for you, you will be judged accordingly.

Jesus cursed the people in His hometown of Capernaum, saying, "If the miracles that were performed in you had

JESUS: OUR SOURCE OF LIFE
When an olive tree that is being cared for becomes too old, it stops bearing fruit and is cut down. From the stump, a new branch is cultivated into a new olive tree. Thousands of years before Jesus came to earth, the prophet Isaiah compared Jesus—the Messiah (the "anointed one")—to a new shoot that will spring out of the unbelieving nation of Israel and revitalize it. When we become Christians, we are in a sense grafted into Jesus—our life-giving branch. We gain our life and energy from Him.

been performed in Sodom, it would have remained to this day. But I tell you that it will be more bearable for Sodom on the day of judgment than for you" (Matthew 11:23–24). They saw Jesus' love in action and knew what to do, yet didn't respond positively to Him and chose to do evil.

But if you submit completely to Jesus and allow God to live through you, you will be spiritually fruitful and derive your life from Him.

What kind of fruit will you produce this week? Will you yield yourself to Jesus daily, or will you be unresponsive to His will for your life?

roll away the stone

before you lead

Synopsis

Jesus' death and resurrection is the defining event in the New Testament—indeed, in all of Scripture. As a result of what God accomplished during those three days in Jerusalem, all of humanity has been given hope for the future.

Jesus' resurrection proclaimed that:

- God has the power to overcome physical death. No tombstone, no grave, no cross, no Roman soldier could stop the work of Jesus Christ.
- God loves us enough to have suffered with us.
- God loves us enough to grant us the power to receive eternal life if we trust in Jesus as our Lord and Savior.

Most participants are probably familiar with the biblical facts surrounding Jesus' death, burial, and resurrection. However, this session reveals fascinating cultural details surrounding these events that most people do not know. Ray Vander Laan's cultural insights heighten the significance of such events as:

- Why Joseph of Arimathea's donation of the hand-hewn tomb was such a great sacrifice. The tomb was brand new and costly (about $100,000 in today's currency). It was a gift, not a loan. Once Jesus was buried in the tomb, it is unlikely that Joseph or any member of his family would ever use it.
- The significance of Jesus dying at 3:00 on the afternoon of the Passover. Jesus, the perfect Lamb of God, was sacrificed for us. He died at the moment the high priest killed the lamb in the temple that would be offered on behalf of the sins of the Jews.
- Why the stone was rolled away from Jesus' tomb. The stone was no barrier to His resurrection. Rather, the stone was removed so that His disciples—and, in a sense, all of humanity—could look in and see that Jesus had risen!

You will help participants visualize the great work of love that God accomplished through the resurrection of Jesus. You will guide them in exploring the significance of Jesus' death, burial, and resurrection . . . and what His sacrifice means to Christians today who seek to live in light of that reality.

Key Points of This Lesson

The following key points are emphasized:

1. *As a result of His great love for us, God unleashed His awesome power in order to accomplish three great works through Jesus' resurrection. He com-*

pleted a promise made to Abraham that He would shed His blood for the sins of Abraham and his descendants.

2. *He made the ultimate sacrifice by offering His sinless life in exchange for ours.* He offered the cup of salvation—His marriage cup, His life—to us. It is up to us to choose whether we will drink from it and thereby declare that we accept His gift and commit our lives to Him.

3. *If we truly believe that Jesus is alive today, we must live accordingly.* It's not enough to know that Jesus was buried. We must, symbolically, look into the tomb for ourselves and say, "I know Jesus is alive!"

4. *Just as the angel rolled away the stone in front of the tomb so that Jesus' disciples could see that He had risen, we must, in effect, be instruments of God and roll the stone away from the doorway so other people can see that the tomb is empty, too!*

Session Outline (55 minutes)

    I. Introduction (5 minutes)
    Welcome
    What's to Come
    Questions to Think About

    II. Video Presentation "Roll Away the Stone" (22 minutes)

    III. Group Discovery (20 minutes)
    Video Highlights
    Small Group Bible Discovery

    IV. Faith Lesson (6 minutes)
    Time for Reflection
    Action Points

    V. Closing Prayer (2 minutes)

Materials

No additional materials are needed for this session. Simply view the video prior to leading the session so you are familiar with its main points.

roll away the stone

introduction

5 minutes

Welcome

Assemble the participants together. Welcome them to session eight of *Faith Lessons on the Death and Resurrection of the Messiah.*

What's to Come

Jesus' death and resurrection is the defining event in the New Testament. As a result of what God accomplished during those three days in Jerusalem, all of humanity has been given eternal hope.

In this session, we will learn fascinating cultural details related to Jesus' death, burial, and resurrection. Rather than dwelling on many of the familiar events that took place during those days, Ray Vander Laan brings to light cultural and spiritual insights that reinforce the significance of those events. He reveals powerful truths that apply to our lives today. Let's begin by thinking about the importance of Jesus' resurrection.

Questions to Think About

Participant's Guide page 134.

Turn to page 134 of the Participant's Guide. Let's consider several questions that will help set the stage for the video we'll see in a few minutes.

Ask each question and solicit a few responses from group members.

1. In what ways has the resurrection of Jesus changed the course of human history?

   Suggested Responses: There are innumerable possibilities because all of Christianity originates with this event. It gave the disciples something to marvel at and proclaim to the world. It provides Christians with the certain hope of eternal life in heaven, led to the establishment of Christian principles of law and order, inspired Christian missionary activities during the past 2,000 years, has caused people to sacrifice themselves for the benefit of others, etc.

2. What hope does the resurrection provide for all of humanity?

   Suggested Responses: It breaks the power of death because Jesus defeated death when He rose from the dead, provides the hope of an afterlife in heaven, proves that life on this earth is not all there is, makes life on earth more meaningful and purposeful.

SESSION EIGHT

roll away the stone

questions to think about

1. In what ways has the resurrection of Jesus changed the course of human history?

2. What hope does the resurrection provide for all of humanity?

3. How would your faith and life be different if Jesus had not been raised from the dead?

134

✏ 3.   How would your faith and life be different if Jesus had not been raised from the dead?

Suggested Responses: My faith would be in vain; there would be no forgiveness of sins, no hope of heaven, no personal relationship with God, etc.

Let's keep these ideas in mind as we view the video.

video presentation

22 minutes

Participant's Guide page 135.

On page 135 of your Participant's Guide, you will find a space in which to take notes on key points as we watch this video.

Leader's Video Observations

Blowing of the Shofar

The Gift of the Tomb

The Stone Rolled Away

The Offering of the Cup

SESSION EIGHT

roll away the stone

questions to think about

1. In what ways has the resurrection of Jesus changed the course of human history?

2. What hope does the resurrection provide for all of humanity?

3. How would your faith and life be different if Jesus had not been raised from the dead?

Session Eight: Roll Away the Stone   135

video notes

Blowing of the Shofar

The Gift of the Tomb

The Stone Rolled Away

The Offering of the Cup

group Discovery

20 minutes

If your group has seven or more members, use the **Video Highlights** with the entire group (five minutes), then break into small groups of three to five to discuss the **Small Group Bible Discovery** (ten minutes). Then reassemble the group to discuss the key points discovered (five minutes).

If your group has fewer than seven members, begin with the **Video Highlights** (five minutes), then do one or more of the topics found in the **Small Group Bible Discovery** as a group (ten minutes). Finally, spend five minutes at the end discussing points that had an impact on participants.

Video Highlights (5 minutes)

Note the map of Jerusalem on page 137 of your Participant's Guide and locate the two possible locations for the crucifixion.

Jerusalem's Districts

A	David's City	1	Eastern Gate	10	Pool of Bethesda	19	Theater
B	New City	2	Southern Stairs	11	First Wall	20	Citadel and Herod's Palace
C	Upper City	3	Royal Stoa	12	Second Wall	21	Essene Quarter
D	Business District	4	Robinson's Arch	13	Garden Gate	22	Mansions
E	Temple Mount	5	Wilson's Arch	14	Towers (Damascus) Gate	23	Mount of Olives
F	Lower City	6	Tyropoeon Street	15	Golgotha (?)	24	Kidron Valley
G	Herod's Palace	7	Warren's Gate	16	Garden Tomb	25	Huldah Gates
		8	Antonia	17	Spring of Gihon		
		9	Tadi Gate	18	Hinnom Valley		

136   The Death and Resurrection of the Messiah

video highlights

1. What insights into Jesus' sacrificial death, burial, and resurrection did you gain by watching this video?

2. Why was the gift of the tomb so remarkable?

3. In what ways might you view the death and resurrection of Jesus as "the defining event in the New Testament"?

4. What did the stone being rolled away from the door of the tomb enable Jesus' disciples to do? Why was this important then? Why is it important today?

Session Eight: Roll Away the Stone   137

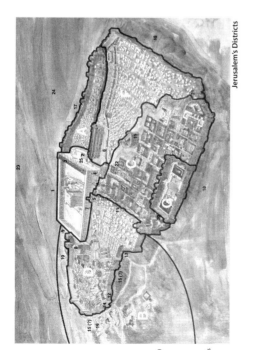

Jerusalem's Districts

A David's City
B New City
C Upper City
D Business District
E Temple Mount
F Lower City
G Herod's Palace
1 Eastern Gate
2 Southern Stairs
3 Royal Stoa
4 Robinson's Arch
5 Wilson's Arch
6 Tyropoeon Street
7 Warren's Gate
8 Antonia
9 Tadi Gate
10 Pool of Bethesda
11 First Wall
12 Second Wall
13 Garden Gate
14 Towers (Damascus) Gate
15 Golgotha (?)
16 Garden Tomb
17 Spring of Gihon
18 Hinnom Valley
19 Theater
20 Citadel and Herod's Palace
21 Essene Quarter
22 Mansions
23 Mount of Olives
24 Kidron Valley
25 Huldah Gates

A typical first-century family tomb

🖎 1. What insights into Jesus' sacrificial death, burial, and resurrection did you gain by watching this video?

🖎 2. Why was the gift of the tomb so remarkable?

Suggested Responses: The rock-hewn tomb had been costly to make; the tomb could never be used again by Joseph of Arimathea or his family; Joseph was an important Jew and stood against the opinions of his peers when he asked for Jesus' body and donated the tomb.

🖎 3. In what ways might you view the death and resurrection of Jesus as "the defining event in the New Testament"?

Suggested Responses: The Christian faith is built upon the reality of Christ's death and resurrection. Jesus' death removed the barrier of sin between humankind and God. It brought into being a new era of relationship between humankind and God. The resurrection demonstrated Jesus' victory over sin and gives us the promise of eternal life if we accept Him as our Savior. Both events dramatically affect all people today. How different life would be if Jesus were not alive and involved in our lives today, and we remained trapped in our sinfulness.

🖎 4. What did the stone being rolled away from the door of the tomb enable Jesus' disciples to do? Why was this important then? Why is it important today?

Suggested Responses: When the angel rolled the stone away from the tomb's entrance, the disciples could see inside, go inside, and know that Jesus was not there. It gave them hope that Jesus was alive as He had promised. Knowing that the tomb was empty, that Jesus is alive, still gives Christians hope.

136   The Death and Resurrection of the Messiah

video Highlights

1. What insights into Jesus' sacrificial death, burial, and resurrection did you gain by watching this video?

2. Why was the gift of the tomb so remarkable?

3. In what ways might you view the death and resurrection of Jesus as "the defining event in the New Testament"?

4. What did the stone being rolled away from the door of the tomb enable Jesus' disciples to do? Why was this important then? Why is it important today?

138   The Death and Resurrection of the Messiah

5. What price did Jesus pay in order to offer the cup of salvation to you and me?

6. How does Jesus want us to respond to His offer of salvation?

A typical first-century family tomb

✏ 5. What price did Jesus pay in order to offer the cup of salvation to you and me?

Suggested Responses: He left His home in heaven to be born a man and to live on earth, He suffered greatly while here on earth, He took the unbearable weight of our sin upon Himself, He was rejected by man, and He was rejected by God the Father as He died on the cross.

✏ 6. How does Jesus want us to respond to His offer of salvation?

Suggested Responses: to love Him and commit ourselves exclusively to Him, to seek Him above all else, to serve Him by sharing the truth of His resurrection with other people.

Small Group Bible Discovery (15 minutes)

Participant's Guide pages 139–47.

During this time, a group with fewer than seven participants will stay together. A group larger than seven participants will break into small groups and reassemble as a large group during the final five minutes. Assign each group one of the following topics. If you have more than five small groups, assign some topics to more than one group.

Let's break into groups of three to five—people sitting near you—and study some of the Bible passages and truths mentioned in the video.

Turn to pages 139–47 in your Participant's Guide. There you'll find a list of five topics. You'll have ten minutes to read and discuss the topic I'll assign to you. Choose one person in your group to be a spokesperson for your group when we discuss these topics later.

Assign each group a topic.

I'll signal you when one minute is left.

To do: During the Small Group Bible Discovery, rewind the video to the beginning of the closing song. You will be replaying this song at the end of the session.

After nine minutes, let participants know that they have one minute remaining. Then reassemble the entire group. After everyone is back together, begin asking one person from each small group to briefly share a key idea with the larger group. In some cases, you may not have time for every group to share their discoveries.

As time allows, let's briefly share the key ideas that your group discussed.

Topic A: Jesus' Crucifixion Prophesied

Compare the actual events surrounding Jesus' crucifixion with the Old Testament prophecies. Record your answers in the chart below:

✏ 1. What did the soldiers do to Jesus? (See Psalm 22:16–18; John 19:23–24; Mark 15:25–32.)

138   The Death and Resurrection of the Messiah

5. What price did Jesus pay in order to offer the cup of salvation to you and me?

6. How does Jesus want us to respond to His offer of salvation?

A typical first-century family tomb

Session Eight: Roll Away the Stone   139

small group bible discovery

Topic A: Jesus' Crucifixion Prophesied
Compare the actual events surrounding Jesus' crucifixion with the Old Testament prophesies. Record your answers in the chart below:

1. What did the soldiers do to Jesus? (See Psalm 22:16–18; John 19:23–24; Mark 15:25–32.)

2. What exception was made in Jesus' case? (See Psalm 34:20; John 19:32–34; Zechariah 12:10.)

3. What was Jesus given to drink while on the cross? (See Psalm 69:21; Matthew 27:48.)

4. What did Isaiah predict would happen to Jesus? (See Isaiah 53:3.)

Old Testament Prophecy	Did it happen?
1.	
2.	
3.	
4.	

2. What exception was made in Jesus' case? (See Psalm 34:20; John 19:32–34; Zechariah 12:10.)

3. What was Jesus given to drink while on the cross? (See Psalm 69:21; Matthew 27:48.)

4. What did Isaiah predict would happen to Jesus? (See Isaiah 53:3.)

Old Testament Prophecy	Did it happen?
1. pierced His hands and feet, cast lots for His clothing, hurled insults at Him.	yes
2. none of His bones would be broken.	yes, the soldiers pierced His side instead of breaking His legs.
3. wine vinegar on a sponge.	yes
4. He would be despised and rejected by men and would experience much sorrow and suffering.	yes

5. Who rejected Jesus, as recorded in each of the following passages?

John 6:66   *many of His disciples*

John 7:47–53   *the Pharisees*

Matthew 26:14–16   *Judas Iscariot*

Matthew 26:56   *all the disciples*

Matthew 26:69–75   *Peter*

Matthew 27:46   *God the Father*

Topic B: Jesus' Sacrifice for Our Sin — He Died as God's Lamb

1. Under which circumstances did the first Passover take place? (See Exodus 12:1–7, 12–14.)

Suggested Response: The final plague God sent to Egypt took the life of the first-born child of every household and the firstborn of the cattle. To escape this plague of death, each Hebrew family ate a portion of a year-old lamb and put some of the lamb's blood on the top and sides of their doorframe. The angel of the Lord then passed through Egypt, killing every firstborn child and cattle in every house on which no blood had been placed.

2. When were subsequent Passovers to be celebrated? (See Leviticus 23:5.)

Suggested Response: at twilight on the fourteenth day of the first month of each year.

small Group Bible Discovery

Topic A: Jesus' Crucifixion Prophesied

Compare the actual events surrounding Jesus' crucifixion with the Old Testament prophesies. Record your answers in the chart below:

1. What did the soldiers do to Jesus? (See Psalm 22:16–18; John 19:23–24; Mark 15:25–32.)

2. What exception was made in Jesus' case? (See Psalm 34:20; John 19:32–34; Zechariah 12:10.)

3. What was Jesus given to drink while on the cross? (See Psalm 69:21; Matthew 27:48.)

4. What did Isaiah predict would happen to Jesus? (See Isaiah 53:3.)

Old Testament Prophecy	Did it happen?
1.	
2.	
3.	
4.	

---

140   The Death and Resurrection of the Messiah

5. Who rejected Jesus, as recorded in each of the following passages?

    John 6:66

    John 7:47–53

    Matthew 26:14–16

    Matthew 26:56

    Matthew 26:69–75

    Matthew 27:46

Topic B: Jesus' Sacrifice for Our Sin—He Died as God's Lamb

1. Under which circumstances did the first Passover take place? (See Exodus 12:1–7, 12–14.)

2. When were subsequent Passovers to be celebrated? (See Leviticus 23:5.)

3. What is the significance of what John the Baptist said about Jesus early in His ministry? (See John 1:29.)

✎ 3.   What is the significance of what John the Baptist said about Jesus early in His ministry? (See John 1:29.)

Suggested Response: He referred to Jesus as "the Lamb of God who takes away the sin of the world." Later, Jesus died on the cross as the sacrificial Lamb of God.

✎ 4.   Which words did Paul use to describe Jesus? (See 1 Corinthians 5:7b.)

Suggested Response: Christ, our Passover Lamb.

✎ 5.   In Hebrews 9:11–15, what do we learn about the importance of Christ's blood?

Suggested Response: Christ came to be our high priest. Instead of sacrificing animals as payment for sin, He sacrificed Himself. He offered His unblemished, sinless life on our behalf, to redeem us from our sin. Through His shed blood, He obtained our eternal redemption.

✎ 6.   What does the timing of Jesus' death say about God's planning? (See Luke 23:44.)

Suggested Response: God's timing is perfect. Jesus died at exactly the moment when the Passover Lamb was being killed.

JESUS, THE LAMB OF THE WORLD

During Old Testament times, perhaps even going back to the time of Moses, the Jewish priests traditionally slaughtered the Passover sacrifice at 3:00 in the afternoon after blowing a shofar—a special horn. They then offered the sacrifice at 3:30, following the daily sacrifice. Both the daily sacrifice and the Passover sacrifice were offered to symbolically cleanse the nation of Israel of its sin.

At exactly 3:00 (the "ninth hour" as the Bible puts it in Luke 23:45), just as the Passover lamb was being killed, Jesus looked up into heaven and said, "Father, into your hands I commit my spirit."

Topic C: The Empty Tomb

Look up Matthew 27:62–65; 28:1–10; Luke 24:9–12.

✎ 1.   When the earthquake occurred, and the angel appeared, and the stone was rolled away, what happened to the Roman guards?

Suggested Response: The guards became so frightened that they became like dead men.

✎ 2.   How did the women respond when they saw the empty tomb and the angel? When they realized the truth of what had happened?

Suggested Responses: They were afraid, but after the angel spoke with them, they were filled with joy. When Jesus appeared to them, they worshiped Him. The women were so joyous and excited that the disciples thought their talk about Jesus' resurrection was nonsense.

4. Which words did Paul use to describe Jesus? (See 1 Corinthians 5:7b.)

5. In Hebrews 9:11–15, what do we learn about the importance of Christ's blood?

6. What does the timing of Jesus' death say about God's planning? (See Luke 23:44.)

JESUS, THE LAMB OF THE WORLD

During Old Testament times, perhaps even going back to the time of Moses, the Jewish priests traditionally slaughtered the Passover sacrifice at 3:00 in the afternoon after blowing a shofar—a special horn. They then offered the sacrifice at 3:30, following the daily sacrifice. Both the daily sacrifice and the Passover sacrifice were offered to symbolically cleanse the nation of Israel of its sin.

At exactly 3:00 (the "ninth hour" as the Bible puts it in Luke 23:45), just as the Passover lamb was being killed, Jesus looked up into heaven and said, "Father, into your hands I commit my spirit."

Topic C: The Empty Tomb

Look up Matthew 27:62–65; 28:1–10; Luke 24:9–12.

1. When the earthquake occurred, and the angel appeared, and the stone was rolled away, what happened to the Roman guards?

2. How did the women respond when they saw the empty tomb and the angel? When they realized the truth of what had happened?

WHAT WAS THE TOMB REALLY LIKE?

- It belonged to a rich Jewish man named Joseph of Arimathea (Matthew 27:57–60), who was a prominent member of the Jewish Council (Mark 15:43).
- It had never been used before. According to Jewish law held by the Pharisees, only people in an immediate family could be buried in the same tomb, so it is likely that no one in the family of Joseph of Arimathea would ever use it again.
- It was cut from rock and sealed with a large stone (Matthew 27:59–60; Mark 16:4). Often the stone for this type of tomb weighed more than two tons and was rolled across the opening of the tomb.
- It was brand new (Luke 23:50–53).
- It had a low door and was large enough to hold more than one person (Luke 24:1–4, 12; Mark 16:1–5).
- It was located near a garden (John 19:38–42).
- People could see into it without entering it (John 20:1–8).

✏ 3.   How did the disciples respond when they heard the news?

Suggested Responses: At first, they did not believe the women, but Peter ran to the tomb to see for himself. When He saw that it was empty, he wondered what had happened.

✏ 4.   Why was it necessary for Jesus' followers to see the empty tomb?

Suggested Response: so that they might know that Jesus had risen.

✏ 5.   What difference should the empty tomb make in our lives today?

Suggested Response: It gives evidence of the truth of Scripture—the claims of Jesus and promises of God. It assures us of forgiveness and of the reality of eternal life.

WHAT WAS THE TOMB REALLY LIKE?
- It belonged to a rich Jewish man named Joseph of Arimathea (Matthew 27:57–60), who was a prominent member of the Jewish Council (Mark 15:43).
- It had never been used before. According to Jewish law held by the Pharisees, only people in an immediate family could be buried in the same tomb, so it is likely that no one in the family of Joseph of Arimathea would ever use it again.
- It was cut from rock and sealed with a large stone (Matthew 27:59–60; Mark 16:4). Often the stone for this type of tomb weighed more than two tons and was rolled across the opening of the tomb.
- It was brand new (Luke 23:50–53).
- It had a low door and was large enough to hold more than one person (Luke 24:1–4, 12; Mark 16:1–5).
- It was located near a garden (John 19:38–42).
- People could see into it without entering it (John 20:1–8).

Topic D: Committing Ourselves to Jesus

As explained in the video, a man and woman in Jesus' day sealed their engagement by exchanging a cup of wine. The bride accepted the cup from her future husband as an indication of her lifelong commitment to him.

✏ 1.   To whom did Jesus compare Himself? (See Mark 2:18–19.)

Suggested Response: to a bridegroom.

✏ 2.   In light of what you learned in the video, what was the significance of Jesus offering the third cup of salvation to His disciples during the Passover celebration in the Upper Room? (See Luke 22:20.)

Suggested Response: The cup of salvation symbolized the blood He would shed for them and for us. He was, in effect, expressing His love for them and inviting them to be His spiritual bride. By accepting the cup and drinking from it, they were accepting His gift and giving Him their lives in return.

Topic C: The Empty Tomb

Look up Matthew 27:62–65; 28:1–10; Luke 24:9–12.

1. When the earthquake occurred, and the angel appeared, and the stone was rolled away, what happened to the Roman guards?

2. How did the women respond when they saw the empty tomb and the angel? When they realized the truth of what had happened?

WHAT WAS THE TOMB REALLY LIKE?

- It belonged to a rich Jewish man named Joseph of Arimathea (Matthew 27:57–60), who was a prominent member of the Jewish Council (Mark 15:43).
- It had never been used before. According to Jewish law held by the Pharisees, only people in an immediate family could be buried in the same tomb, so it is likely that no one in the family of Joseph of Arimathea would ever use it again.
- It was cut from rock and sealed with a large stone (Matthew 27:59–60; Mark 16:4). Often the stone for this type of tomb weighed more than two tons and was rolled across the opening of the tomb.
- It was brand new (Luke 23:50–53).
- It had a low door and was large enough to hold more than one person (Luke 24:1–4, 12; Mark 16:1–5).
- It was located near a garden (John 19:38–42).
- People could see into it without entering it (John 20:1–8).

3. How did the disciples respond when they heard the news?

4. Why was it necessary for Jesus' followers to see the empty tomb?

5. What difference should the empty tomb make in our lives today?

Topic D: Committing Ourselves to Jesus

As explained in the video, a man and woman in Jesus' day sealed their engagement by exchanging a cup of wine. The bride accepted the cup from her future husband as an indication of her lifelong commitment to him.

1. To whom did Jesus compare Himself? (See Mark 2:18–19.)

2. In light of what you learned in the video, what was the significance of Jesus offering the third cup of salvation to His disciples during the Passover celebration in the Upper Room? (See Luke 22:20.)

✎ 3.   In Revelation 19:6–8, what do the "Lamb" and "his bride" symbolize?

Suggested Response: The "Lamb" represents Jesus. The "bride" represents the individual believer and the Church as a whole.

✎ 4.   In light of the symbolism of the cup, what are we, in effect, saying to God when we drink the cup during Communion? How do you live out that commitment in your daily life?

Suggested Response: We are in effect saying to God, "I accept Your gift, and I give You my life in return." Encourage participants to seriously consider their answer to the second question!

DATA FILE

The Symbolism of the Cup

The Marriage Cup. During biblical times, a young man who wanted to marry would accompany his father to the chosen woman's house, where she and her father would be present. They'd negotiate a steep "bride price"—the money or physical items that the woman's father would ask for in exchange for giving up his valuable daughter.

Then the young man's father would hand his son a cup of wine. The son, in turn, would offer it to the woman and say, "This cup I offer to you." In effect he was saying, "I love you, and I offer you my life. Will you marry me?" If she drank it (sealing their engagement), she accepted his life and gave him hers. If not, she simply declined.

The Passover Cup. During the Passover liturgy of Jesus' day, participants would drink from four cups of wine at different times. The third cup was called the cup of salvation. While celebrating the Passover with His disciples in the Upper Room, Jesus offered them the cup of salvation and said, "This cup is a new covenant in My blood." He was saying, in effect, "I love you. I give you My life. Will you marry Me? Will you be My spiritual bride? Will you give your life to Me?"

So, every time we drink from the Communion cup when the minister says, "This cup is a new covenant in my blood," God is saying to us, "I love you. I invite you to be My spiritual bride." And every time we drink it, we are in effect saying to Him, "I accept Your gift, and I give You my life in return."

The Cup from Which Jesus Drank in Order to Become Our Spiritual Husband. Jesus asked His Father the night before He died, "If it is possible, may this cup be taken from me" (Matthew 26:39). He knew the high price He would have to pay to purchase His bride and become our spiritual husband.

144   The Death and Resurrection of the Messiah

DATA FILE

The Symbolism of the Cup

The Marriage Cup. During biblical times, a young man who wanted to marry would accompany his father to the chosen woman's house, where she and her father would be present. They'd negotiate a steep "bride price"—the money or physical items that the woman's father would ask for in exchange for giving up his valuable daughter.

Then the young man's father would hand his son a cup of wine. The son, in turn, would offer it to the woman and say, "This cup I offer to you." In effect he was saying, "I love you, and I offer you my life. Will you marry me?" If she drank it (sealing their engagement), she accepted his life and gave him hers. If not, she simply declined.

The Passover Cup. During the Passover liturgy of Jesus' day, participants would drink from four cups of wine at different times. The third cup was called the cup of salvation. While celebrating the Passover with His disciples in the Upper Room, Jesus offered them the cup of salvation and said, "This cup is a new covenant in My blood." He was saying, in effect, "I love you. I give you My life. Will you marry Me? Will you be My spiritual bride? Will you give your life to Me?"

So, every time we drink from the Communion cup when the minister says, "This cup is a new covenant in my blood," God is saying to us, "I love you. I invite you to be My spiritual bride." And every time we drink it, we are in effect saying to Him, "I accept Your gift, and I give You my life in return."

The Cup from Which Jesus Drank in Order to Become Our Spiritual Husband. Jesus asked His Father the night before He died, "If it is possible, may this cup be taken from me" (Matthew 26:39). He knew the high price He would have to pay to purchase His bride and become our spiritual husband.

Session Eight: Roll Away the Stone   145

3. In Revelation 19:6–8, what do the "Lamb" and "his bride" symbolize?

4. In light of the symbolism of the cup, what are we, in effect, saying to God when we drink the cup during Communion? How do you live out that commitment in your daily life?

Topic E: The Torn Curtain in the Temple

1. Where did God make His presence known to the people of Israel? (See Leviticus 16:2; Hebrews 9:1–4.)

2. Who was the only person who could enter the inner room behind the curtain? (See Hebrews 9:7.)

3. Why did the high priest offer a blood offering? (See Hebrews 9:7–9.)

Topic E: The Torn Curtain in the Temple

✏ 1. Where did God make His presence known to the people of Israel? (See Leviticus 16:2; Hebrews 9:1–4.)

Suggested Response: In the inner part of the temple—the Holy of Holies.

✏ 2. Who was the only person who could enter the inner room behind the curtain? (See Hebrews 9:7.)

Suggested Response: The high priest.

✏ 3. Why did the high priest offer a blood offering? (See Hebrews 9:7–9.)

Suggested Response: He offered it as a sin sacrifice to obtain the forgiveness of the people's sins.

✏ 4. What did Jesus' death accomplish through the shedding of His blood? (See Hebrews 9:12.)

Suggested Response: It obtained our eternal redemption.

COMPELLING EVIDENCE

There is an abundance of evidence in Scripture and in the religious practices of the Jews that God carefully planned the timing of Jesus' death and resurrection. The following are just a few examples of God's planning:

- Prophecies given hundreds of years before Jesus was even born were precisely fulfilled when Jesus died.
- The high priest's practice of killing the Passover Lamb had been in force for hundreds, perhaps a thousand, years. On Friday of the year Jesus died, the Jews celebrated Passover and killed a lamb for the temple sacrifice. Jesus, the Lamb of God, died at that same time in order to take our sins upon Himself.
- The year that Jesus died, Saturday—the Sabbath—was also the day on which the Jews celebrated the Feast of Unleavened Bread. This feast reminded the Jews of the bread that God provided for the Israelites when they left Egypt. Consider the significant parallels between this feast and Jesus' death:

Wheat seeds must die in order to bring forth their crop.	Jesus had to die and be buried in order to accomplish His ministry and be raised to new life.
Unleavened bread was made without yeast, because yeast represented sin (1 Corinthians 5:7–8).	Jesus, the Lamb of God, was sinless.

- On the Sunday following Jesus' death, the Israelites celebrated the Feast of Firstfruits, which in this case celebrated the beginning of the barley harvest. The Israelites returned to God the "first part" of everything they had been given to indicate: their thankfulness for the harvest; their acknowledgment that God had given them the gifts; and their faith that God would continue to provide (Numbers 15:17–21; Deuteronomy 26:1–11). They gave the best first part of what they received to God (Exodus 23:19). Also, on that day Jesus came to life as God's Firstfruits—the guarantee that the rest would follow—including the resurrection of the dead (1 Corinthians 15:20–23).

Session Eight: Roll Away the Stone   145

3. In Revelation 19:6–8, what do the "Lamb" and "his bride" symbolize?

4. In light of the symbolism of the cup, what are we, in effect, saying to God when we drink the cup during Communion? How do you live out that commitment in your daily life?

Topic E: The Torn Curtain in the Temple

1. Where did God make His presence known to the people of Israel? (See Leviticus 16:2; Hebrews 9:1–4.)

2. Who was the only person who could enter the inner room behind the curtain? (See Hebrews 9:7.)

3. Why did the high priest offer a blood offering? (See Hebrews 9:7–9.)

---

146   The Death and Resurrection of the Messiah

COMPELLING EVIDENCE

There is an abundance of evidence in Scripture and in the religious practices of the Jews that God carefully planned the timing of Jesus' death and resurrection. The following are just a few examples of God's planning:

• Prophecies given hundreds of years before Jesus was even born were precisely fulfilled when Jesus died.

• The high priest's practice of killing the Passover Lamb had been in force for hundreds, perhaps a thousand, years. On Friday of the year Jesus died, the Jews celebrated Passover and killed a lamb for the temple sacrifice. Jesus, the Lamb of God, died at that same time in order to take our sins upon Himself.

• The year that Jesus died, Saturday—the Sabbath—was also the day on which the Jews celebrated the Feast of Unleavened Bread. This feast reminded the Jews of the bread that God provided for the Israelites when they left Egypt. Consider the significant parallels between this feast and Jesus' death:

Wheat seeds must die in order to bring forth their crop.	Jesus had to die and be buried in order to accomplish His ministry and be raised to new life.
Unleavened bread was made without yeast, because yeast represented sin (1 Corinthians 5:7–8).	Jesus, the Lamb of God, was sinless.

• On the Sunday following Jesus' death, the Israelites celebrated the Feast of Firstfruits, which in this case celebrated the beginning of the barley harvest. The Israelites returned to God the "first part" of everything they had been given to indicate: their thankfulness for the harvest; their acknowledgment that God had given them the gifts; and their faith that God would continue to provide (Numbers 15:17–21; Deuteronomy 26:1–11). They gave the best first part of what they received to God (Exodus 23:19). Also, on that day Jesus came to life as God's Firstfruits—the guarantee that the rest would follow—including the resurrection of the dead (1 Corinthians 15:20–23).

✏ 5. What did Jesus—the unblemished Lamb of God—do to make the temple curtain obsolete? (See Matthew 27:50–51; Hebrews 9:14.)

Suggested Responses: He offered Himself, sinless, to God as our sacrifice. He bore the sins of the world upon Himself, died, and rose again. By sacrificing Himself, He broke down the sin barrier between God and humankind. Thus the temple curtain that hung between God and His people was no longer necessary.

✏ 6. How did Jesus' death and resurrection affect our access to the very presence of God?

Suggested Response: Through the blood of Christ, God's people could now approach Him directly.

faith Lesson

6 minutes

Time for Reflection (3 minutes)

It's time for each of us to think quietly about how we can apply what we've learned today. On page 148 of the Participant's Guide, you'll find a passage of Scripture. Let's each read this passage silently and take the next few minutes to consider some of the questions that follow the Scripture passage.

Please do not talk during this time. It's a time when we all can reflect on today's lesson and how it applies to our lives.

The Scripture passage and questions are reproduced in their entirety in the Participant's Guide on pages 148–49.

As evening approached, there came a rich man from Arimathea, named Joseph, who had himself become a disciple of Jesus. Going to Pilate, he asked for Jesus' body, and Pilate ordered that it be given to him. Joseph took the body, wrapped it in a clean linen cloth, and placed it in his own new tomb that he had cut out of the rock. He rolled a big stone in front of the entrance to the tomb and went away. Mary Magdalene and the other Mary were sitting there opposite the tomb.

MATTHEW 27:57–61

After the Sabbath, at dawn on the first day of the week, Mary Magdalene and the other Mary went to look at the tomb. There was a violent earthquake, for an angel of the Lord came down from heaven and, going to the tomb, rolled back the stone and sat on it. His appearance was like lightning, and his clothes were white as snow. The guards were so afraid of him that they shook and became like dead men. The angel said to the women, "Do not be afraid, for I know that you are looking for Jesus, who was crucified. He is not here; he has risen, just as he said. Come and see the place where he lay. Then go quickly and tell his disciples: 'He has risen from the dead and is going ahead of you into Galilee. There you will see him.' Now I have told you." So the women hurried away from the tomb, afraid yet filled with joy, and ran to tell his disciples. Suddenly Jesus met them. "Greetings," he

4. What did Jesus' death accomplish through the shedding of His blood? (See Hebrews 9:12.)

5. What did Jesus—the unblemished Lamb of God—do to make the temple curtain obsolete? (See Matthew 27:50–51; Hebrews 9:14.)

6. How did Jesus' death and resurrection affect our access to the very presence of God?

faith lesson

Time for Reflection

The following Scripture passage describes the responses of some of Jesus' followers to His death and resurrection. Read this passage silently and consider your own response to God's great work of salvation.

As evening approached, there came a rich man from Arimathea, named Joseph, who had himself become a disciple of Jesus. Going to Pilate, he asked for Jesus' body, and Pilate ordered that it be given to him. Joseph took the body, wrapped it in a clean linen cloth, and placed it in his own new tomb that he had cut out of the rock. He rolled a big stone in front of the entrance to the tomb and went away. Mary Magdalene and the other Mary were sitting there opposite the tomb.

MATTHEW 27:57–61

After the Sabbath, at dawn on the first day of the week, Mary Magdalene and the other Mary went to look at the tomb. There was a violent earthquake, for an angel of the Lord came down from heaven and, going to the tomb, rolled back the stone and sat on it. His appearance was like lightning, and his clothes were white as snow. The guards were so afraid of him that they shook and became like dead men. The angel said to the women, "Do not be afraid, for I know that you are looking for Jesus, who was crucified. He is not here; he has risen, just as he said. Come and see the place where he lay. Then go quickly and tell his disciples: 'He has risen from the dead and is going ahead of you into Galilee. There you will see him.' Now I have told you." So the women hurried away from the tomb, afraid yet filled with joy, and ran to tell his disciples. Suddenly Jesus met them. "Greetings," he said. They came to him, clasped his feet and worshiped him. Then Jesus said to them, "Do not be afraid. Go and tell my brothers to go to Galilee; there they will see me."

MATTHEW 28:1–10

said. They came to him, clasped his feet and worshiped him. Then Jesus said to them, "Do not be afraid. Go and tell my brothers to go to Galilee; there they will see me."

MATTHEW 28:1–10

1. When Joseph of Arimathea—a public figure—asked for Jesus' body and willingly placed it in his costly new tomb, he made a great sacrifice that expressed deep devotion. In what way could you demonstrate a similar level of sacrificial devotion to Jesus?

2. When Joseph of Arimathea boldly asked Pilate for Jesus' body, his expression of love for Jesus went against the tide of the other members of the Jewish council. Have you ever spoken out for Jesus in a setting where your views were unpopular? In what ways are you willing to stand against the tide—of your friends? Of your family? Of the culture in which you live?

3. If you could go back in time and see the empty tomb of Jesus, how might you live your life differently? What does your answer reveal about your faith?

4. What effect does the reality of Jesus' resurrection have on your life today? In what specific ways do you live differently because Jesus is alive today?

> As soon as participants have spent three minutes reflecting on the above questions, get the entire group's attention and move to the next section.

Action Points (3 minutes)

> The following points are reproduced on page 150 of the Participant's Guide:

Now it's time to wrap up our session.

> Give participants a moment to transition from their thoughtfulness to giving you their full attention.

I'd like to take a moment to summarize the key points we explored. After I have reviewed these points, I will give you a moment to jot down an action step (or steps) that you will commit to this week as a result of what you have learned today.

> Read each point and pause after the final point so that participants can consider and write out their commitment.

1. *Jesus made the ultimate sacrifice for us by offering up His sinless life.* He has offered us the cup of salvation—His marriage cup, His life. He invites us to accept the cup of salvation. It is up to us to choose whether or not we will drink from it and thereby accept His gift and commit our lives to Him each day.

   In what ways has Jesus proven His love to you? What must you do this week to faithfully live out your commitment to Him?

1. When Joseph of Arimathea—a public figure—asked for Jesus' body and willingly placed it in his costly new tomb, he made a great sacrifice that expressed deep devotion. In what way could you demonstrate a similar level of sacrificial devotion to Jesus?

2. When Joseph of Arimathea boldly asked Pilate for Jesus' body, his expression of love for Jesus went against the tide of the other members of the Jewish council. Have you ever spoken out for Jesus in a setting where your views were unpopular? In what ways are you willing to stand against the tide—of your friends? Of your family? Of the culture in which you live?

3. If you could go back in time and see the empty tomb of Jesus, how might you live your life differently? What does your answer reveal about your faith?

4. What effect does the reality of Jesus' resurrection have on your life today? In what specific ways do you live differently because Jesus is alive today?

Action Points

Take a moment to review the key points you explored today. Then write down an action step or steps that you will commit to this week as a result of what you have discovered.

1. *Jesus made the ultimate sacrifice for us by offering up His sinless life.* He has offered us the cup of salvation—His marriage cup, His life. He invites us to accept the cup of salvation. It is up to us to choose whether or not we will drink from it and thereby accept His gift and commit our lives to Him each day.

   In what ways has Jesus proven His love to you? What must you do this week to faithfully live out your commitment to Him?

2. *Jesus' resurrection proclaimed God's power over everything— Roman soldiers, the cross, even physical death.* But it's not enough to know that Jesus was buried. We must, symbolically, look into the tomb for ourselves and say, "I know Jesus is alive!" We must believe that and live accordingly.

   Are you living as if Jesus were still in the tomb? How might you tap into the power of God that raised Jesus from the dead and live more fully as a child of the risen Lord?

3. *Just as the angel rolled away the stone in front of the tomb so that Jesus' disciples could see that He had risen, we must, in effect, be instruments of God and roll the stone away so that other people can see that the tomb is empty, too!*

✏ 2.   *Jesus' resurrection proclaimed God's power over everything—Roman soldiers,*
       the cross, even physical death. But it's not enough to know that Jesus was
       buried. We must, symbolically, look into the tomb for ourselves and say, "I
       know Jesus is alive!" We must believe that and live accordingly.

       Are you living as if Jesus were still in the tomb? How might you tap into
       the power of God that raised Jesus from the dead and live more fully as a
       child of the risen Lord?

✏ 3.   *Just as the angel rolled away the stone in front of the tomb so that Jesus' dis-*
       ciples could see that He had risen, we must, in effect, be instruments of God
       and roll the stone away so that other people can see that the tomb is empty,
       too!

       Which person has God brought into your life who needs to meet the res-
       urrected Christ? How might God want you to respond to him or her this
       week?

       In light of the fact that Jesus sacrificed His life for me, in light of the fact
       that the stone has been rolled away, I will: .

closing prayer

2 minutes

I hope that this lesson has given you, as it has me, a new appreciation of the
great depth of God's love for us. I'd like to close by replaying the song from the
video. As you listen, meditate on the great work God accomplished for you
through Jesus' death and resurrection. When the song is finished, our session
today is over.

> Play the song at the end of the video. This song replaces the closing prayer that
> often ends the session.

How beautiful the hands that served,
The wine and the bread and the sons of the earth.
How beautiful the feet that walked,
The long dusty road and the hill to the cross.
How beautiful the heart that bled,
That took all my sin and bore it instead.
And as he lay down his life,
We offer this sacrifice,
That we should give, live just as he died.
Willing to pay the price.
Willing to pay the price.
How beautiful the radiant bride,
Who waits for her groom with his light in her eyes.
How beautiful, how beautiful, how beautiful,
Is the body of Christ.

150   The Death and Resurrection of the Messiah

Action Points

Take a moment to review the key points you explored today. Then write down an action step or steps that you will commit to this week as a result of what you have discovered.

1. *Jesus made the ultimate sacrifice for us by offering up His sinless life.* He has offered us the cup of salvation—His marriage cup, His life. He invites us to accept the cup of salvation. It is up to us to choose whether or not we will drink from it and thereby accept His gift and commit our lives to Him each day.

   In what ways has Jesus proven His love to you? What must you do this week to faithfully live out your commitment to Him?

2. *Jesus' resurrection proclaimed God's power over everything—Roman soldiers, the cross, even physical death.* But it's not enough to know that Jesus was buried. We must, symbolically, look into the tomb for ourselves and say, "I know Jesus is alive!" We must believe that and live accordingly.

   Are you living as if Jesus were still in the tomb? How might you tap into the power of God that raised Jesus from the dead and live more fully as a child of the risen Lord?

3. *Just as the angel rolled away the stone in front of the tomb so that Jesus' disciples could see that He had risen, we must, in effect, be instruments of God and roll the stone away so that other people can see that the tomb is empty, too!*

Session Eight: Roll Away the Stone   151

Which person has God brought into your life who needs to meet the resurrected Christ? How might God want you to respond to him or her this week?

In light of the fact that Jesus sacrificed His life for me, in light of the fact that the stone has been rolled away, I will:

As you make this commitment, meditate on the great work God accomplished for you through Jesus' death and resurrection as expressed in the words of the closing song of the video.

> *How beautiful the hands that served,*
> *The wine and the bread and the sons of the earth.*
> *How beautiful the feet that walked,*
> *The long dusty road and the hill to the cross.*
> *How beautiful the heart that bled,*
> *That took all my sin and bore it instead.*
> *And as he lay down his life,*
> *We offer this sacrifice,*
> *That we should give, live just as he died.*
> *Willing to pay the price.*
> *Willing to pay the price.*
> *How beautiful the radiant bride,*
> *Who waits for her groom with his light in her eyes.*
> *How beautiful, how beautiful, how beautiful,*
> *Is the body of Christ.*

PLANNING NOTES:

power to the people

before you lead

Synopsis

Following His resurrection, Jesus taught His disciples about the kingdom of God. On the fortieth day, He took His disciples up to the Mount of Olives. There He promised that they would receive power and become His witnesses to the world. Then the disciples watched in awe as Jesus was caught up in a cloud and ascended to His Father in heaven (Acts 1:3–12). As they watched, two men in shining white appeared and promised that Jesus would someday come back in the same way He had disappeared.

The ecstatic disciples returned to Jerusalem to await the baptism Jesus had promised. For ten days they prayed and praised God in the temple, but they had little idea of the dramatic transfer of God's indwelling power that would soon take place.

Meanwhile, all around them, the entire Jewish world waited and rejoiced. This was the time of *Shavuot,* one of three annual feasts celebrated in Jerusalem—Passover (*Pesach*), Tabernacles (*Sukkot*), and Pentecost (*Shavuot*)—in which every Jewish male was required to participate. So, more than a million Jews from all parts of the world were streaming into the city to celebrate and worship in the magnificent marble temple. The city was filled to capacity, and throngs of celebrants filled the streets.

Suddenly, at about 9:00 A.M., during the temple service of Pentecost, a sound like the blowing of a violent wind came from heaven and filled the house where the disciples were. The disciples were filled with the Holy Spirit. Tongues of fire sat on their heads, and they spoke in other languages. Immediately, bewildered people "from every nation under heaven" gathered around them (Acts 2:5). The people marveled that they could understand the disciples, and although some people mocked, about 3,000 others believed and were baptized.

It is likely that this event occurred in the immediate vicinity of the temple—the "house" of God—perhaps on the Southern Stairs, the huge staircase over which hundreds of thousands of Jewish pilgrims made their way to the main processional entrance of the temple. Built by Herod the Great, this unusual staircase had steps of varying widths and was an ideal location for rabbis to teach their disciples. Near the stairs were *mikvoth,* or ritual baths, where Jewish pilgrims purified themselves before worship. These baths may well have been where the 3,000 new Christian believers were baptized on Pentecost.

On this special day of Pentecost, God gave His power to His people. The Holy Spirit, who had filled the temple for so many years, moved into a new "temple"—the temple of individual Christian believers. God was demonstrating that He was beginning a new age, an age rooted in His people—people like you and me who have invited Christ into our lives and will allow Him to live through us and empower us to do His will.

Key Points of This Lesson

This session explores the Jewish setting of Acts 2 and the Pentecost story. Ray Vander Laan adds the element of Jewish tradition to the meaning of Pentecost that Christians have always stressed: the miracle of tongues, gifts of the Spirit, and Peter's empowered preaching. You will guide participants in understanding:

1. *The historical roots of the Feast of Pentecost.* Pentecost was (and is) a Jewish feast instituted by God through Moses. It had been celebrated for more than 1,200 years before the Holy Spirit came upon the disciples.

2. *The spiritual impact of Pentecost.* The Holy Spirit worked a great miracle on the day of Pentecost. The presence of God left the temple and entered the new "temple"—the community of Christian believers. As Christians, we are God's temple. His Spirit fills us and empowers us to do that which He calls us to do.

3. *An evidence of Pentecost.* Pentecost was a holiday of thanksgiving during which Jews celebrated the wheat harvest and the giving of the *Torah* on Mount Sinai. As part of the celebration, the people were to demonstrate their thanksgiving by caring for needy people. When God fulfilled Pentecost by sending His Holy Spirit upon the disciples, the early Christians responded immediately by meeting one another's material needs.

Session Outline (53 minutes)

I. Introduction (4 minutes)
Welcome
What's to Come
Questions to Think About

II. Video Presentation "Power to the People" (17 minutes)

III. Group Discovery (20 minutes)
Video Highlights
Small Group Bible Discovery

IV. Faith Lesson (10 minutes)
Time for Reflection
Action Points

V. Closing Prayer (2 minutes)

Materials

No additional materials are needed for this session. Simply view the video prior to leading the session so you are familiar with its main points.

power to the people

introduction

4 minutes

Welcome

> Assemble the participants together. Welcome them to session nine of *Faith Lessons on the Death and Resurrection of the Messiah*.

What's to Come

During the Feast of Pentecost, the Holy Spirit filled and empowered Jesus' disciples, and the church of Jesus Christ began. God moved His presence on earth from the Holy of Holies in the temple into a new "temple"—the hearts of His people.

In this session, we'll learn about the temple, the Feast of Pentecost, and what took place when God sent His Holy Spirit upon Jesus' disciples. Ray Vander Laan will share keen insights into Jewish culture and the Scriptures that will encourage us to demonstrate the Holy Spirit's power in our lives today. Let's begin by thinking about the ways we approach the challenges of life and how the Holy Spirit is demonstrated through our lives.

Questions to Think About

> *Participant's Guide page 152.*

Turn to page 152 of the Participant's Guide. Let's consider two questions that will help set the stage for the video we'll see.

> Ask each question and solicit a few responses from group members.

1. Think about a time when you faced what seemed like an insurmountable challenge. What or who gave you the courage and willpower to keep going?

   If you feel comfortable doing so, I hope several of you will briefly share a specific experience from your own lives.

   > Listen to the responses. If no one answers, share about a time in your life when you faced a great challenge.

   Suggested Responses may focus on: faith in my abilities, other people's encouragement, fear of failure, God meeting me where I was, the hope that things would get better, the confidence that God had called me to complete the task, etc.

SESSION NINE

power to the people

questions to think about

1. Think about a time when you faced what seemed like an insurmountable challenge. What or who gave you the courage and willpower to keep going?

2. How would you describe a *Pentecost* Christian? What is the evidence of the Holy Spirit within that person?

152

✏ 2. How would you describe a *Pentecost* Christian? What is the evidence of the Holy Spirit within that person?

Suggested Responses for this question are very broad: demonstrates the fruit of the Spirit—love, joy, peace, patience, kindness, goodness, faithfulness, gentleness, self-control; speaks in tongues; has a powerful prayer life; witnesses to others; demonstrates spiritual gifts such as healing, prophecy; etc.

As we view the video, let's consider how our concept of the Holy Spirit and the evidence of His work in our lives line up with the testimony of Scripture.

video presentation

17 minutes

Participant's Guide page 153.

On page 153 of your Participant's Guide you will find a space in which to take notes on key points as we watch this video.

Leader's Video Observations

The Southern Stairs on Pentecost (Shavuot) Morning

The Disciples After Jesus' Ascension

Evidence of God's Indwelling Presence

SESSION NINE

power to the people

questions to think about

1. Think about a time when you faced what seemed like an insurmountable challenge. What or who gave you the courage and willpower to keep going?

2. How would you describe a *Pentecost* Christian? What is the evidence of the Holy Spirit within that person?

Session Nine: Power to the People   153

video notes

The Southern Stairs on Pentecost (Shavuot) Morning

The Disciples After Jesus' Ascension

Evidence of God's Indwelling Presence

Group Discovery

20 minutes

If your group has seven or more members, use the **Video Highlights** with the entire group (five minutes), then break into small groups of three to five to discuss the **Small Group Bible Discovery** (ten minutes). Then reassemble the group to discuss the key points discovered (five minutes).

If your group has fewer than seven members, begin with the **Video Highlights** (five minutes), then do one or more of the topics found in the **Small Group Bible Discovery** as a group (ten minutes). Finally, spend five minutes at the end discussing points that had an impact on participants.

Video Highlights (5 minutes)

Here you'll ask one or more of the following questions that directly relate to the video the participants have just seen.

1. What impact does the possibility that the "house" in which the disciples gathered on Pentecost morning was the temple have on your understanding of God's work at Pentecost?

   Suggested Responses: Allow people to share their perspectives with the group.

2. How do you think the disciples felt when they found themselves filled with the Holy Spirit and realized that God's power—the power they had seen Jesus demonstrate time and again—was within them?

   Suggested Responses: surprised, excited, motivated and filled with zeal, relieved, compelled to testify, filled with hope, overflowing with God's grace and power, etc.

3. What did God command the celebrants of the Feast of Pentecost to do in order to express their thanksgiving?

   Suggested Responses: to care for the needy, to let the poor gather the crops left in the corners of the fields and/or left on the ground after the harvest.

4. What immediately happened after the disciples received the Holy Spirit?

   Suggested Responses: The disciples had the courage and willpower to begin to change the world. The community of believers shared with one another so that no one was in need.

Small Group Bible Discovery (15 minutes)

Participant's Guide pages 155–64.

During this time, a group with fewer than seven participants will stay together. A group larger than seven participants will break into small groups and reassemble as a large group during the final five minutes. Assign each group one of the following topics. If you have more than five small groups, assign some topics to more than one group.

154 The Death and Resurrection of the Messiah

video Highlights

1. What impact does the possibility that the "house" in which the disciples gathered on Pentecost morning was the temple have on your understanding of God's work at Pentecost?

2. How do you think the disciples felt when they found themselves filled with the Holy Spirit and realized that God's power—the power they had seen Jesus demonstrate time and again—was within them?

3. What did God command the celebrants of the Feast of Pentecost to do in order to express their thanksgiving?

4. What immediately happened after the disciples received the Holy Spirit?

Session Nine: Power to the People 155

small Group Bible Discovery

Topic A: Remembering God's Faithfulness During Difficult Times

1. Immediately after Jesus' crucifixion, what was the mood of the disciples? What happened to their faith? (See Luke 24:1–4, 9–22; Mark 16:8–14; Luke 24:36–37; John 20:19.)

2. How did the disciples' mood change after Jesus' resurrection? (See Matthew 28:8–10, 16–17; Luke 24:36–42; John 20:19–20.)

3. What was the disciples' mood after Jesus' ascension? What happened to their faith? (See Luke 24:50–53.)

4. Why did the disciples' mood improve after Jesus' ascension?

PLANNING NOTES:

Let's break into groups of three to five—people sitting near you—and study some of the Bible passages and truths mentioned in the video.

Turn to pages 155–64 in your Participant's Guide. There you'll find a list of five topics. You'll have ten minutes to read and discuss the topic I'll assign to you. Choose one person in your group to be a spokesperson for your group when we discuss these topics later.

> Assign each group a topic.

I'll signal you when one minute is left.

> After nine minutes, let participants know that they have one minute remaining. Then reassemble the entire group. After everyone is back together, begin asking one person from each small group to briefly share a key idea with the larger group. In some cases, you may not have time for every group to share their discoveries.

As time allows, let's briefly share the key ideas that your group discussed.

Topic A: Remembering God's Faithfulness During Difficult Times

1. Immediately after Jesus' crucifixion, what was the mood of the disciples? What happened to their faith? (See Luke 24:1–4, 9–22; Mark 16:8–14; Luke 24:36–37; John 20:19.)

   Suggested Responses: sad, disbelieving of what the women saw at the tomb, fearful, unsure of what to do next, doubtful, confused, bewildered, etc. Their faith was shattered.

2. How did the disciples' mood change after Jesus' resurrection? (See Matthew 28:8–10, 16–17; Luke 24:36–42; John 20:19–20.)

   Suggested Responses: They were filled with joy, worshiped Jesus, became obedient to Jesus again, their fear and despair vanished, etc.

3. What was the disciples' mood after Jesus' ascension? What happened to their faith? (See Luke 24:50–53.)

   Suggested Responses: They prayed and joyfully praised God in the temple. They did these things continually. Their faith was strengthened.

4. Why did the disciples' mood improve after Jesus' ascension?

   Suggested Responses: They realized that God will accomplish His work, no matter how desperate the circumstances might appear to be; they realized that God is faithful to His promises and that Jesus was the fulfillment of what God had been doing in the Hebrew people all along; their hope had been restored.

5. Which truths and principles from the disciples' experience can we cling to today when we face seemingly impossible difficulties, when we feel as if God has abandoned us, or when we don't know which way to turn?

   Suggested Responses: God keeps His promises; we need to trust Him no matter what; God wants to help us to fulfill His purposes for our lives; God's timing is perfect; sometimes we have to walk in faith without knowing what the outcome will be; etc.

Session Nine: Power to the People   155

small Group Bible Discovery

Topic A: Remembering God's Faithfulness During Difficult Times

1. Immediately after Jesus' crucifixion, what was the mood of the disciples? What happened to their faith? (See Luke 24:1–4, 9–22; Mark 16:8–14; Luke 24:36–37; John 20:19.)

2. How did the disciples' mood change after Jesus' resurrection? (See Matthew 28:8–10, 16–17; Luke 24:36–42; John 20:19–20.)

3. What was the disciples' mood after Jesus' ascension? What happened to their faith? (See Luke 24:50–53.)

4. Why did the disciples' mood improve after Jesus' ascension?

---

156   The Death and Resurrection of the Messiah

5. Which truths and principles from the disciples' experience can we cling to today when we face seemingly impossible difficulties, when we feel as if God has abandoned us, or when we don't know which way to turn?

Topic B: When the Church Was Born
On the map of the city of Jerusalem locate the temple and the Southern Stairs. Imagine the whole city filled with visitors and thousands upon thousands of worshippers going into the temple on Pentecost morning.

1. After Jesus ascended to heaven, what did the disciples do? What does their activity reveal about them? (See Luke 24:50–53.)

2. After the Holy Spirit came upon Jesus' disciples, why were the nearby Jews who had come from many lands bewildered? (See Acts 2:5–12.)

3. What was the result of Peter's preaching? (See Acts 2:37–41.)

PLANNING NOTES:

Topic B: When the Church Was Born

On your map of the city of Jerusalem, page 157, locate the temple and the Southern Stairs. Imagine the whole city filled with visitors and thousands upon thousands of worshipers going into the temple on Pentecost morning.

1. After Jesus ascended to heaven, what did the disciples do? What does their activity reveal about them? (See Luke 24:50–53.)

   Suggested Responses: In obedience to Jesus, they returned to Jerusalem filled with joy; they continued their Jewish practices and went into the temple to praise God. They expected something to happen during this special feast time.

2. After the Holy Spirit came upon Jesus' disciples, why were the nearby Jews who had come from many lands bewildered? (See Acts 2:5–12.)

   Suggested Response: Each person in the crowd heard the disciples speaking his or her particular language and wondered how this could be possible, especially since most of the disciples were common Galileans who were not well educated.

3. What was the result of Peter's preaching? (See Acts 2:37–41.)

   Suggested Response: About 3,000 people repented and were baptized.

Jerusalem's Districts

A David's City	1 Eastern Gate	9 Tadi Gate	17 Spring of Gihon
B New City	2 Southern Stairs	10 Pool of Bethesda	18 Hinnom Valley
C Upper City	3 Royal Stoa	11 First Wall	19 Theater
D Business District	4 Robinson's Arch	12 Second Wall	20 Citadel and Herod's Palace
E Temple Mount	5 Wilson's Arch	13 Garden Gate	21 Essene Quarter
F Lower City	6 Tyropoeon Street	14 Towers (Damascus) Gate	22 Mansions
G Herod's Palace	7 Warren's Gate	15 Golgotha (?)	23 Mount of Olives
	8 Antonia	16 Garden Tomb	24 Kidron Valley
			25 Huldah Gates

Power to the People

---

156 The Death and Resurrection of the Messiah

5. Which truths and principles from the disciples' experience can we cling to today when we face seemingly impossible difficulties, when we feel as if God has abandoned us, or when we don't know which way to turn?

Topic B: When the Church Was Born

On the map of the city of Jerusalem locate the temple and the Southern Stairs. Imagine the whole city filled with visitors and thousands upon thousands of worshippers going into the temple on Pentecost morning.

1. After Jesus ascended to heaven, what did the disciples do? What does their activity reveal about them? (See Luke 24:50–53.)

2. After the Holy Spirit came upon Jesus' disciples, why were the nearby Jews who had come from many lands bewildered? (See Acts 2:5–12.)

3. What was the result of Peter's preaching? (See Acts 2:37–41.)

Session Nine: Power to the People 157

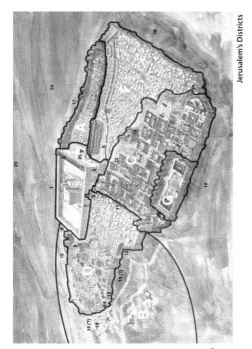

Jerusalem's Districts

David's City
New City
Upper City
Business District
Temple Mount
Lower City
Herod's Palace
Eastern Gate
Southern Stairs
Royal Stoa
Robinson's Arch
Wilson's Arch
Tyropoeon Street
Warren's Gate
Antonia
Tadi Gate
Pool of Bethesda
First Wall
Second Wall
Garden Gate
Towers (Damascus) Gate
Golgotha (?)
Garden Tomb
Spring of Gihon
Hinnom Valley
Theater
Citadel and Herod's Palace
Mansions
Essene Quarter
Mount of Olives
Kidron Valley
Huldah Gates

P L A N N I N G   N O T E S :

4. What continued to occur in the young church during the days immediately following Pentecost? (See Acts 4:4; 5:14; 6:7.)

    Suggested Responses: The apostles continued preaching and doing miracles, and thousands more people (primarily Jews) became believers—even some from among the priesthood.

5. Why were the Jews scattered throughout the world at this period in time? (See 2 Kings 17:23; 2 Chronicles 36:20.)

    Suggested Responses: Assyria had destroyed the ten tribes and Babylon had placed Judah in captivity, so Jews lived throughout these empires.

6. Why was it important in God's plan that Jews from every nation become followers of Jesus?

    Suggested Responses: These Jews were free to go back to the countries in which they resided and preach the message of Jesus the Messiah, thereby taking the gospel throughout the world.

7. In what way did the events of Pentecost fulfill Shavuot? (See Matthew 9:37–38; Luke 10:1–3; John 4:34–38.)

    Suggested Response: It produced the firstfruits of the harvest of Christians.

Topic C: The Physical Evidence of God's Spirit

God's presence had been physically evident prior to the birth of the church at Pentecost. Let's take a closer look at several significant manifestations of God's Spirit that occurred at the giving of the law, the setting up of the tabernacle, and the dedication of the temple.

1. In what ways was the Spirit of God evident when Moses was on Mount Sinai? (See Exodus 19:16–19.)

    Suggested Responses: through thunder and lightning, a thick cloud that descended over the mountain, a loud trumpet blast, billowing smoke, an earthquake, etc.

2. How did God make His presence known in the Tent of Meeting, or tabernacle, during the Israelites' travels to the Promised Land? (See Exodus 40:34–38.)

    Suggested Responses: His cloud of glory filled and covered the Tent of Meeting; it so filled the tabernacle that Moses couldn't go into it. The cloud was always visible to all the people—as a cloud during the day, and as a cloud with fire by night. The Israelites followed the cloud whenever it lifted from the tabernacle.

3. At the dedication of Solomon's temple, how did the Israelites know that God had taken up residence there?

    2 Chronicles 5:7, 11–14:

    > *Suggested Response:* The temple was so filled with the cloud of God's glory that the priests couldn't go into it.

158 The Death and Resurrection of the Messiah

4. What continued to occur in the young church during the days immediately following Pentecost? (See Acts 4:4; 5:14; 6:7.)

5. Why were the Jews scattered throughout the world at this period in time? (See 2 Kings 17:23; 2 Chronicles 36:20.)

6. Why was it important in God's plan that Jews from every nation become followers of Jesus?

7. In what way did the events of Pentecost fulfill Shavuot? (See Matthew 9:37–38; Luke 10:1–3; John 4:34–38.)

Topic C: The Physical Evidence of God's Spirit

God's presence had been physically evident prior to the birth of the church at Pentecost. Let's take a closer look at several significant manifestations of God's Spirit that occurred at the giving of the law, the setting up of the tabernacle, and the dedication of the temple.

1. In what ways was the Spirit of God evident when Moses was on Mount Sinai? (See Exodus 19:16–19.)

160 The Death and Resurrection of the Messiah

2. How did God make His presence known in the Tent of Meeting, or tabernacle, during the Israelites' travels to the Promised Land? (See Exodus 40:34–38.)

3. At the dedication of Solomon's temple, how did the Israelites know that God had taken up residence there? 2 Chronicles 5:7, 11–14:

2 Chronicles 7:1–3:

2 Chronicles 7:11–12, 15–16:

4. Describe what it was like when the Holy Spirit moved from the temple building into a new temple—that of Jesus' disciples. (See Acts 2:1–5.)

Topic D: The History of the Feast of Weeks (Pentecost)

1. When, as God spoke through Moses, was the Feast of Weeks (Pentecost) to take place? (See Leviticus 23:15–22; Deuteronomy 16:9–12.)

2. The Feast of Weeks was celebrated during the month Sivan—the third month. Which other significant event occurred during the third month? (See Exodus 19:1).

2 Chronicles 7:1–3:

> *Suggested Responses:* Fire came down from heaven and consumed the sacrifices; the glory of the Lord so filled the temple that the priests couldn't go into it.

2 Chronicles 7:11–12, 15–16:

> *Suggested Responses:* God appeared to Solomon and said that He had chosen and consecrated the temple for His name, that His eyes and heart would always be there.

✏ 4. Describe what it was like when the Holy Spirit moved from the temple building into a new temple—that of Jesus' disciples. (See Acts 2:1–5.)

Suggested Responses: There was a sound from heaven like a violent wind; fire appeared and divided into tongues, which came to rest on each disciple; all the disciples began to speak in other tongues; crowds of people gathered around them; etc.

COMPELLING EVIDENCE

Consider the similarities in the manifestations of God's presence on Mount Sinai and during Pentecost. Is it simply a coincidence?

On Mount Sinai	During Pentecost
God's presence was accompanied by fire, smoke, and the sound of thunder (Exodus 19:16–19).	God's presence was accompanied by the sound of wind, tongues of fire, and the gift of languages (Acts 2:1–3). The Hebrew term translated "Holy Spirit," *Ruach HaKodesh*, means "Holy Wind."
When God gave the Torah to Moses, the people were worshiping the golden calf. About 3,000 people died as punishment for their sins (Exodus 32:1–4, 19–20, 27–28).	When Jesus' Spirit was given, the people repented, and about 3,000 people believed and found spiritual life (Acts 2:41).
The Law was written on stone tablets (Exodus 31:18).	The Law was written on the hearts of the people (2 Corinthians 3:3; Jeremiah 31:33).
God's presence was symbolized by a cloud and fire, which had led the Israelites out of Egypt. Later, God moved His presence into the temple (2 Chronicles 5:7–8, 13–14).	God's presence moved from the temple into a "new temple"—the followers of Jesus (Romans 8:9; 1 Corinthians 3:16–17).
The Torah (*Torah* means "teaching") provided God's teachings for the Old Testament community of people.	The Holy Spirit became the Teacher of believers (John 14:26).
God met Moses—the Israelites' leader—on Mount Sinai, "the mountain of God" (Exodus 24:13).	Jerusalem was built on a mountain called "the mountain of the Lord" (Isaiah 2:3; 66:20).

160The Death and Resurrection of the Messiah

2. How did God make His presence known in the Tent of Meeting, or tabernacle, during the Israelites' travels to the Promised Land? (See Exodus 40:34–38.)

3. At the dedication of Solomon's temple, how did the Israelites know that God had taken up residence there?
2 Chronicles 5:7, 11–14:

2 Chronicles 7:1–3:

2 Chronicles 7:11–12, 15–16:

4. Describe what it was like when the Holy Spirit moved from the temple building into a new temple—that of Jesus' disciples. (See Acts 2:1–5.)

Topic D: The History of the Feast of Weeks (Pentecost)

1. When, as God spoke through Moses, was the Feast of Weeks (Pentecost) to take place? (See Leviticus 23:15–22; Deuteronomy 16:9–12.)

2. The Feast of Weeks was celebrated during the month Sivan—the third month. Which other significant event occurred during the third month? (See Exodus 19:1).

Session Nine: Power to the People159

COMPELLING EVIDENCE
Consider the similarities in the manifestations of God's presence on Mount Sinai and during Pentecost. Is it simply a coincidence?

On Mount Sinai	During Pentecost
God's presence was accompanied by fire, smoke, and the sound of thunder (Exodus 19:16–19).	God's presence was accompanied by the sound of wind, tongues of fire, and the gift of languages (Acts 2:1–3). The Hebrew term translated "Holy Spirit," *Ruach HaKodesh*, means "Holy Wind."
When God gave the Torah to Moses, the people were worshiping the golden calf. About 3,000 people died as punishment for their sins (Exodus 32:1–4, 19–20, 27–28).	When Jesus' Spirit was given, the people repented, and about 3,000 people believed and found spiritual life (Acts 2:41).
The Law was written on stone tablets (Exodus 31:18).	The Law was written on the hearts of the people (2 Corinthians 3:3; Jeremiah 31:33).
God's presence was symbolized by a cloud and fire, which had led the Israelites out of Egypt. Later, God moved His presence into the temple (2 Chronicles 5:7–8, 13–14).	God's presence moved from the temple into a "new temple"—the followers of Jesus (Romans 8:9; 1 Corinthians 3:16–17).
The Torah (*Torah* means "teaching") provided God's teachings for the Old Testament community of people.	The Holy Spirit became the Teacher of believers (John 14:26).
God met Moses—the Israelites' leader—on Mount Sinai, "the mountain of God" (Exodus 24:13).	Jerusalem was built on a mountain called "the mountain of the Lord" (Isaiah 2:3; 66:20).

Topic D: The History of the Feast of Weeks (Pentecost)

1. When, as God spoke through Moses, was the Feast of Weeks (Pentecost) to take place? (See Leviticus 23:15–22; Deuteronomy 16:9–12.)

   Suggested Response: fifty days after Passover (Greek-speaking Jews referred to the feast as "Pentecost," which is derived from the Greek word translated "fifty days").

2. The Feast of Weeks was celebrated during the month Sivan—the third month. Which other significant event occurred during the third month? (See Exodus 19:1.)

   Suggested Response: The Israelites reached Mount Sinai, where the Law was given, in the third month after leaving Egypt.

3. What were celebrants to present to God during the Feast of Weeks—the feast in honor of the end of the wheat harvest? (See Leviticus 23:16–22; Numbers 28:26–31.)

   Suggested Responses: an offering of new grain, two loaves of bread that were made from the finest flour ground from the newly harvested wheat, and a basket of seven spices. In addition, special sacrifices were made to provide burnt offerings, a male goat was offered as a sin offering, and two lambs were offered as a fellowship offering.

4. Who was required to attend Pentecost—and the other two feasts—and appear before God in the temple? (See Deuteronomy 16:16.)

   Suggested Response: all Jewish men.

5. List the subjects of the Scriptures that were read in the synagogue and temple on Pentecost:

Scripture Reading	Subject
Exodus 19:1–20:26	*The story of God giving the Law.*
Ezekiel 1:22–28	*A description of God's appearance with sound and fire.*
The Book of Ruth	*A story of Pentecost in action, set at harvest time.*

6. What insights do these readings provide concerning the events of the Christian Pentecost?

   Suggested Responses: Allow participants to share their ideas.

160   The Death and Resurrection of the Messiah

2. How did God make His presence known in the Tent of Meeting, or tabernacle, during the Israelites' travels to the Promised Land? (See Exodus 40:34–38.)

3. At the dedication of Solomon's temple, how did the Israelites know that God had taken up residence there? 2 Chronicles 5:7, 11–14:

   2 Chronicles 7:1–3:

   2 Chronicles 7:11–12, 15–16:

4. Describe what it was like when the Holy Spirit moved from the temple building into a new temple—that of Jesus' disciples. (See Acts 2:1–5.)

Topic D: The History of the Feast of Weeks (Pentecost)

1. When, as God spoke through Moses, was the Feast of Weeks (Pentecost) to take place? (See Leviticus 23:15–22; Deuteronomy 16:9–12.)

2. The Feast of Weeks was celebrated during the month Sivan—the third month. Which other significant event occurred during the third month? (See Exodus 19:1).

---

3. What were celebrants to present to God during the Feast of Weeks—the feast in honor of the end of the wheat harvest? (See Leviticus 23:16–22; Numbers 28:26–31.)

4. Who was required to attend Pentecost—and the other two feasts—and appear before God in the temple? (See Deuteronomy 16:16.)

5. List the subjects of the Scriptures that were read in the synagogue and temple on Pentecost:

Scripture Reading	Subject
Exodus 19:1–20:26	
Ezekiel 1:22–28	
The Book of Ruth	

6. What insights do these readings provide concerning the events of the Christian Pentecost?

Topic E: A Call to Action—The Evidence of Pentecost

1. In addition to bringing offerings to the temple, how were the celebrants of the Feast of Weeks (Pentecost) to demonstrate their thankfulness? (See Leviticus 19:9–10; 23:22.)

DATA FILE

Pentecost — The History of the Feast

The Feast of Weeks (also called *Shavuot,* in Hebrew; *Pentecoste,* by Greek-speaking Jews; and "the day of first-fruits") celebrated the end of the wheat harvest. It was a time to bring thank offerings to God and, according to Jewish tradition, the time when God gave Moses the Torah on Mount Sinai.

- Instituted by God more than 1,200 years before Jesus sent His Spirit to indwell the disciples, the Feast of Weeks was one of three feasts during which all Jewish men were required to appear before God in the temple (Deuteronomy 16:16).
- The Feast of Weeks was celebrated fifty days after Passover Sabbath (Leviticus 23:16). Because of this, it was called *Pentecost,* a word derived from the Greek word translated "fifty days" (Acts 2:1).
- People who celebrated Pentecost were to show concern for the poor by not harvesting the edges of their fields and leaving the grain they dropped during the harvest for those in need to gather (Leviticus 19:9–10; 23:22).

Pentecost — The Birthplace of the Church

For Christians, Pentecost is considered to be the day when the Holy Spirit left the temple and came in visible, audible form and miraculously filled the disciples with God's power. It is the day on which the Christian church — the community of believers — was born.

Although it is commonly believed that the disciples were in the Upper Room when they were filled with the Holy Spirit, that is unlikely. Here's why:

- Crowds of people were present (Acts 2:5–6). These people would not have fit into a small room. Clearly masses of people would have been in the temple on Pentecost.
- The disciples were continually in the temple (Luke 24:53) and would have been there during the day of Pentecost.
- Pentecost was one of the holiest days of the year, and it is likely that they were in the temple for worship and to hear the readings at 9:00 A.M. (Acts 2:15).
- The disciples were in "the house" (Acts 2:1–2) when the Holy Spirit came upon them. Many Old Testament passages referred to the temple as "the house." However, the English translation is rendered "temple." (See Ezekiel 40:5, 42:15, and 43:10 in the King James Version.)
- Peter described his location as being near the tomb of David (Acts 2:29). According to 1 Kings 2:10, David was buried in the "City of David" — the part of Jerusalem near the Temple Mount.

So where were the disciples? No one knows for sure, but they were in the vicinity of the temple, perhaps in the temple courts or on the Southern Stairs where thousands of Jewish pilgrims would have gathered. Consider the evidence:

- The Southern Stairs led from the valley below, where David's City was located, to the double gates by the main processional entrance to the temple. Many thousands of pilgrims at a time walked up the Southern Stairs to the huge temple platform (about 900 by 1,500 feet) that surrounded the marble temple.
- The Southern Stairs were also known as the "Rabbi's Teaching Staircase" because they were a prime location for rabbis to teach their disciples. (Some scholars believe that Jesus' final discourse on the end of the world, found in Luke 21, took place as He left the temple by the Southern Stairs.) Listeners could sit on the broad, stone steps, and passersby could gather and listen, too.
- Nearby ceremonial baths would have made it convenient for the disciples to baptize the approximately 3,000 people who became believers after the Holy Spirit came upon the disciples. These baths were one of the few places where there would have been sufficient water to baptize that many people.

DATA FILE
Pentecost—The History of the Feast
The Feast of Weeks (also called *Shavuot*, in Hebrew; *Pentecoste,* by Greek-speaking Jews; and "the day of firstfruits") celebrated the end of the wheat harvest. It was a time to bring thank offerings to God and, according to Jewish tradition, the time when God gave Moses the Torah on Mount Sinai.
- Instituted by God more than 1,200 years before Jesus sent His Spirit to indwell the disciples, the Feast of Weeks was one of three feasts during which all Jewish men were required to appear before God in the temple (Deuteronomy 16:16).
- The Feast of Weeks was celebrated fifty days after Passover Sabbath (Leviticus 23:16). Because of this, it was called *Pentecost,* a word derived from the Greek word translated "fifty days" (Acts 2:1).
- People who celebrated Pentecost were to show concern for the poor by not harvesting the edges of their fields and leaving the grain they dropped during the harvest for those in need to gather (Leviticus 19:9–10; 23:22).

Pentecost—The Birthplace of the Church
For Christians, Pentecost is considered to be the day when the Holy Spirit left the temple and came in visible, audible form and miraculously filled the disciples with God's power. It is the day on which the Christian church—the community of believers—was born.

Although it is commonly believed that the disciples were in the Upper Room when they were filled with the Holy Spirit, that is unlikely. Here's why:
- Crowds of people were present (Acts 2:5–6). These people would not have fit into a small room. Clearly masses of people would have been in the temple on Pentecost.
- The disciples were continually in the temple (Luke 24:53) and would have been there during the day of Pentecost.

- Pentecost was one of the holiest days of the year, and it is likely that they were in the temple for worship and to hear the readings at 9:00 A.M. (Acts 2:15).
- The disciples were in "the house" (Acts 2:1–2) when the Holy Spirit came upon them. Many Old Testament passages referred to the temple as "the house." However, the English translation is rendered "temple." (See Ezekiel 40:5, 42:15, and 43:10 in the King James Version.)
- Peter described his location as being near the tomb of David (Acts 2:29). According to 1 Kings 2:10, David was buried in the "City of David"—the part of Jerusalem near the Temple Mount.

So where were the disciples? No one knows for sure, but they were in the vicinity of the temple, perhaps in the temple courts or on the Southern Stairs where thousands of Jewish pilgrims would have gathered. Consider the evidence:
- The Southern Stairs led from the valley below, where David's City was located, to the double gates by the main processional entrance to the temple. Many thousands of pilgrims at a time walked up the Southern Stairs to the huge temple platform (about 900 by 1,500 feet) that surrounded the marble temple.
- The Southern Stairs were also known as the "Rabbi's Teaching Staircase" because they were a prime location for rabbis to teach their disciples. (Some scholars believe that Jesus' final discourse on the end of the world, found in Luke 21, took place as He left the temple by the Southern Stairs.) Listeners could sit on the broad, stone steps, and passersby could gather and listen, too.
- Nearby ceremonial baths would have made it convenient for the disciples to baptize the approximately 3,000 people who became believers after the Holy Spirit came upon the disciples. These baths were one of the few places where there would have been sufficient water to baptize that many people.

Topic E: A Call to Action—The Evidence of Pentecost

✎ 1. In addition to bringing offerings to the temple, how were the celebrants of the Feast of Weeks (Pentecost) to demonstrate their thankfulness? (See Leviticus 19:9–10; 23:22.)

Suggested Responses: The Jews were to not reap to the very edges of their fields or gather all the gleanings of the harvest. This left food for less-fortunate people to gather.

✎ 2. When the early Christians were filled with the Holy Spirit, how did they respond to one another and to the needs of other people? (See Acts 2:44–47.)

Suggested Responses: They shared what they had with needy people, met together every day in the temple courts, ate together with glad hearts, praised God, etc.

✎ 3. What is the fruit of the Spirit? (See Galatians 5:22–26.)

Suggested Responses: love, joy, peace, patience, kindness, goodness, faithfulness, gentleness, and self-control.

✎ 4. In what ways does this list relate to the fulfillment of Pentecost?

Suggested Responses: Like the Old Testament fulfillment of Shavuot, the fulfillment of Pentecost includes concern for others, particularly for those in need. Many of the gifts of the Spirit involve concern for and response to others. Being filled with the Spirit affects how we treat others.

PENTECOST PROFILE

Boaz—His Love for One Needy Person Changed the World

Each year on Pentecost, the Jews read the Old Testament book of Ruth. It tells the story of an Israelite couple who moved to Moab during a famine in Canaan. The husband and two sons died, leaving the mother (Naomi) and her two daughters-in-law alone. Naomi chose to return to Israel, and one of her daughters-in-law, Ruth, insisted on accompanying her.

Naomi had a relative on her husband's side named Boaz, and Ruth began picking up the barley left in his fields after harvest. Boaz had compassion on the destitute Gentile woman and provided generously for her. Eventually he recognized his God-given responsibility and married her.

Little did Boaz know how the help he provided changed the world! Ruth had a son, who became the father of Jesse, who was the father of David—the lineage from which Jesus came! (See Matthew 1—the genealogy of Jesus.)

By helping just one needy person in Jesus' name, you could truly make an eternal impact.

3. What were celebrants to present to God during the Feast of Weeks—the feast in honor of the end of the wheat harvest? (See Leviticus 23:16–22; Numbers 28:26–31.)

4. Who was required to attend Pentecost—and the other two feasts—and appear before God in the temple? (See Deuteronomy 16:16.)

5. List the subjects of the Scriptures that were read in the synagogue and temple on Pentecost:

Scripture Reading	Subject
Exodus 19:1–20:26	
Ezekiel 1:22–28	
The Book of Ruth	

6. What insights do these readings provide concerning the events of the Christian Pentecost?

Topic E: A Call to Action—The Evidence of Pentecost

1. In addition to bringing offerings to the temple, how were the celebrants of the Feast of Weeks (Pentecost) to demonstrate their thankfulness? (See Leviticus 19:9–10; 23:22.)

2. When the early Christians were filled with the Holy Spirit, how did they respond to one another and to the needs of other people? (See Acts 2:44–47.)

3. What is the fruit of the Spirit? (See Galatians 5:22–26.)

4. In what ways does this list relate to the fulfillment of Pentecost?

PENTECOST PROFILE:

Boaz—His Love for One Needy Person Changed the World
Each year on Pentecost, the Jews read the Old Testament book of Ruth. It tells the story of an Israelite couple who moved to Moab during a famine in Canaan. The husband and two sons died, leaving the mother (Naomi) and her two daughters-in-law alone. Naomi chose to return to Israel, and one of her daughters-in-law, Ruth, insisted on accompanying her.

Naomi had a relative on her husband's side named Boaz, and Ruth began picking up the barley left in his fields after harvest. Boaz had compassion on the destitute Gentile woman and provided generously for her. Eventually he recognized his God-given responsibility and married her.

Little did Boaz know how the help he provided changed the world! Ruth had a son, who became the father of Jesse, who was the father of David—the lineage from which Jesus came! (See Matthew 1—the genealogy of Jesus.)

By helping just one needy person in Jesus' name, you could truly make an eternal impact.

faith Lesson

Time for Reflection (5 minutes)

It's time for each of us to think quietly about how we can apply what we've learned today. On pages 165–66 of the Participant's Guide, you'll find a passage of Scripture. Let's each read this passage silently and take the next few minutes to consider the significance of what happened on that marvelous Pentecost day.

Please do not talk during this time. It's a time when we can reflect on today's lesson and consider how the indwelling Spirit of God affects our lives.

> *The Scripture passage and questions are reproduced in their entirety in the Participant's Guide on pages 165–67.*

But you will receive power when the Holy Spirit comes on you; and you will be my witnesses in Jerusalem, and in all Judea and Samaria, and to the ends of the earth.

ACTS 1:8

All of them were filled with the Holy Spirit and began to speak in other tongues as the Spirit enabled them. Now there were staying in Jerusalem God-fearing Jews from every nation under heaven. When they heard this sound, a crowd came together in bewilderment, because each one heard them speaking in his own language. Utterly amazed, they asked: "Are not all these men who are speaking Galileans? Then how is it that each of us hears them in his own native language?" . . . Amazed and perplexed, they asked one another, "What does this mean?"

ACTS 2:4–8, 12

"Therefore let all Israel be assured of this: God has made this Jesus, whom you crucified, both Lord and Christ." When the people heard this, they were cut to the heart and said to Peter and the other apostles, "Brothers, what shall we do?" Peter replied, "Repent and be baptized, every one of you, in the name of Jesus Christ for the forgiveness of your sins. And you will receive the gift of the Holy Spirit. The promise is for you and your children and for all who are far off—for all whom the Lord our God will call." With many other words he warned them; and he pleaded with them, "Save yourselves from this corrupt generation." Those who accepted his message were baptized, and about three thousand were added to their number that day.

ACTS 2:36–41

All the believers were one in heart and mind. No one claimed that any of his possessions was his own, but they shared everything they had. With great power the apostles continued to testify to the resurrection of the Lord Jesus, and much grace was upon them all.

ACTS 4:32–33

faith Lesson

Time for Reflection
The following passages of Scripture reveal the work of the Holy Spirit in the lives of early believers. Read these passages silently and consider the significance of what happened on Pentecost and how the indwelling Spirit of God affects your life.

> But you will receive power when the Holy Spirit comes on you; and you will be my witnesses in Jerusalem, and in all Judea and Samaria, and to the ends of the earth.
>
> ACTS 1:8

> All of them were filled with the Holy Spirit and began to speak in other tongues as the Spirit enabled them. Now there were staying in Jerusalem God-fearing Jews from every nation under heaven. When they heard this sound, a crowd came together in bewilderment, because each one heard them speaking in his own language. Utterly amazed, they asked: "Are not all these men who are speaking Galileans? Then how is it that each of us hears them in his own native language?" . . . Amazed and perplexed, they asked one another, "What does this mean?"
>
> ACTS 2:4–8, 12

> "Therefore let all Israel be assured of this: God has made this Jesus, whom you crucified, both Lord and Christ." When the people heard this, they were cut to the heart and said to Peter and the other apostles, "Brothers, what shall we do?" Peter replied, "Repent and be baptized, every one of you, in the name of Jesus Christ for the forgiveness of your sins. And you will receive the gift of the Holy Spirit. The promise is for you and your children and for all who are far off— for all whom the Lord our God will call." With many other words he warned them; and he pleaded with them, "Save yourselves from this

corrupt generation." Those who accepted his message were baptized, and about three thousand were added to their number that day.

> ACTS 2:36–41

> All the believers were one in heart and mind. No one claimed that any of his possessions was his own, but they shared everything they had. With great power the apostles continued to testify to the resurrection of the Lord Jesus, and much grace was upon them all.
>
> ACTS 4:32–33

1. As Christians, we are to be to our world what the temple was to the world of the Old Testament. We are to reflect God's indwelling presence. Think about what this meant— in terms of practical, day-to-day living—for the early Christians and what it produced in their lives.

   a. What does it mean for you to reflect God's presence to your world?

   b. What might be the result?

   c. Think about what it means to be a *Pentecost* Christian. What evidence of the Spirit's presence can be seen in your desire to help other people in need?

1. As Christians, we are to be to our world what the temple was to the world of the Old Testament. We are to reflect God's indwelling presence. Think about what this meant—in terms of practical, day-to-day living—for the early Christians and what it produced in their lives.

   a. What does it mean for you to reflect God's presence to your world?

   b. What might be the result?

   c. Think about what it means to be a *Pentecost* Christian. What evidence of the Spirit's presence can be seen in your desire to help other people in need?

   A PENTECOST CHRISTIAN:
   - Asks God to indwell him or her in order to reflect God's presence to the world.
   - Brings a spiritual harvest to God by testifying of Him to other people.
   - Demonstrates the presence of God's Spirit by caring for people in need.

2. At Pentecost, God empowered His disciples to be His witnesses, and with great power they testified to the resurrection of the Lord Jesus.

   a. What has God empowered you to do?

   b. Are you trusting Him to lead you to accomplish His purposes through you?

   c. How might you seek out God's Spirit and become a more powerful witness to your needy world?

   As soon as participants have spent five minutes reflecting on the above questions, get the entire group's attention and move to the next section.

Action Points (5 minutes)

The following points are reproduced on pages 168–69 of the Participant's Guide:

Now it's time to wrap up our session.

Give participants a moment to transition from their thoughtfulness to giving you their full attention.

Jesus frequently used the image of the "harvest" to describe those who would come to believe in Him. Some places where He used the term "harvest" are Matthew 9:37–38; 13:24–29, 36–43; Luke 10:1–2; John 4:34–38. On Pentecost—the day when the Jewish people celebrated the end of the wheat harvest—His promise came true. God called and empowered His people to reap the harvest, and thousands of people believed in Jesus.

Today, if we have God's Spirit, God calls us to be His witnesses and to bring in the spiritual harvest. Empowered by His Holy Spirit, we are to share Him with other people so that they, too, can develop a personal relationship with Him and reflect Him to the world.

corrupt generation." Those who accepted his message were baptized, and about three thousand were added to their number that day.

ACTS 2:36–41

All the believers were one in heart and mind. No one claimed that any of his possessions was his own, but they shared everything they had. With great power the apostles continued to testify to the resurrection of the Lord Jesus, and much grace was upon them all.

ACTS 4:32–33

1. As Christians, we are to be to our world what the temple was to the world of the Old Testament. We are to reflect God's indwelling presence. Think about what this meant—in terms of practical, day-to-day living—for the early Christians and what it produced in their lives.

   a. What does it mean for you to reflect God's presence to your world?

   b. What might be the result?

   c. Think about what it means to be a *Pentecost* Christian. What evidence of the Spirit's presence can be seen in your desire to help other people in need?

A PENTECOST CHRISTIAN:
· Asks God to indwell him or her in order to reflect God's presence to the world.
· Brings a spiritual harvest to God by testifying of Him to other people.
· Demonstrates the presence of God's Spirit by caring for people in need.

2. At Pentecost, God empowered His disciples to be His witnesses, and with great power they testified to the resurrection of the Lord Jesus.

   a. What has God empowered you to do?

   b. Are you trusting Him to lead you to accomplish His purposes through you?

   c. How might you seek out God's Spirit and become a more powerful witness to your needy world?

PLANNING NOTES:

I'd like to take a moment to highlight what we have explored today. After I have reviewed each point, I will give you a moment to jot down a step (or steps) of commitment or action that you are willing to make as a result of what you have learned today.

> Read each point and pause after each one so that participants can consider and write out their commitment or action.

1. *God has called and empowered His people—the church—to be His witnesses.* On Pentecost, God gave His power to His people so that they might be His witnesses "in Jerusalem, and in all Judea and Samaria, and to the ends of the earth" (Acts 1:8).

   In what ways can you be a more powerful witness for God in your world? At home? At work? In your neighborhood?

2. *Christians are God's temple.* The Holy Spirit worked a great miracle on the day of Pentecost. The presence of God entered a new "temple"—the community of believers. His Spirit has filled this new temple and empowers us to do what He calls us to do.

   What are you willing to do in order to obediently and courageously reflect God's presence and impact a world that desperately needs Him?

3. *The reality of Pentecost is made evident by the way in which we care for other people.* Pentecost was a holiday of thanksgiving to God. In addition to worshiping in the temple, the people demonstrated their thanksgiving by caring for needy people. When God fulfilled Pentecost by sending His Holy Spirit upon the disciples, the early Christians immediately began meeting one another's needs. When you and I are filled with God's Spirit, our response will be to willingly and gratefully share our resources and our lives with people in need.

   Whose needs will you seek to meet this week? This month? This year?

   What will you share with those individuals?

closing prayer

2 minutes

Dear God, we are so thankful that You are willing to dwell in each of us. We ask You to live through us, to make the power of Your presence overflow our lives and into the lives of people around us. Thank You for the privilege of bringing the presence of Jesus into our world—speaking His words and demonstrating His love to those who need Him. Help us to faithfully demonstrate Your presence to our hurting world, to the many people who need Your healing, caring, correcting touch. Guide us as we seek to meet the needs of others—one person at a time. Amen.

168   The Death and Resurrection of the Messiah

Action Points

If we have God's Spirit, God calls us to be His witnesses and to bring in the spiritual harvest. Empowered by His Holy Spirit, we are to share Him with other people so that they, too, can develop a personal relationship with Him and reflect Him to the world. Take a moment to highlight the key points you have explored today. Then write down the step or steps of commitment or action that you are willing to make as a result of what you have discovered.

1. *God has called and empowered His people—the church—to be His witnesses.* On Pentecost, God gave His power to His people so that they might be His witnesses "in Jerusalem, and in all Judea and Samaria, and to the ends of the earth" (Acts 1:8).

   In what ways can you be a more powerful witness for God in your world? At home? At work? In your neighborhood?

2. *Christians are God's temple.* The Holy Spirit worked a great miracle on the day of Pentecost. The presence of God entered a new "temple"—the community of believers. His Spirit has filled this new temple and empowers us to do what He calls us to do.

   What are you willing to do in order to obediently and courageously reflect God's presence and impact a world that desperately needs Him?

3. *The reality of Pentecost is made evident by the way in which we care for other people.* Pentecost was a holiday of thanksgiving to God. In addition to worshiping in the temple, the

Session Nine: Power to the People   169

people demonstrated their thanksgiving by caring for needy people. When God fulfilled Pentecost by sending His Holy Spirit upon the disciples, the early Christians immediately began meeting one another's needs. When you and I are filled with God's Spirit, our response will be to willingly and gratefully share our resources and our lives with people in need.

Whose needs will you seek to meet this week? This month? This year?

What will you share with those individuals?

Total commitment

Before You Lead

Synopsis

King Herod the Great, one of the most powerful people who ever lived in the land of Israel, was a construction genius. He completed glorious building projects that incorporated amazing features for that time in history—sewers, running water, a man-made harbor, a stadium, a palace hung on the edge of an 1,800-foot mountain, a freshwater swimming pool in the Mediterranean Sea, and an outdoor theater with engineered acoustics. Why did he build? He wanted to create a lasting legacy to himself.

This video focuses on what Herod built in Caesarea, a seacoast city strategically located by the Via Maris at the northern end of the coastal plain of Israel. It examines the importance of using our talents and energies to build the right things with our lives. You'll view the ruins of Herod's man-made seaport, the largest of his day—even larger than the port of Alexandria—that made his realm a great commercial center. You'll see an aqueduct, amphitheater, and other impressive ruins and catch a glimpse of what life was like in that important city.

In addition to being Herod's crowning accomplishment, the pagan city of Caesarea was the entryway for the Roman worldview into the land of Israel. It was in Caesarea, where the humanistic views of Hellenism were widely accepted, that the early believers first shared the message of Jesus with non-Jews—both the common people and influential leaders.

Although Herod had a self-serving perspective on life, God used what he accomplished in Caesarea between 22 and 9 B.C. to give early believers a launching point from which to share the message of Jesus the Messiah with the Gentile world. Thus Christians today remember Caesarea as the seaport through which Paul traveled on his missionary journeys.

Little of Caesarea's glory remains, however, and participants will visualize the contrast between the city's former splendor and its present ruins. Following a Jewish riot in A.D. 64, the Roman army came to Caesarea and virtually leveled the city, which they considered to be a "symbol of Jewish arrogance." The Roman army then went on to destroy the temple in Jerusalem in A.D. 70.

Today, one can find fragments of marble and stone—the remains of Herod's genius—along the seashore. Most people remember him only as the cruel king who had many babies killed while trying to kill the baby Jesus. In contrast, Ray Vander Laan points out, small stones remind us of another person of the Bible—a youth named David who also became a great king of Israel. We remember David as the shepherd-warrior who killed a giant named Goliath with a common stone so "that the whole world will know that there is a God in Israel" (1 Samuel 17:46).

Key Points of This Lesson

1. *Herod built beautiful and amazing buildings and a seaport in Caesarea, yet all that's left of Herod's legacy are broken pieces of marble and stone—broken pieces of his dreams.* He lived to promote himself, and his greatness is of no consequence today.

2. *God used what Herod, a self-centered genius, had built in Caesarea in order to spread the gospel.* First, He poured His Spirit upon influential Gentiles in that city with whom Peter had shared the gospel. Then, Paul and other missionaries used Herod's seaport as a departure or returning point for their missionary journeys, which spread the gospel message to distant lands more quickly than was possible over land.

3. *Caesarea stood at the crossroads of culture, near the ancient trade route called the Via Maris.* There, the first Christians shared the message of Jesus with powerful people who shaped their culture. These first Christians were like standing stones placed by God on the crossroads of the world so that their lives could point people to God. In that pagan city, these Christians spoke and acted boldly, even though they were sometimes ridiculed and persecuted. As a result, many people came to know Israel's God and His Messiah.

Session Outline (54 minutes)

I. Introduction (4 minutes)
Welcome
What's to Come
Questions to Think About

II. Video Presentation "Total Commitment" (18 minutes)

III. Group Discovery (20 minutes)
Video Highlights
Small Group Bible Discovery

IV. Faith Lesson (10 minutes)
Time for Reflection
Action Points

V. Closing Prayer (2 minutes)

Materials

No additional materials are needed for this session. Simply view the video prior to leading the session so you are familiar with its main points.

total commitment

introduction

4 minutes

Welcome

> Assemble the participants together. Welcome them to session ten of *Faith Lessons on the Death and Resurrection of the Messiah.*

What's to Come

King Herod the Great lived to promote himself. In the influential Judean city of Caesarea, one of his greatest accomplishments, he built the greatest seaport in his world, a beautiful palace on the edge of the sea, aqueducts, a sewer system, an amphitheater, and other wonders.

Today, we'll learn about Herod and see footage of what remains of his handiwork in Caesarea. More important, however, Ray Vander Laan will challenge us to carefully consider the dreams we pursue. What will we live for? Will we live for ourselves? Or will we live for God? Let's begin this session by thinking about the things people pursue in order to promote themselves—to gain fame and fortune.

Questions to Think About

> *Participant's Guide page 170.*

Turn to page 170 of the Participant's Guide. Let's consider several questions that will help set the stage for the video we'll see in a few minutes.

> Ask each question and solicit a few responses from group members.

✏ 1. What do people today pursue in order to appear successful? What kinds of monuments to themselves do they build?

Suggested Responses: money, fame, great job title, having the "right" appearance, being seen with the "right" people, owning certain kinds of possessions. They build "empires" of power and influence, real estate and business; they amass great collections of art or artifacts; they make extensive donations to charities or the arts, etc.

✏ 2. What are some of the false truths that motivate people to spend lots of money, time, and energy to promote themselves and/or to build monuments to themselves?

Suggested Responses: They believe that promoting humankind is of greater importance than submission to God and the truths of the Bible; they consider what's here on earth to be of greatest importance; they desire to live life to the

SESSION TEN

total commitment

questions to think about

1. What do people today pursue in order to appear success-
    ful? What kinds of monuments to themselves do they
    build?

2. What are some of the false truths that motivate people to
    spend lots of money, time, and energy to promote them-
    selves and/or to build monuments to themselves?

3. What kind of legacy do you want to leave? What would
    you like other people to say about you after you die? Be
    specific. Write down your answer.

170

fullest; they are driven to do whatever is necessary to prove their worth in this life because to them that's all there is; they need to leave a monumental legacy in order for others to think highly of them; they believe they are what they do; they want the best for themselves; they believe that accumulating toys is what's really important; etc.

✏ **3.** What kind of legacy do you want to leave? What would you like other people to say about you after you die? Be specific. Write down your answer.

> Don't ask participants to share their responses to this question. Just give them a moment to think about it, encourage them to write down their answers, and start the video.

Keep in mind the legacy you would like to leave as we view the video.

video presentation

18 minutes   *Participant's Guide page 171.*

On page 171 of your Participant's Guide, you will find a space in which to take notes on key points as we watch this video.

Leader's Video Observations

The Wonders of Caesarea

Caesarea: The Gospel's Gateway to the Gentile World

The Stones Symbolizing Herod and David

SESSION TEN

total commitment

questions to think about

1. What do people today pursue in order to appear successful? What kinds of monuments to themselves do they
   build?

2. What are some of the false truths that motivate people to
   spend lots of money, time, and energy to promote themselves and/or to build monuments to themselves?

3. What kind of legacy do you want to leave? What would
   you like other people to say about you after you die? Be
   specific. Write down your answer.

Session Ten: Total Commitment   171

video notes

The Wonders of Caesarea

Caesarea: The Gospel's Gateway to the Gentile World

The Stones Symbolizing Herod and David

PLANNING NOTES:

Group Discovery

20 minutes

If your group has seven or more members, use the **Video Highlights** with the entire group (five minutes), then break into small groups of three to five to discuss the **Small Group Bible Discovery** (ten minutes). Then reassemble the group to discuss the key points discovered (five minutes).

If your group has fewer than seven members, begin with the **Video Highlights** (five minutes), then do one or more of the topics found in the **Small Group Bible Discovery** as a group (ten minutes). Finally, spend five minutes at the end discussing points that had an impact on participants.

Video Highlights (5 minutes)

Here you'll ask one or more of the following questions that directly relate to the video the participants have just seen.

1. What was so remarkable about Caesarea during Herod's time?

   Suggested Responses: the city's magnificence, its beautiful and modern public buildings, its seaside palace, its man-made harbor and seaport, its water and sewer system, its location at the crossroads of civilization, being the first place where many Gentiles heard the gospel, etc.

2. What were your thoughts about the way people today (including yourself) live as you discovered what Herod lived for and then saw the ruins of his great city?

   Suggested Responses: that nothing earthly lasts, that we must choose what we pursue carefully, that man can accomplish so much in life yet accomplish so little of eternal value, the perils of pride, etc.

3. Which truths stood out to you as Ray Vander Laan compared the two stones—the marble fragment and the ordinary sling stone—to Herod and David?

   Suggested Responses: only what's done for God is truly significant; when we live only for ourselves, our accomplishments have only temporal value; God can use anything—even that which is built in defiance of Him—to accomplish His work on earth; etc.

video highlights

1. What was so remarkable about Caesarea during Herod's time?

2. What were your thoughts about the way people today (including yourself) live as you discovered what Herod lived for and then saw the ruins of his great city?

3. Which truths stood out to you as Ray Vander Laan compared the two stones—the marble fragment and the ordinary sling stone—to Herod and David?

DATA FILE

The Glory of Caesarea

The Harbor

- No natural harbor existed, so Herod constructed a harbor using two breakwaters. The south breakwater was 600 yards (1800 feet) long, the north breakwater was 300 yards long.
- The base for these breakwaters was built of 40-foot by 50-foot concrete blocks that were poured under water at depths up to 100 feet.
- The towering lighthouse at the harbor entrance could be seen for miles.
- Harbor facilities included vaulted storage rooms along the breakwaters.

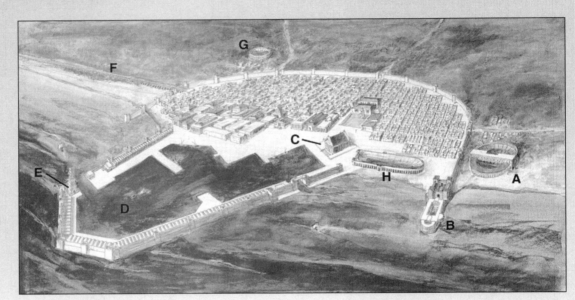

A Theater
B Palace
C Temple of
   Augustus
D Harbor (Sebastos)
E Lighthouse
F Aqueduct
G Amphitheater
H Hippodrome

The Palace

- Located on its own peninsula, the palace included a small port so that Herod's visitors could enter the palace without stepping into the city.
- Its pool—115 feet long, 60 feet wide, and 8 feet deep—extended into the salty Mediterranean Sea, yet it most likely held fresh water.
- Herod welcomed his guests with luxurious rooms that included a large dining hall, hot and cold baths, and a semicircular colonnade that extended out into the sea.

The Remains of the Pool in the Palace at Caesarea

- Most likely, Paul was held prisoner here for at least two years before he departed for Rome to appeal to the emperor.

DATA FILE

The Glory of Caesarea

A Theater	D Harbor (Sebastos)	G Amphitheater
B Palace	E Lighthouse	H Hippodrome
C Temple of Augustus	F Aqueduct	

The Harbor

- No natural harbor existed, so Herod constructed a harbor using two breakwaters. The south breakwater was 600 yards (1800 feet) long, the north breakwater was 300 yards long.
- The base for these breakwaters was built of 40-foot by 50-foot concrete blocks that were poured under water at depths up to 100 feet.
- The towering lighthouse at the harbor entrance could be seen for miles.
- Harbor facilities included vaulted storage rooms along the breakwaters.

The Remains of the Pool in the Palace at Caesarea

The Palace

- Located on its own peninsula, the palace included a small port so that Herod's visitors could enter the palace without stepping into the city.
- Its pool—115 feet long, 60 feet wide, and 8 feet deep—extended into the salty Mediterranean Sea, yet it most likely held fresh water.
- Herod welcomed his guests with luxurious rooms that included a large dining hall, hot and cold baths, and a semicircular colonnade that extended out into the sea.
- Most likely, Paul was held prisoner here for at least two years before he departed for Rome to appeal to the emperor.

The Theater

- It was located outside the city, probably because the bawdy and obscene performances that took place there were so offensive to Jewish residents.
- It was an important tool in promoting Hellenism—a people-centered lifestyle that glorified human knowledge, accomplishment, and experience.

The Theater

- It was located outside the city, probably because the bawdy and obscene performances that took place there were so offensive to Jewish residents.
- It was an important tool in promoting Hellenism—a people-centered lifestyle that glorified human knowledge, accomplishment, and experience.
- Positioned so that prevailing breezes provided amazingly good acoustics, the theater could hold about 4,000 spectators, who sat on stone benches.
- It may have been the site where Paul presented his magnificent defense of the gospel to Felix, Festus, Agrippa II, and Bernice.

The Temple of Augustus

- Dedicated to the goddess Roma and the "divine" emperor Augustus, it was one of the largest temples in the world at that time.
- Built on a great platform, the temple itself towered an additional 100 feet.
- It was coated with plaster made from marble dust, which made it gleam white in the sun.

The Hippodrome and Amphitheater

- It is not yet known if Herod actually built these facilities, but it is known that he promoted Hellenism by sponsoring sports festivals such as those that would take place in such facilities.
- The games that took place in these facilities were dedicated to pagan gods, were performed in the nude, at times involved human bloodshed, and were considered by religious Jews to be immoral.

The Aqueduct

- Since there was no fresh-water source in Caesarea, it provided the city and Herod's palace with water from springs on the slopes of Mount Carmel.
- It extended nearly nine miles from the city to the base of Mount Carmel, plus had an additional six miles of shafts and tunnels that burrowed into the mountain itself.
- It was an amazing engineering feat. It carried water in a plastered channel (much of which rested on a series of arches) across a river and through a channel cut into the sandstone hills.

The Palace
- Located on its own peninsula, the palace included a small port so that Herod's visitors could enter the palace without stepping into the city.
- Its pool—115 feet long, 60 feet wide, and 8 feet deep—extended into the salty Mediterranean Sea, yet it most likely held fresh water.
- Herod welcomed his guests with luxurious rooms that included a large dining hall, hot and cold baths, and a semicircular colonnade that extended out into the sea.
- Most likely, Paul was held prisoner here for at least two years before he departed for Rome to appeal to the emperor.

The Theater

- It was located outside the city, probably because the bawdy and obscene performances that took place there were so offensive to Jewish residents.
- It was an important tool in promoting Hellenism—a people-centered lifestyle that glorified human knowledge, accomplishment, and experience.

- Positioned so that prevailing breezes provided amazingly good acoustics, the theater could hold about 4,000 spectators, who sat on stone benches.
- It may have been the site where Paul presented his magnificent defense of the gospel to Felix, Festus, Agrippa II, and Bernice.

The Temple of Augustus
- Dedicated to the goddess Roma and the "divine" emperor Augustus, it was one of the largest temples in the world at that time.
- Built on a great platform, the temple itself towered an additional 100 feet.
- It was coated with plaster made from marble dust, which made it gleam white in the sun.

The Hippodrome and Amphitheater
- It is not yet known if Herod actually built these facilities, but it is known that he promoted Hellenism by sponsoring sports festivals such as those that would take place in such facilities.
- The games that took place in these facilities were dedicated to pagan gods, were performed in the nude, at times involved human bloodshed, and were considered by religious Jews to be immoral.

The Aqueduct
- Since there was no fresh-water source in Caesarea, it provided the city and Herod's palace with water from springs on the slopes of Mount Carmel.
- It extended nearly nine miles from the city to the base of Mount Carmel, plus had an additional six miles of shafts and tunnels that burrowed into the mountain itself.
- It was an amazing engineering feat. It carried water in a plastered channel (much of which rested on a series of arches) across a river and through a channel cut into the sandstone hills.

PLANNING NOTES:

small Group Bible Discovery

Participant's Guide pages 176–82.

During this time, a group with fewer than seven participants will stay together. A group larger than seven participants will break into small groups and reassemble as a large group during the final five minutes. Assign each group one of the following topics. If you have more than four small groups, assign some topics to more than one group.

Let's break into groups of three to five—people sitting near you—and study some of the Bible passages and truths mentioned in the video.

Turn to pages 176–82 in your Participant's Guide. There you'll find a list of four topics. You'll have ten minutes to read and discuss the topic I'll assign to you. Choose one person in your group to be a spokesperson for your group when we discuss these topics later.

Assign each group a topic.

I'll signal you when one minute is left.

After nine minutes, let participants know that they have one minute remaining. Then reassemble the entire group. After everyone is back together, begin asking one person from each small group to briefly share a key idea with the larger group. In some cases, you may not have time for every group to share their discoveries.

As time allows, let's briefly share the key ideas that your group discussed.

Topic A: Caesarea—Where Gentiles First Received God's Spirit

1. Who was Cornelius? Where did he live? What do we know about his lifestyle? (See Acts 10:1–2.)

    Suggested Responses: He was a Roman centurion in charge of one hundred troops. He lived in Caesarea. He prayed regularly, helped people in need, and was devout and God fearing.

2. Which unusual spiritual events happened to Cornelius and to Peter? (See Acts 10:3–16.)

    Suggested Responses: They both saw visions. Cornelius was instructed to send men to Joppa to bring Peter back to Caesarea. Meanwhile, Peter had a perplexing vision in which he saw heaven open and something like a large sheet being let down to earth. It contained all kinds of animals, reptiles, and birds that Peter, as a Jew, would have considered to be unclean. God's voice then told him to kill and eat them and said, "Do not call anything impure that God has made clean." As Peter pondered his vision, the men sent by Cornelius came to his door, and the Spirit instructed Peter to go with them.

3. After Cornelius's messengers found Peter, what unusual thing did Peter do? (See Acts 10:23–33.)

    Suggested Responses: He invited them into the home in which he was staying, and the next day he went with them to Caesarea (about thirty miles away) and

small group bible discovery

Topic A: Caesarea—Where Gentiles First Received God's Spirit

1. Who was Cornelius? Where did he live? What do we know about his lifestyle? (See Acts 10:1–2.)

2. Which unusual spiritual events happened to Cornelius and to Peter? (See Acts 10:3–16.)

3. After Cornelius's messengers found Peter, what unusual thing did Peter do? (See Acts 10:23–33.)

4. What happened as Peter shared the message of Jesus with the Gentiles in Caesarea? What was the response of the Jews who were with Peter? (See Acts 10:44–48.)

spoke to a large gathering of Gentiles in Cornelius's home. This was unusual because it was against Jewish law for a Jew to associate with Gentiles, but God had now commanded Peter—and thus the early Christians—to share the message of Jesus with the Gentiles.

4. What happened as Peter shared the message of Jesus with the Gentiles in Caesarea? What was the response of the Jews who were with Peter? (See Acts 10:44–48.)

Suggested Responses: God gave the Gentiles the Holy Spirit, which utterly amazed the Jews. Because the Gentiles had received the Holy Spirit just as the apostles had, the Jews baptized the Gentiles. People who are not Jewish would not have received the gospel unless God had opened the way, as He did in Caesarea.

Topic B: The Herods—A Legacy of Rejection

1. How did Herod Agrippa, grandson of Herod the Great who built Caesarea, respond to the message of Jesus being spread throughout his realm? (See Acts 12:1–4.)

Suggested Responses: He clearly didn't like it because he persecuted the believers; he had James put to death; when he saw that his persecution pleased the Jews, he arrested Peter with the intent of putting him on trial.

2. How did God thwart Herod Agrippa's plan? (See Acts 12:5–10, 18–19.)

Suggested Responses: An angel of the Lord freed Peter from prison, and Herod executed the soldiers who had been guarding Peter.

3. How would you describe Herod Agrippa's relationship to God? What was the result of his attitude? (See Acts 12:21–24.)

Suggested Responses: He apparently had little respect for God and even considered himself equal with God. Because he refused to give God the glory, an angel of God struck him down, and the Word of God continued to be multiplied.

4. What had Herod the Great done that no doubt influenced his grandson? (See Matthew 2:13–16.)

Suggested Response: In an effort to kill the infant Jesus, Herod the Great had killed all the boys in Bethlehem and its vicinity who were two years of age and younger.

5. What does this example of Herod emphasize concerning the legacy each of us will leave and the way in which the values of parents and grandparents can influence their children?

Suggested Responses: We each are influential in our own way; we won't know the full impact we'll have on other people and our culture as a whole. Herod the Great's values impacted his children and grandchildren deeply; he taught them to pursue paths of defiance against God.

small Group Bible Discovery

Topic A: Caesarea—Where Gentiles First Received God's Spirit

1. Who was Cornelius? Where did he live? What do we know about his lifestyle? (See Acts 10:1–2.)

2. Which unusual spiritual events happened to Cornelius and to Peter? (See Acts 10:3–16.)

3. After Cornelius's messengers found Peter, what unusual thing did Peter do? (See Acts 10:23–33.)

4. What happened as Peter shared the message of Jesus with the Gentiles in Caesarea? What was the response of the Jews who were with Peter? (See Acts 10:44–48.)

Topic B: The Herods—A Legacy of Rejection

1. How did Herod Agrippa, grandson of Herod the Great who built Caesarea, respond to the message of Jesus being spread throughout his realm? (See Acts 12:1–4.)

2. How did God thwart Herod Agrippa's plan? (See Acts 12:5–10, 18–19.)

3. How would you describe Herod Agrippa's relationship to God? What was the result of his attitude? (See Acts 12:21–24.)

4. What had Herod the Great done that no doubt influenced his grandson? (See Matthew 2:13–16.)

5. What does this example of Herod emphasize concerning the legacy each of us will leave and the way in which the values of parents and grandparents can influence their children?

PLANNING NOTES:

THE HEROD FAMILY TREE

Antipater (Idumaean)

HEROD THE GREAT

- Died in 4 B.C.
- Effective administrator, cruel, supported by Rome
- Visited by wise men, killed Bethlehem babies
- Greatest builder the ancient Near East ever knew
- Had 10 wives, three of whom were:

Cleopatra	Miriam		Malthace
PHILIP		**ANTIPAS**	**ARCHELAUS**

PHILIP

- Effective, popular king
- Ruled north and east of Galilee
- Built Caesarea Philippi

(Luke 3:1)

ANTIPAS

- Effective king
- Ruled Galilee and Perea
- Killed John the Baptist
- Built Tiberias and Sepphoris
- Tried Jesus before crucifixion

(Luke 3:19; Luke 23:7–12; Luke 9:7–9; Matthew 14:1–12; Luke 13:32)

ARCHELAUS

- Poor ruler, deposed by Romans
- Ruled Judea
- Mary and Joseph settle in Nazareth to avoid him

(Matthew 2:22)

HEROD AGRIPPA I

(Grandson of Herod the Great)

- King of Judea
- Killed James, put Peter in prison
- Struck down by an angel

(Acts 12:1–24)

AGRIPPA II

- King of Judea
- Paul defends his faith before him

(Acts 25:13–26:32)

DRUSILLA

(Sisters of Agrippa II)

- Married Felix, the Roman governor

(Acts 24:24)

BERNICE

- With her brother at Paul's defense

(Acts 25:13)

THE HEROD FAMILY TREE

Antipater (Idumaean)

HEROD THE GREAT

- Died in 4 B.C.
- Effective administrator, cruel, supported by Rome
- Visited by wise men, killed Bethlehem babies
- Greatest builder the ancient Near East ever knew
- Had 10 wives, three of whom were:

Cleopatra	Miriam	Malthace
PHILIP		**ANTIPAS**	**ARCHELAUS**

PHILIP

- Effective, popular king
- Ruled north and east of Galilee
- Built Caesarea Philippi

(Luke 3:1)

ANTIPAS

- Effective king
- Ruled Galilee and Perea
- Killed John the Baptist
- Built Tiberias and Sepphoris
- Tried Jesus before crucifixion

(Luke 3:19; Luke 23:7–12; Luke 9:7–9; Matthew 14:1–12; Luke 13:32)

ARCHELAUS

- Poor ruler, deposed by Romans
- Ruled Judea
- Mary and Joseph settle in Nazareth to avoid him

(Matthew 2:22)

HEROD AGRIPPA I

(Grandson of Herod the Great)

- King of Judea
- Killed James, put Peter in prison
- Struck down by an angel

(Acts 12:1–24)

AGRIPPA II

- King of Judea
- Paul defends his faith before him

(Acts 25:13–26:32)

DRUSILLA

Sisters of Agrippa II

- Married Felix, the Roman governor

(Acts 24:24)

BERNICE

- With her brother at Paul's defense

(Acts 25:13)

DATA FILE

The Legacy of the Herods: Generations of Hardened Hearts
The Herod family had many encounters with Jesus and His message, yet no one in this family believed.

Herod the Great	Learned about Jesus' birth from the wise men. Responded by trying to kill the infant Jesus (Matthew 2:1–16).
Antipas (Herod the Great's son)	Heard about Jesus; listened to John the Baptist's teachings; met Jesus but sent Him to Pilate (Mark 6:14–20; Luke 23:8–12).
Agrippa I (grandson of Herod the Great) to whom Emperor Claudius gave Herod the Great's entire kingdom.	Arrested Christians; had James put to death; imprisoned Peter; had to figure out how Peter escaped (Acts 12:1–5, 18–19). Died when he allowed people to treat him like a god (Acts 12:21–23).
Drusilla (daughter of Agrippa I)	Listened to Paul as he spoke about faith in Christ Jesus (Acts 24:24–26).
Agrippa II (great-grandson of Herod the Great)	Discussed Paul's case in Caesarea with governor Festus; heard Paul's conversion testimony; recognized that Paul was trying to persuade him to become a Christian (Acts 25:13–14, 23; 26:1–29).
Bernice (great-granddaughter of Herod the Great)	Accompanied Agrippa II and heard Paul's conversion testimony (Acts 25:13–14, 23; 26:1–29).

Topic C: Jesus' Testimony to a Culture Shaper

✏ 1.   Who was Pilate? (See Matthew 27:11.)

Suggested Response: The Roman governor of Judea.

✏ 2.   What do the questions Pilate asked of Jesus in the following verses reveal about Pilate?

Matthew 27:11

Suggested Responses: He wanted to hear Jesus testify about His identity, showing relative indifference to Jesus' claims and the miracles Jesus had done.

Matthew 27:13

Suggested Responses: Pilate couldn't understand why Jesus wouldn't defend Himself against the chief priests' and elders' accusations; he was insecure and ready to defend himself at all costs and protect his position.

178   The Death and Resurrection of the Messiah

DATA FILE

The Legacy of the Herods: Generations of Hardened Hearts
The Herod family had many encounters with Jesus and His message, yet no one in this family believed.

Herod the Great	Learned about Jesus' birth from the wise men. Responded by trying to kill the infant Jesus (Matthew 2:1–16).
Antipas (Herod the Great's son)	Heard about Jesus; listened to John the Baptist's teachings; met Jesus but sent Him to Pilate (Mark 6:14–20; Luke 23:8–12).
Agrippa I (grandson of Herod the Great) to whom Emperor Claudius gave Herod the Great's entire kingdom.	Arrested Christians; had James put to death; imprisoned Peter; had to figure out how Peter escaped (Acts 12:1–5, 18–19). Died when he allowed people to treat him like a god (Acts 12:21–23).
Drusilla (daughter of Agrippa I)	Listened to Paul as he spoke about faith in Christ Jesus (Acts 24:24–26).
Agrippa II (great-grandson of Herod the Great)	Discussed Paul's case in Caesarea with governor Festus; heard Paul's conversion testimony; recognized that Paul was trying to persuade him to become a Christian (Acts 25:13–14, 23; 26:1–29).
Bernice (great-granddaughter of Herod the Great)	Accompanied Agrippa II and heard Paul's conversion testimony (Acts 25:13–14, 23; 26:1–29).

180   The Death and Resurrection of the Messiah

Topic C: Jesus' Testimony to a Culture Shaper

1. Who was Pilate? (See Matthew 27:11.)

2. What do the questions Pilate asked of Jesus in the following verses reveal about Pilate?
   Matthew 27:11

   Matthew 27:13

   Matthew 27:17

   Matthew 27:19–21

   John 18:36–38

3. What do Jesus' answers to Pilate (John 18:33–37) reveal about His desire to tailor His message to fit Pilate's pagan worldview?

4. To whom are Jesus' followers called to be witnesses? (See Matthew 28:19–20; Acts 1:8; Luke 21:10–13.)

Matthew 27:17

> *Suggested Response:* Pilate made key decisions based upon their popularity among the mobs.

Matthew 27:19–21

> *Suggested Response:* Even after his wife's urging, Pilate refused to make his own ruling and again asked the people what they wanted him to do.

John 18:36–38

> *Suggested Responses:* Pilate was skeptical about Jesus and cynical about truth. A believer in Hellenism, Pilate believed that truth was dependent on human reason. Thus "truth" to him was constantly changing and to be questioned.

3. What do Jesus' answers to Pilate (John 18:33–37) reveal about His desire to tailor His message to fit Pilate's pagan worldview?

> *Suggested Responses:* Jesus' questions reveal His desire to cause Pilate to think for himself; He was asking Pilate to make a commitment about what he knew to be true; He introduced the fact that what's on earth is not all there is and emphasized the reality of the supernatural realm of which He was King; He also testified of the truth, something about which Pilate was curious but cynical.

4. To whom are Jesus' followers called to be witnesses? (See Matthew 28:19–20; Acts 1:8; Luke 21:10–13.)

> *Suggested Responses:* to all nations; to the ends of the earth; in churches and prisons, to kings and governors.

Topic D: Caesarea — Launching Point for Spreading the News of Jesus

Herod built a seaport and cosmopolitan city that would play a vital role in spreading the news of Jesus throughout the Gentile world, even though Herod built them solely to bolster his ego and glorify himself.

1. Where did Philip share Jesus' message? (See Acts 8:40; 21:8.)

> *Suggested Response:* in Caesarea.

2. Where did the Gospel first reach the Gentiles? (See Acts 10:1, 24–33, 44–48.)

> *Suggested Response:* in Caesarea.

3. What role did Caesarea play in each of Paul's missionary journeys?

Acts 9:30; 13–14	*began at Caesarea*
Acts 15–18	*began and ended at Caesarea*
Acts 18–21	*ended at Caesarea*
Acts 27–28	*began and ended at Caesarea*

4. Because of a plot against Paul's life, he was sent to which city where he was able to share Christ with two Roman governors and Herod Agrippa II? (See Acts 23:23–24, 27; 25:1–6, 23.)

> *Suggested Response:* Caesarea.

180   The Death and Resurrection of the Messiah

Topic C: Jesus' Testimony to a Culture Shaper

1. Who was Pilate? (See Matthew 27:11.)

2. What do the questions Pilate asked of Jesus in the following verses reveal about Pilate?

   Matthew 27:11

   Matthew 27:13

   Matthew 27:17

   Matthew 27:19–21

   John 18:36–38

3. What do Jesus' answers to Pilate (John 18:33–37) reveal about His desire to tailor His message to fit Pilate's pagan worldview?

4. To whom are Jesus' followers called to be witnesses? (See Matthew 28:19–20; Acts 1:8; Luke 21:10–13.)

Session Ten: Total Commitment   181

Topic D: Caesarea—Launching Point for Spreading the News of Jesus

Herod built a seaport and cosmopolitan city that would play a vital role in spreading the news of Jesus throughout the Gentile world, even though Herod built them solely to bolster his ego and glorify himself.

1. Where did Philip share Jesus' message? (See Acts 8:40; 21:8.)

2. Where did the Gospel first reach the Gentiles? (See Acts 10:1, 24–33, 44–48.)

3. What role did Caesarea play in each of Paul's missionary journeys?

   Acts 9:30; 13–14

   Acts 15–18

   Acts 18–21

   Acts 27–28

4. Because of a plot against Paul's life, he was sent to which city where he was able to share Christ with two Roman governors and Herod Agrippa II? (See Acts 23:23–24, 27; 25:1–6, 23.)

PLANNING NOTES:

DATA FILE

Herod Built the Seaport at Caesarea Because He:

- Needed a port on the Mediterranean because existing ones were outside his kingdom or hostile to him.
- Recognized Caesarea's strategic location along the Via Maris, the trade route between Rome and such regions as Persia, Babylonia, the Orient, and the Arabian Peninsula.
- Needed a vast source of revenue to fund his great building projects, such as the Temple Mount in Jerusalem, his palace at Masada, and Jericho.
- Sought to expand his influence, both to curry favor with Rome and to bring Roman culture and military support to Judea.
- Wanted to demonstrate his greatness.
- Needed to create a buffer zone to keep the Parfians and Idumeans out of the Roman Empire.

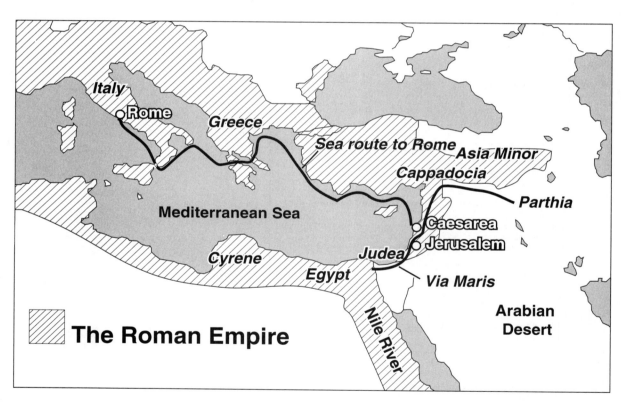

182   The Death and Resurrection of the Messiah

DATA FILE

Herod Built the Seaport at Caesarea Because He:

- Needed a port on the Mediterranean because existing ones were outside his kingdom or hostile to him.
- Recognized Caesarea's strategic location along the Via Maris, the trade route between Rome and such regions as Persia, Babylonia, the Orient, and the Arabian Peninsula.
- Needed a vast source of revenue to fund his great building projects, such as the Temple Mount in Jerusalem, his palace at Masada, and Jericho.
- Sought to expand his influence, both to curry favor with Rome and to bring Roman culture and military support to Judea.
- Wanted to demonstrate his greatness.
- Needed to create a buffer zone to keep the Parfians and Idumeans out of the Roman Empire.

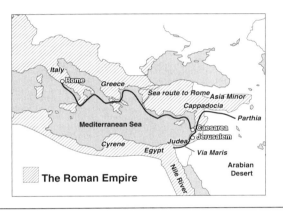

The Roman Empire

faith Lesson

Time for Reflection (6 minutes)

It's time for each of us to think quietly about how we can apply what we've learned today. On pages 183–84 of the Participant's Guide, you'll find a passage of Scripture. Let's each read this passage silently and take the next few minutes to consider how the apostle Paul used his time and energy while imprisoned in Caesarea to proclaim the truth of the gospel to the surrounding secular culture.

Please do not talk during this time. It's a time when we all can reflect on how God might have each of us bring Jesus' message to our world.

> *The Scripture passage and questions are reproduced in their entirety in the Participant's Guide on pages 183–85.*

Then he called two of his centurions and ordered them, "Get ready a detachment of two hundred soldiers, seventy horsemen and two hundred spearmen to go to Caesarea at nine tonight. Provide mounts for Paul so that he may be taken safely to Governor Felix."

ACTS 23:23–24

More than two years later:

. . . Agrippa and Bernice came with great pomp and entered the audience room with the high ranking officers and the leading men of the city. At the command of Festus, Paul was brought in. . . . Then Agrippa said to Paul, "You have permission to speak for yourself." So Paul motioned with his hand and began his defense: "King Agrippa, I consider myself fortunate to stand before you today as I make my defense against all the accusations of the Jews, and especially so because you are well acquainted with all the Jewish customs and controversies. Therefore, I beg you to listen to me patiently. . . . "So then, King Agrippa, I was not disobedient to the vision from heaven. First to those in Damascus, then to those in Jerusalem and in all Judea, and to the Gentiles also, I preached that they should repent and turn to God and prove their repentance by their deeds. That is why the Jews seized me in the temple courts and tried to kill me. But I have had God's help to this very day, and so I stand here and testify to small and great alike. I am saying nothing beyond what the prophets and Moses said would happen—that the Christ would suffer and, as the first to rise from the dead, would proclaim light to his own people and to the Gentiles." At this point Festus interrupted Paul's defense. "You are out of your mind, Paul!" he shouted. "Your great learning is driving you insane." "I am not insane, most excellent Festus," Paul replied. "What I am saying is true and reasonable. The king is familiar with these things, and I can speak freely to him. I am convinced that none of this has escaped his notice, because it was not done in a corner. King Agrippa, do you believe the prophets? I know you do." Then Agrippa said to Paul, "Do you think that in such a short time you can persuade me to be a Christian?" Paul replied, "Short time or long—I pray God that not only

faith Lesson

Time for Reflection

Read the following passage of Scripture silently and consider how the apostle Paul used his time and energy while imprisoned in Caesarea to proclaim the truth of the gospel to the surrounding secular culture. Then reflect on how God might have you bring Jesus' message to your world.

> Then he called two of his centurions and ordered them, "Get ready a detachment of two hundred soldiers, seventy horsemen and two hundred spearmen to go to Caesarea at nine tonight. Provide mounts for Paul so that he may be taken safely to Governor Felix."

> ACTS 23:23–24

More than two years later:

> . . . Agrippa and Bernice came with great pomp and entered the audience room with the high ranking officers and the leading men of the city. At the command of Festus, Paul was brought in. . . . Then Agrippa said to Paul, "You have permission to speak for yourself." So Paul motioned with his hand and began his defense: "King Agrippa, I consider myself fortunate to stand before you today as I make my defense against all the accusations of the Jews, and especially so because you are well acquainted with all the Jewish customs and controversies. Therefore, I beg you to listen to me patiently. . . . So then, King Agrippa, I was not disobedient to the vision from heaven. First to those in Damascus, then to those in Jerusalem and in all Judea, and to the Gentiles also, I preached that they should repent and turn to God and prove their repentance by their deeds. That is why the Jews seized me in the temple courts and tried to kill me. But I have had God's help to this very day, and so I stand here and testify to small and great alike. I am saying nothing beyond what the prophets and Moses said would happen—that the

> Christ would suffer and, as the first to rise from the dead, would proclaim light to his own people and to the Gentiles." At this point Festus interrupted Paul's defense. "You are out of your mind, Paul!" he shouted. "Your great learning is driving you insane." "I am not insane, most excellent Festus," Paul replied. "What I am saying is true and reasonable. The king is familiar with these things, and I can speak freely to him. I am convinced that none of this has escaped his notice, because it was not done in a corner. King Agrippa, do you believe the prophets? I know you do." Then Agrippa said to Paul, "Do you think that in such a short time you can persuade me to be a Christian?" Paul replied, "Short time or long—I pray God that not only you but all who are listening to me today may become what I am, except for these chains."

> ACTS 25:23; 26:1–3, 19–29

1. Paul, even though he was a prisoner, boldly presented Jesus' message to the Gentile authorities in Caesarea. Are you eager to testify of the truth of the gospel to non-Christians, or do you tend to "hide" from secular culture?

2. In Caesarea, as in our culture today, a war for the souls of people was being fought. Note the many ways in which Paul sought to convince his listeners of the truth of the gospel message. How might you bring Jesus' message to the people around you this week? In what ways can you present the gospel?

you but all who are listening to me today may become what I am, except for these chains."

ACTS 25:23; 26:1–3, 19–29

1. Paul, even though he was a prisoner, boldly presented Jesus' message to the Gentile authorities in Caesarea. Are you eager to testify of the truth of the gospel to non-Christians, or do you tend to "hide" from secular culture?

2. In Caesarea, as in our culture today, a war for the souls of people was being fought. Note the many ways in which Paul sought to convince his listeners of the truth of the gospel message. How might you bring Jesus' message to the people around you this week? In what ways can you present the gospel?

3. God gave Paul education, intelligence, eloquence, boldness—wonderful stones with which to build a legacy. Even when he was imprisoned and his sphere of influence was limited by others, he used every opportunity to deliver the message of Jesus the Messiah to the secular culture. What limits your sphere of influence? Given that limitation, what opportunities do you have to deliver the gospel message?

> As soon as participants have spent six minutes reflecting on the above questions, get the entire group's attention and move to the next section.

Action Points (4 minutes)

> *The following points are reproduced on pages 185–87 of the Participant's Guide:*

Now it's time to wrap up our session.

> Give participants a moment to transition from their thoughtfulness to giving you their full attention.

I'd like to take a moment to summarize the key points we explored. After I have reviewed these points, I will give you a moment to jot down an action step (or steps) that you will commit to this week as a result of what you have learned today.

> Read each point and pause after the final point so that participants can consider and write out their commitment.

1. *Herod built magnificent buildings, a harbor, and a seaport in Caesarea, yet all that's left of Herod's legacy are broken pieces of marble and stone—broken pieces of his dreams.* He lived to promote himself, and his greatness is of no consequence today.

In contrast, a boy named David used a common stone to kill Goliath and honor God. What David did to Goliath in the valley of Elah is a witness to what happens when a person uses his or her life to honor God and point other people toward Him. David lived in obedience to God . . . and his memory lives on. In fact, Jesus was born into the lineage of David—and lives today as the "chosen and precious cornerstone" of our faith (1 Peter 2:6).

Christ would suffer and, as the first to rise from the dead, would proclaim light to his own people and to the Gentiles." At this point Festus interrupted Paul's defense. "You are out of your mind, Paul!" he shouted. "Your great learning is driving you insane." "I am not insane, most excellent Festus," Paul replied. "What I am saying is true and reasonable. The king is familiar with these things, and I can speak freely to him. I am convinced that none of this has escaped his notice, because it was not done in a corner. King Agrippa, do you believe the prophets? I know you do." Then Agrippa said to Paul, "Do you think that in such a short time you can persuade me to be a Christian?" Paul replied, "Short time or long—I pray God that not only you but all who are listening to me today may become what I am, except for these chains."

ACTS 25:23; 26:1–3, 19–29

1. Paul, even though he was a prisoner, boldly presented Jesus' message to the Gentile authorities in Caesarea. Are you eager to testify of the truth of the gospel to non-Christians, or do you tend to "hide" from secular culture?

2. In Caesarea, as in our culture today, a war for the souls of people was being fought. Note the many ways in which Paul sought to convince his listeners of the truth of the gospel message. How might you bring Jesus' message to the people around you this week? In what ways can you present the gospel?

3. God gave Paul education, intelligence, eloquence, boldness—wonderful stones with which to build a legacy. Even when he was imprisoned and his sphere of influence was limited by others, he used every opportunity to deliver the message of Jesus the Messiah to the secular culture. What limits your sphere of influence? Given that limitation, what opportunities do you have to deliver the gospel message?

Action Points

Take a moment to review the key points you explored today. Then write down an action step (or steps) that you will commit to this week as a result of what you have discovered.

1. *Herod built magnificent buildings, a harbor, and a seaport in Caesarea, yet all that's left of Herod's legacy are broken pieces of marble and stone—broken pieces of his dreams.* He lived to promote himself, and his greatness is of no consequence today.

   In contrast, a boy named David used a common stone to kill Goliath and honor God. What David did to Goliath in the valley of Elah is a witness to what happens when a person uses his or her life to honor God and point other people toward Him. David lived in obedience to God . . . and his memory lives on. In fact, Jesus was born into the lineage of David—and lives today as the "chosen and precious cornerstone" of our faith (1 Peter 2:6).

   God has given each of us "stones" with which to build a legacy—talents, opportunities, resources, training, intelligence, networks. How are you using the life-building "stones" God has given you? For whom are you building? Are you building your life around yourself, in which case other people will someday pick up the broken pieces of

PLANNING NOTES:

God has given each of us "stones" with which to build a legacy—talents, opportunities, resources, training, intelligence, networks. How are you using the life-building "stones" God has given you? For whom are you building? Are you building your life around yourself, in which case other people will someday pick up the broken pieces of your dreams? Or are you building for God, honoring Him with your life and building something that will last for eternity?

2. *God used what Herod—a self-centered genius who rejected God and highly esteemed pagan values—built in Caesarea in order to spread the gospel.* First, God poured His Spirit upon influential Gentiles in that city with whom Peter had shared the gospel. Then Paul stood in the city that Herod had built and proclaimed the gospel to the highest rulers of that region. Paul and other early missionaries used Herod's seaport in their travels, which spread the gospel message to more distant lands.

Just as God used Caesarea to promote His kingdom, He has used technological and man-made advances to help spread the gospel. Which resources available to you could be used to further the kingdom of God, to address the pagan values and practices in our own culture?

How will you use your resources to honor God and draw other people closer to Him this week?

3. *Caesarea stood at the crossroads of culture, near the ancient trade route called the Via Maris.* There, the first Christians shared the message of Jesus with powerful people who shaped their culture. Those first Christians were like standing stones. God placed them on the crossroads of the world so that their lives could point people toward God. In that pagan city, the Christians spoke and acted boldly, even though they were sometimes ridiculed and persecuted. As a result, many people around the world—including modern-day non-Jewish Christians—came to know Israel's God and His Messiah.

Now it's your turn. You live at a crossroads. The world is watching you. You must make a choice. Will you succumb to the self-indulgent and self-glorifying culture of our day? Will you allow your culture to woo you away from God and encourage you to seek pleasure apart from God? Or will you act as a standing stone, boldly proclaiming God's message? Will you live out your commitment to Him to a watching world?

Where do you stand? What is your choice?

closing prayer

2 minutes

I hope this lesson has caused you, as it has me, to think more about the legacy we each are building with the stones God has given to us. I hope it will prompt each of us to discover how God wants us to use what He has provided in our culture to impact people for Christ—just as the early Christians used the seaport in Caesarea. Let's close in prayer.

your dreams? Or are you building for God, honoring Him with your life and building something that will last for eternity?

2. *God used what Herod—a self-centered genius who rejected God and highly esteemed pagan values—built in Caesarea in order to spread the gospel.* First, God poured His Spirit upon influential Gentiles in that city with whom Peter had shared the gospel. Then Paul stood in the city that Herod had built and proclaimed the gospel to the highest rulers of that region. Paul and other early missionaries used Herod's seaport in their travels, which spread the gospel message to more distant lands.

    Just as God used Caesarea to promote His kingdom, He has used technological and man-made advances to help spread the gospel. Which resources available to you could be used to further the kingdom of God, to address the pagan values and practices in our own culture?

    How will you use your resources to honor God and draw other people closer to Him this week?

3. *Caesarea stood at the crossroads of culture, near the ancient trade route called the Via Maris.* There, the first Christians shared the message of Jesus with powerful people who shaped their culture. Those first Christians

were like standing stones. God placed them on the cross-roads of the world so that their lives could point people toward God. In that pagan city, the Christians spoke and acted boldly, even though they were sometimes ridiculed and persecuted. As a result, many people around the world—including modern-day non-Jewish Christians—came to know Israel's God and His Messiah.

Now it's your turn. You live at a crossroads. The world is watching you. You must make a choice. Will you succumb to the self-indulgent and self-glorifying culture of our day? Will you allow your culture to woo you away from God and encourage you to seek pleasure apart from God? Or will you act as a standing stone, boldly proclaiming God's message? Will you live out your commitment to Him to a watching world?

Where do you stand? What is your choice?

Dear God, thank You for giving us various talents, abilities, and opportunities. We are all different, yet each of us has the opportunity to use what You've given to build a lasting legacy. Help us to make the right choices about what's important in this life. Help us to use what You've given us to share the message of Jesus with other people who need You so much. Amen.

additional resources

History

Connolly, Peter. *Living in the Time of Jesus of Nazareth.* Tel Aviv: Steimatzky, 1983.

Ward, Kaari. *Jesus and His Times.* New York: Reader's Digest, 1987.

Whiston, William, trans. *The Works of Josephus: Complete and Unabridged.* Peabody, Mass.: Hendrikson Publishers, 1987.

Wood, Leon. Revised by David O'Brien. *A Survey of Israel's History.* Grand Rapids: Zondervan, 1986.

Jewish Roots of Christianity

Stern, David H. *Jewish New Testament Commentary.* Clarksville, Md.: Jewish New Testament Publications, 1992.

Wilson, Marvin R. *Our Father Abraham: Jewish Roots of the Christian Faith.* Grand Rapids: Eerdmans, 1986.

Young, Brad H. *Jesus the Jewish Theologian.* Peabody, Mass.: Hendrickson Publishers, 1995.

Geography

Beitzel, Barry J. *The Moody Atlas of Bible Lands.* Chicago: Moody Press, 1993.

Gardner, Joseph L. *Reader's Digest Atlas of the Bible.* New York: Reader's Digest, 1993.

General Background

Alexander, David, and Pat Alexander, eds. *Eerdmans' Handbook to the Bible.* Grand Rapids: Eerdmans, 1983.

Butler, Trent C., ed. *Holman Bible Dictionary.* Nashville: Holman Bible Publishers, 1991.

Edersheim, Alfred. *The Life and Times of Jesus the Messiah.* Peabody, Mass.: Hendrickson Publishers, 1994.

Archaeological Background

Charlesworth, James H. *Jesus Within Judaism: New Light from Exciting Archaeological Discoveries.* New York: Doubleday, 1988.

Finegan, Jack. *The Archaeology of the New Testament: The Life of Jesus and the Beginning of the Early Church.* Princeton: Princeton University Press, 1978.

Mazar, Amihai. *Archaeology of the Land of the Bible: 10,000–586 B.C.E.* New York: Doubleday, 1990.

To learn more about the specific backgrounds of this set of videos, consult the following resources:

Avigad, Nahman. "Jerusalem in Flames—The Burnt House Captures a Moment in Time." *Biblical Archaeology Review* (November-December 1983).

Barkey, Gabriel. "The Garden Tomb—Was Jesus Buried Here?" *Biblical Archaeology Review* (March-April 1986).

Ben Dov, Meir. "Herod's Mighty Temple Mount." *Biblical Archaeology Review* (November-December 1986).

Bivin, David. "The Miraculous Catch." *Jerusalem Perspective* (March-April 1992).

Burrell, Barbara, Kathryn Gleason, and Ehud Netzer. "Uncovering Herod's Seaside Palace." *Biblical Archaeology Review* (May-June 1993).

Edersheim, Alfred. *The Temple*. London: James Clarke & Co., 1959.

Edwards, William D., Wesley J. Gabel, and Floyd E. Hosmer. "On the Physical Death of Jesus Christ." *Journal of American Medical Association (JAMA)* (March 21, 1986).

Flusser, David. "To Bury Caiaphas, Not to Praise Him." *Jerusalem Perspective* (July-October 1991).

Greenhut, Zvi. "Burial Cave of the Caiaphas Family." *Biblical Archaeology Review* (September-October 1992).

Hareuveni, Nogah. *Nature in Our Biblical Heritage*. Kiryat Ono, Israel: Neot Kedumim, Ltd., 1980.

Hepper, F. Nigel. *Baker Encyclopedia of Bible Plants: Flowers and Trees, Fruits and Vegetables, Ecology*. Ed. by J. Gordon Melton. Grand Rapids: Baker, 1993.

"The 'High Priest' of the Jewish Quarter." *Biblical Archaeology Review* (May-June 1992).

Hirschfeld, Yizhar, and Giora Solar. "Sumptuous Roman Baths Uncovered Near Sea of Galilee." *Biblical Archaeology Review* (November-December 1984).

Hohlfelder, Robert L. "Caesarea Maritima: Herod the Great's City on the Sea." *National Geographic* (February 1987).

Holum, Kenneth G. *King Herod's Dream: Caesarea on the Sea*. New York: W. W. Norton, 1988.

Mazar, Benjamin. "Excavations Near Temple Mount Reveal Splendors of Herodian Jerusalem." *Biblical Archaeology Review* (July-August 1980).

Nun, Mendel. *Ancient Stone Anchors and Net Sinkers from the Sea of Galilee*. Israel: Kibbutz Ein Gev, 1993. (Also available from *Jerusalem Perspective*.)

_____. "Fish, Storms, and a Boat." *Jerusalem Perspective* (March-April 1990).

_____. "The Kingdom of Heaven Is Like a Seine." *Jerusalem Perspective* (November-December 1989).

_____. "Net Upon the Waters: Fish and Fishermen in Jesus' Time." *Biblical Archaeology Review* (November-December 1993).

_____. *The Sea of Galilee and Its Fishermen in the New Testament*. Israel: Kibbutz Ein Gev, 1993. (Also available from *Jerusalem Perspective*.)

Pileggi, David. "A Life on the Kinneret." *Jerusalem Perspective* (November-December 1989).

Pixner, Bargil. *With Jesus Through Galilee According to the Fifth Gospel*. Rosh Pina, Israel: Corazin Publishing, 1992.

Pope, Marvin, H. "Hosanna: What It Really Means." *Bible Review* (April 1988).

Riech, Ronny. "Ossuary Inscriptions from the Caiaphas Tomb." *Jerusalem Perspective* (July-October 1991).

_____. "Six Stone Water Jars." *Jerusalem Perspective* (July-September 1995).

Ritmeyer, Kathleen. "A Pilgrim's Journey." *Biblical Archaeology Review* (November-December 1989).

Ritmeyer, Kathleen, and Leen Ritmeyer. "Reconstructing Herod's Temple Mount in Jerusalem." *Biblical Archaeology Review* (November-December 1989).

_____. "Reconstructing the Triple Gate." *Biblical Archaeology Review* (November-December 1989).

Ritmeyer, Leen. "The Ark of the Covenant: Where It Stood in Solomon's Temple." *Biblical Archaeology Review* (January-February 1996).

_____. "Quarrying and Transporting Stones for Herod's Temple Mount." *Biblical Archaeology Review* (November-December 1989).

Ritmeyer, Leen, and Kathleen Ritmeyer. "Akeldama: Potter's Field of High Priest's Tomb." *Biblical Archaeology Review.* (November–December 1994).

Sarna, Nahum M. *The JPS Torah Commentary: Exodus.* New York: Jewish Publication Society, 1991.

"Sea of Galilee Museum Opens Its Doors." *Jerusalem Perspective* (July-September 1995).

Shanks, Hershel. "Excavating in the Shadow of the Temple Mount." *Biblical Archaeology Review* (November-December 1986).

"Shavuot." *Encyclopedia Judaica,* Volume 14. Jerusalem: Keter Publishing House, 1980.

Stern, David. *Jewish New Testament Commentary.* Clarksville, Md.: Jewish New Testament Publications, 1992.

Taylor, Joan E. "The Garden of Gethsemane." *Biblical Archaeology Review* (July-August 1995).

Tzaferis, Vassilios. "Crucifixion—The Archaeological Evidence." *Biblical Archaeology Review* (January-February 1985).

_____. "A Pilgrimage to the Site of the Swine Miracle." *Biblical Archaeology Review* (March-April 1989).

_____. "Susita." *Biblical Archaeology Review* (September-October 1990).

Vann, Lindley. "Herod's Harbor Construction Recovered Underwater." *Biblical Archaeology Review* (May-June 1983).

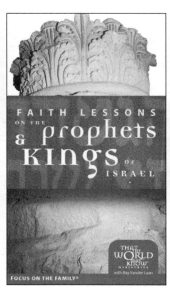
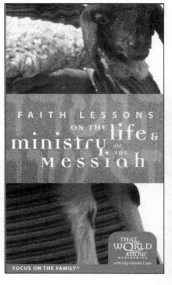

Travel back in time to see the sights, hear the sounds, and experience the wonder of Jesus— all through the power of interactive CD-ROM.

Jesus
An Interactive Journey

CD-ROM

0-310-67888-9

Imagine traveling back in time for a life-changing encounter with Christ . . . meeting the people who knew him . . . retracing his footsteps . . . seeing firsthand what his life was like.

Now, through the cutting-edge technology of interactive CD-ROM, you can make that incredible voyage—back to the life and times of Jesus! This exciting multimedia adventure takes you there, giving you an entirely new appreciation for the fascinating historical, geographical, and cultural backdrop that will enhance your understanding of the Gospel.

An innovative "Visitor's Center" is your gateway to more than 180 different avenues of study, from Christ's birth to his resurrection. With a click of the mouse, you'll be guided to dozens of colorful locales, where you'll experience through the eyes and ears of ancient Jews and Romans what Christ's world was really like.

Or take a self-guided tour and stroll at your own pace through the lively marketplace to learn about trade and commerce, pause to listen in on the people, or go to the synagogue to gain a better understanding of the religious practices of the day.

The high technology and vast amount of material in this unique presentation will captivate you for hours, while providing a solid understanding of the Gospel and its relevance to today's believer. It's great for personal and family Bible study, Christian schools, and a wide variety of church uses.

Compatible with Windows® 95 and Windows® 3.1

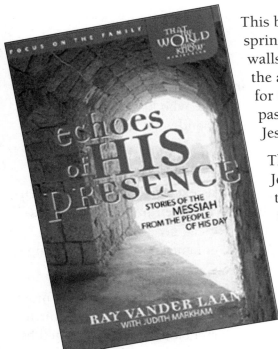